STAR WARS®
LEGACY

LEGACY

(Forty years after the Battle of Yavin and beyond)

As this era began, Luke Skywalker had unified the Jedi Order into a cohesive group of powerful Jedi Knights. It was a time of relative peace, yet darkness approached on the horizon. Now, Skywalker's descendants face new and resurgent threats to the galaxy, and to the balance of the Force.

The events in this story begin approximately 138 years after the Battle of Yavin.

STAR WARS®
LEGACY

VOLUME TEN
❖ EXTREMES ❖

STORY
John Ostrander and Jan Duursema

SCRIPT
John Ostrander

PENCILS
Jan Duursema

INKS
Dan Parsons

COLORS
Brad Anderson

FRONT COVER ART
Jan Duursema

BACK COVER ART
Sean Cooke

LETTERING
Michael Heisler

DARK HORSE BOOKS®

PRESIDENT & PUBLISHER
Mike Richardson

EDITOR
Randy Stradley

COLLECTION DESIGNER
Kat Larson

ASSISTANT EDITOR
Freddye Lins

Special thanks to Jann Moorhead, David Anderman, Troy Alders,
Leland Chee, Sue Rostoni, and Carol Roeder at Lucas Licensing.

STAR WARS: LEGACY VOLUME TEN—EXTREMES

This volume collects issues #47–#50 of the
Dark Horse comic-book series *Star Wars: Legacy*.

Published by
Dark Horse Books
A division of Dark Horse Comics, Inc.
10956 SE Main Street
Milwaukie, OR 97222

darkhorse.com
starwars.com

To find a comics shop in your area, call the Comic Shop Locator Service toll-free at 1-888-266-4226

Library of Congress Cataloging-in-Publication Data

Ostrander, John.
Star wars, legacy. volume ten : extremes / story, John Ostrander and Jan Duursema ; script, John Ostrander ; pencils, Jan Duursema ; inks, Dan Parsons ; colors, Brad Anderson ; lettering, Michael Heisler ; front cover art, Jan Duursema ; back cover art, Sean Cooke. -- 1st ed.
   p. cm.
ISBN 978-1-59582-631-2
1. Graphic novels. 2. Star Wars fiction--Comic books, strips, etc. I. Duursema, Jan. II. Title. III. Title: Extremes.
PN6728.S73O8854 2011
741.5'973--dc22

            2010031785

First edition: January 2011
ISBN 978-1-59582-631-2

1 3 5 7 9 10 8 6 4 2
Printed at Midas Printing International, Ltd., Huizhou, China

As a result of Emperor Darth Krayt's apparent coma following an encounter with Cade Skywalker, Darth Wyyrlok has assumed the Imperial throne and the leadership of the "One Sith."

Wyyrlok is moving forward with Krayt's plans for the extermination of the Mon Calamari—despite dissent among other Sith Lords and the Imperial Moffs.

Meanwhile, the Galactic Alliance and deposed emperor Roan Fel's "true" Imperials have allied themselves with the Jedi. The low-level conflicts that have marked the time since the Sith Empire was established are about to erupt into galaxy-wide war . . .

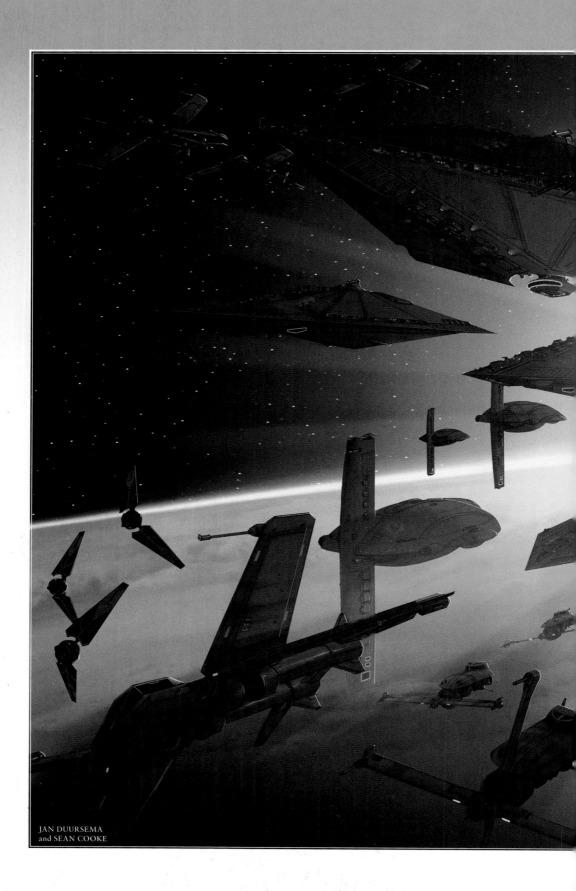

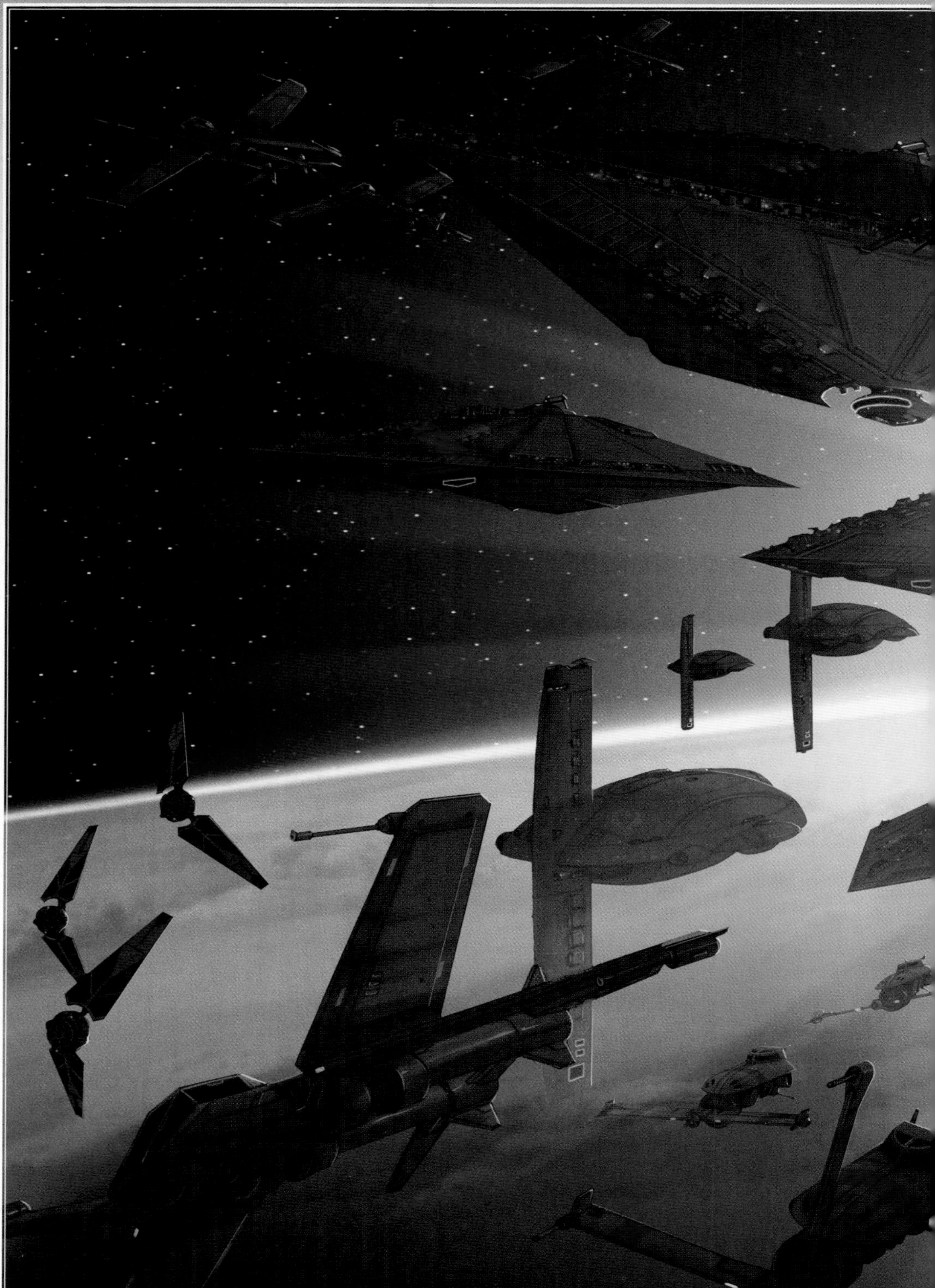
JAN DUURSEMA
and SEAN COOKE

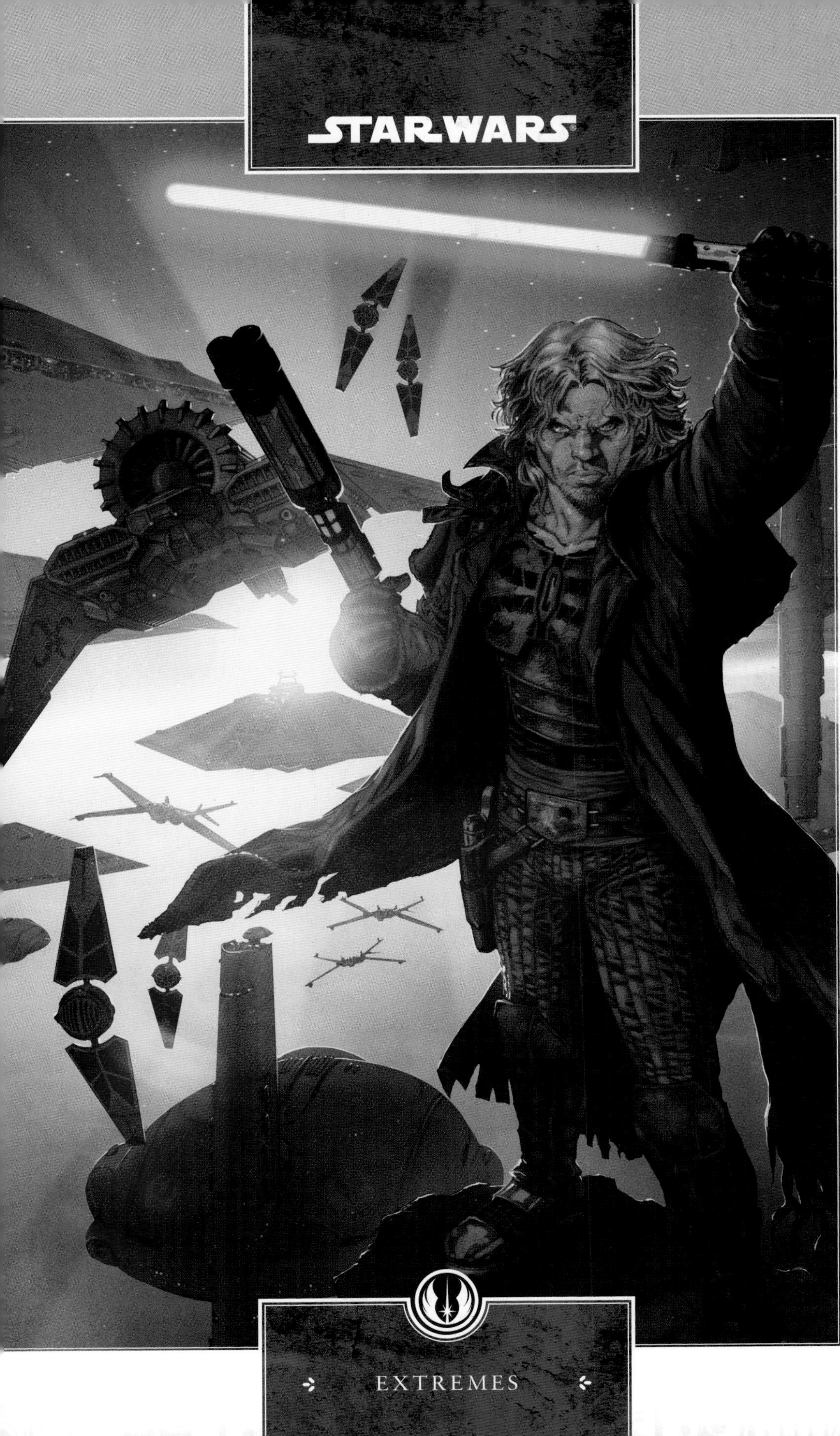
STAR WARS
EXTREMES

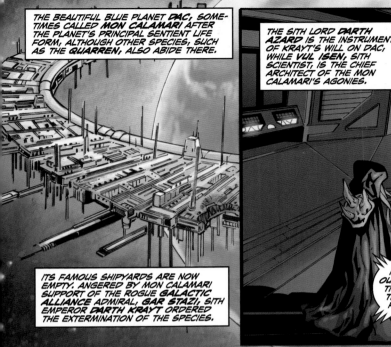

THE BEAUTIFUL BLUE PLANET **DAC**, SOMETIMES CALLED **MON CALAMARI** AFTER THE PLANET'S PRINCIPAL SENTIENT LIFE FORM, ALTHOUGH OTHER SPECIES, SUCH AS THE **QUARREN**, ALSO ABIDE THERE.

ITS FAMOUS SHIPYARDS ARE NOW EMPTY. ANGERED BY MON CALAMARI SUPPORT OF THE ROGUE **GALACTIC ALLIANCE** ADMIRAL, **GAR STAZI**, SITH EMPEROR **DARTH KRAYT** ORDERED THE EXTERMINATION OF THE SPECIES.

THE SITH LORD **DARTH AZARD** IS THE INSTRUMENT OF KRAYT'S WILL ON DAC, WHILE **VUL ISEN**, SITH SCIENTIST, IS THE CHIEF ARCHITECT OF THE MON CALAMARI'S AGONIES.

AND DARTH WYYRLOK IS THE VOICE OF LORD KRAYT -- THE VOICE OF DOOM FOR DAC.

LORD KRAYT NO LONGER WISHES OUR RESOURCES TO BE TIED UP ON DAC. IT IS TIME OTHER PLANETS FELT THE WRATH OF THE SITH.

VUL ISEN, EXECUTE THE **FINAL PROTOCOL**.

WHAT OF THE OTHER SPECIES, LORD WYYRLOK? THE QUARREN HAVE BEEN ALLIES AND THE OTHER SPECIES, LARGELY NEUTRAL.

NO ONE IS NEUTRAL. THEY WILL SHARE THE FATE OF THE MON CALAMARI. THE QUARREN'S "HELP" HAS BEEN NOTHING. ALLOW THEM TO FLEE, BUT OFFER THEM NO AID.

THIS IS LORD KRAYT'S WILL.

GOOD, GOOD, GOOD! IT'S ABOUT TIME! I'VE HAD THE VIRAL SPORES PLACED FOR MONTHS.

ONCE I RELEASE THEM, THE CURRENTS WILL CARRY THE SPORE THROUGHOUT THE PLANET. WITHIN A WEEK, EVERYTHING ON DAC WILL BE DEAD, AND WE CAN BOTH GO ON TO PRODUCTIVE WORK ELSEWHERE.

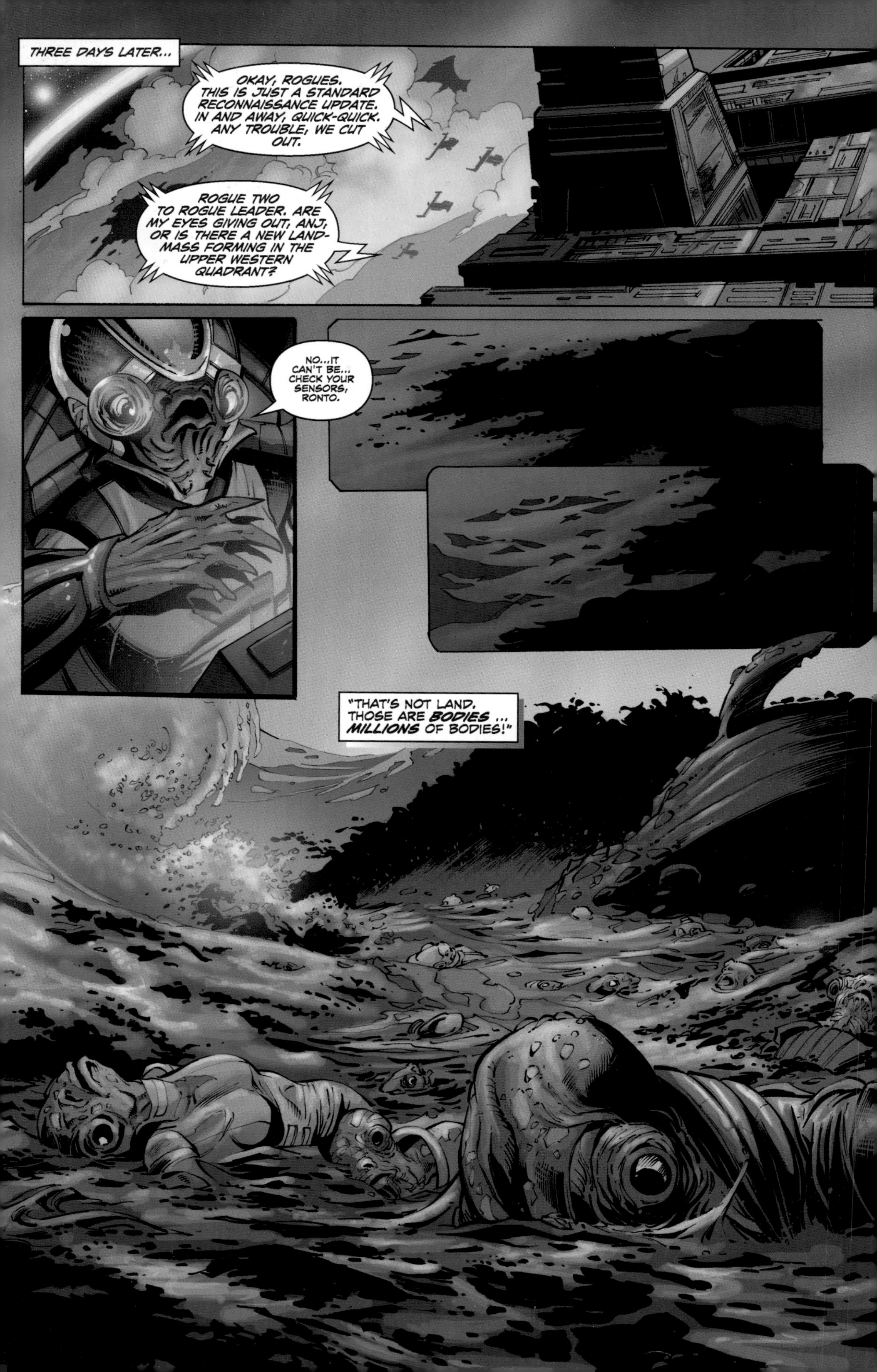
THREE DAYS LATER...
OKAY, ROGUES. THIS IS JUST A STANDARD RECONNAISSANCE UPDATE. IN AND AWAY, QUICK-QUICK. ANY TROUBLE, WE CUT OUT.
ROGUE TWO TO ROGUE LEADER. ARE MY EYES GIVING OUT, ANJ, OR IS THERE A NEW LAND-MASS FORMING IN THE UPPER WESTERN QUADRANT?
NO...IT CAN'T BE... CHECK YOUR SENSORS, RONTO.
"THAT'S NOT LAND. THOSE ARE BODIES ... MILLIONS OF BODIES!"

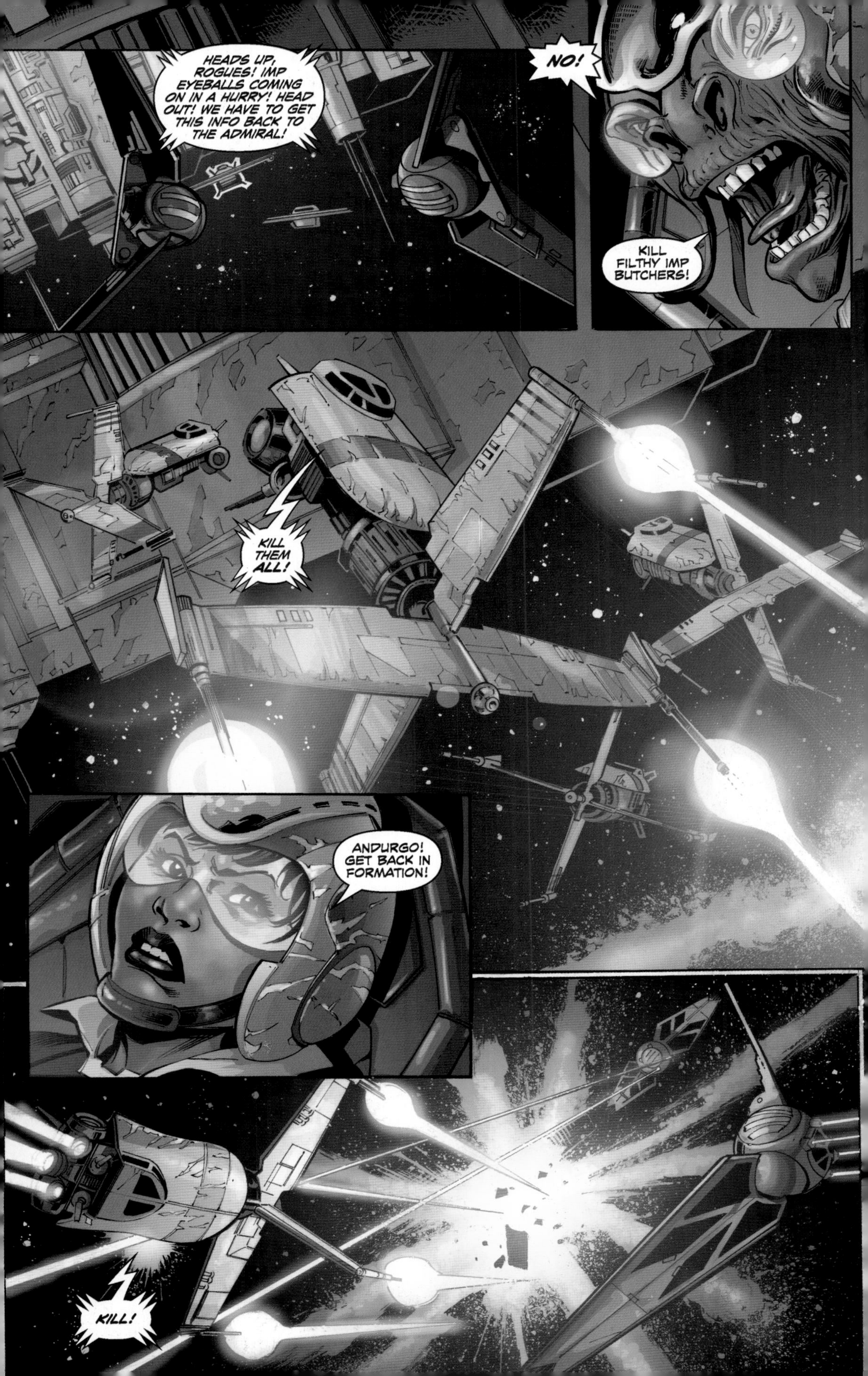
HEADS UP, ROGUES! IMP EYEBALLS COMING ON IN A HURRY! HEAD OUT! WE HAVE TO GET THIS INFO BACK TO THE ADMIRAL!
NO!
KILL FILTHY IMP BUTCHERS!
KILL THEM ALL!
ANDURGO! GET BACK IN FORMATION!
KILL!

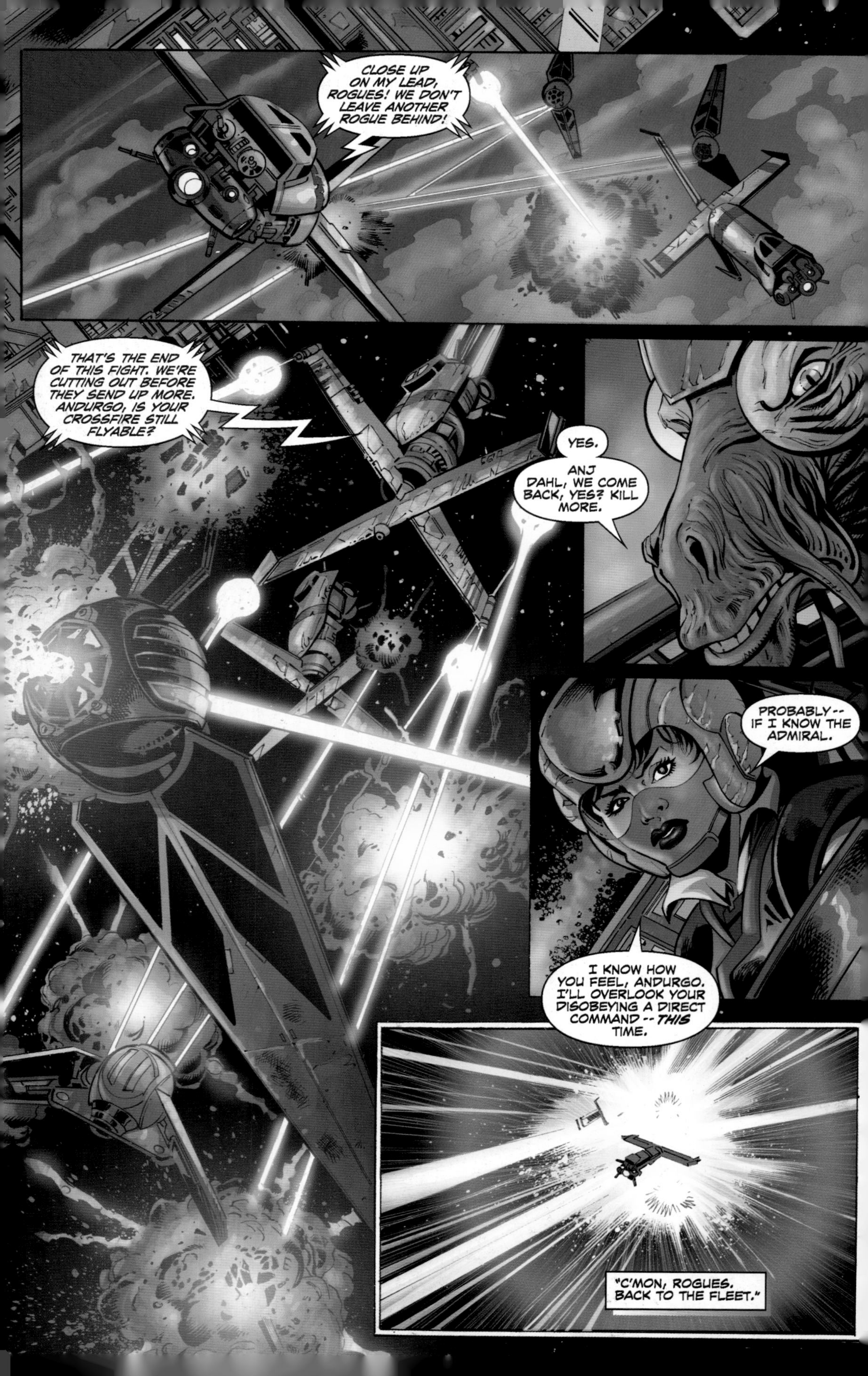
CLOSE UP ON MY LEAD, ROGUES! WE DON'T LEAVE ANOTHER ROGUE BEHIND!
THAT'S THE END OF THIS FIGHT. WE'RE CUTTING OUT BEFORE THEY SEND UP MORE. ANDURGO, IS YOUR CROSSFIRE STILL FLYABLE?
YES. ANJ DAHL, WE COME BACK, YES? KILL MORE.
PROBABLY-- IF I KNOW THE ADMIRAL.
I KNOW HOW YOU FEEL, ANDURGO. I'LL OVERLOOK YOUR DISOBEYING A DIRECT COMMAND --*THIS* TIME.
"C'MON, ROGUES. BACK TO THE FLEET."

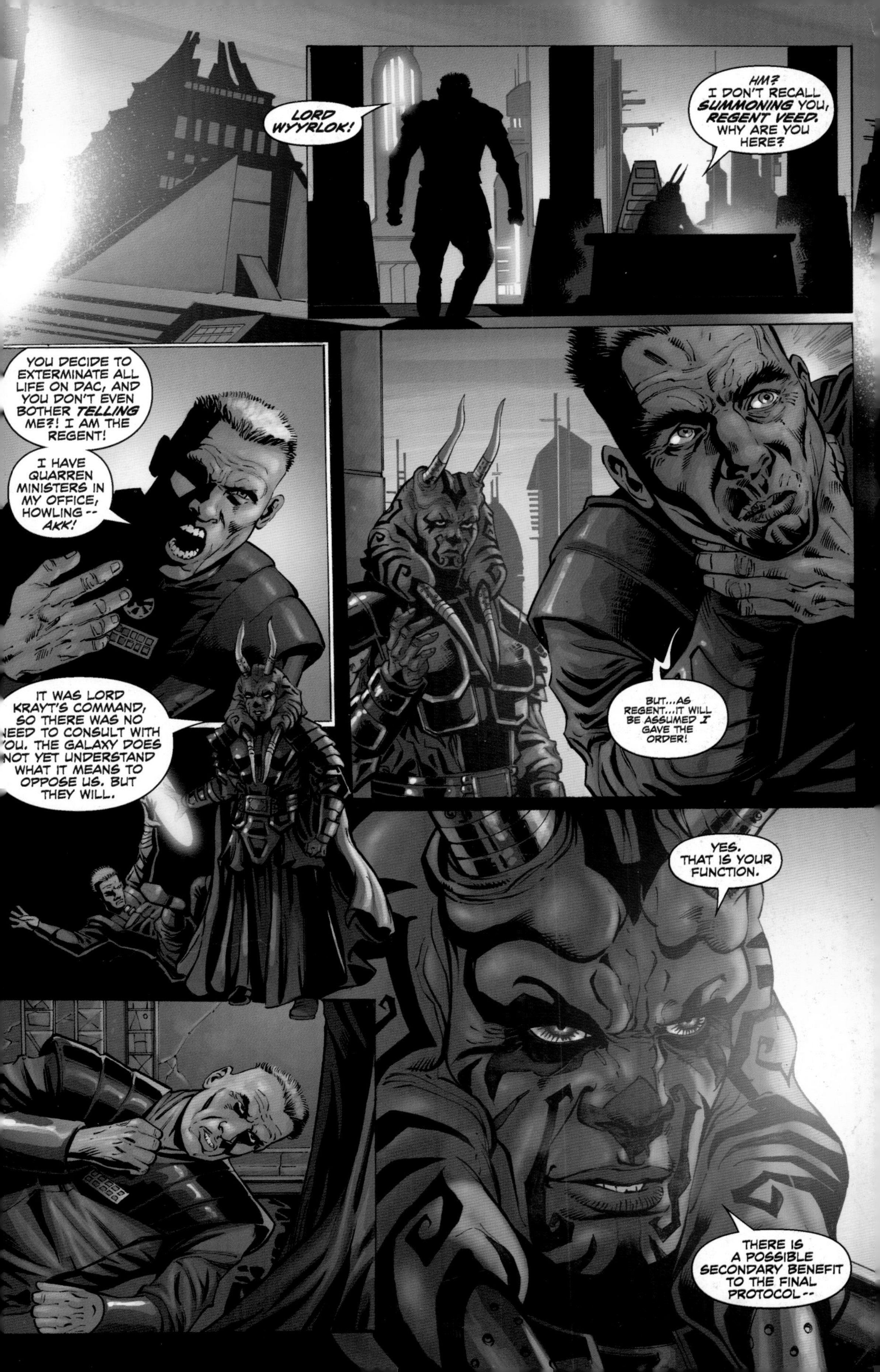
LORD WYYRLOK!
HM? I DON'T RECALL SUMMONING YOU, REGENT VEED. WHY ARE YOU HERE?
YOU DECIDE TO EXTERMINATE ALL LIFE ON DAC, AND YOU DON'T EVEN BOTHER TELLING ME?! I AM THE REGENT!
I HAVE QUARREN MINISTERS IN MY OFFICE, HOWLING-- AKK!
IT WAS LORD KRAYT'S COMMAND, SO THERE WAS NO NEED TO CONSULT WITH YOU. THE GALAXY DOES NOT YET UNDERSTAND WHAT IT MEANS TO OPPOSE US. BUT THEY WILL.
BUT...AS REGENT...IT WILL BE ASSUMED I GAVE THE ORDER!
YES. THAT IS YOUR FUNCTION.
THERE IS A POSSIBLE SECONDARY BENEFIT TO THE FINAL PROTOCOL--

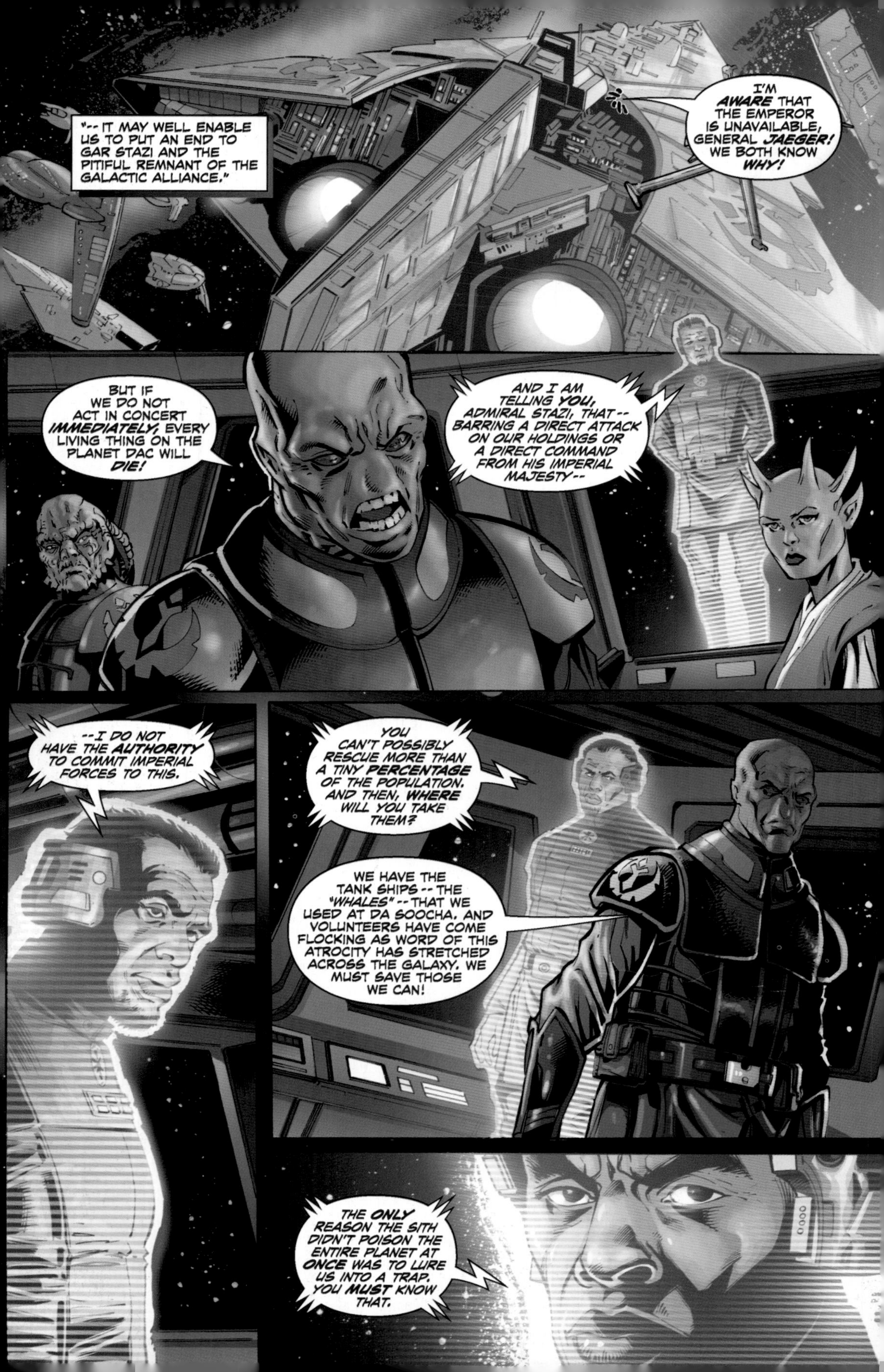
"-- IT MAY WELL ENABLE US TO PUT AN END TO GAR STAZI AND THE PITIFUL REMNANT OF THE GALACTIC ALLIANCE."
I'M AWARE THAT THE EMPEROR IS UNAVAILABLE, GENERAL JAEGER! WE BOTH KNOW WHY!
BUT IF WE DO NOT ACT IN CONCERT IMMEDIATELY, EVERY LIVING THING ON THE PLANET DAC WILL DIE!
AND I AM TELLING YOU, ADMIRAL STAZI, THAT -- BARRING A DIRECT ATTACK ON OUR HOLDINGS OR A DIRECT COMMAND FROM HIS IMPERIAL MAJESTY --
--I DO NOT HAVE THE AUTHORITY TO COMMIT IMPERIAL FORCES TO THIS.
YOU CAN'T POSSIBLY RESCUE MORE THAN A TINY PERCENTAGE OF THE POPULATION. AND THEN, WHERE WILL YOU TAKE THEM?
WE HAVE THE TANK SHIPS -- THE "WHALES" -- THAT WE USED AT DA SOOCHA. AND VOLUNTEERS HAVE COME FLOCKING AS WORD OF THIS ATROCITY HAS STRETCHED ACROSS THE GALAXY. WE MUST SAVE THOSE WE CAN!
THE ONLY REASON THE SITH DIDN'T POISON THE ENTIRE PLANET AT ONCE WAS TO LURE US INTO A TRAP. YOU MUST KNOW THAT.

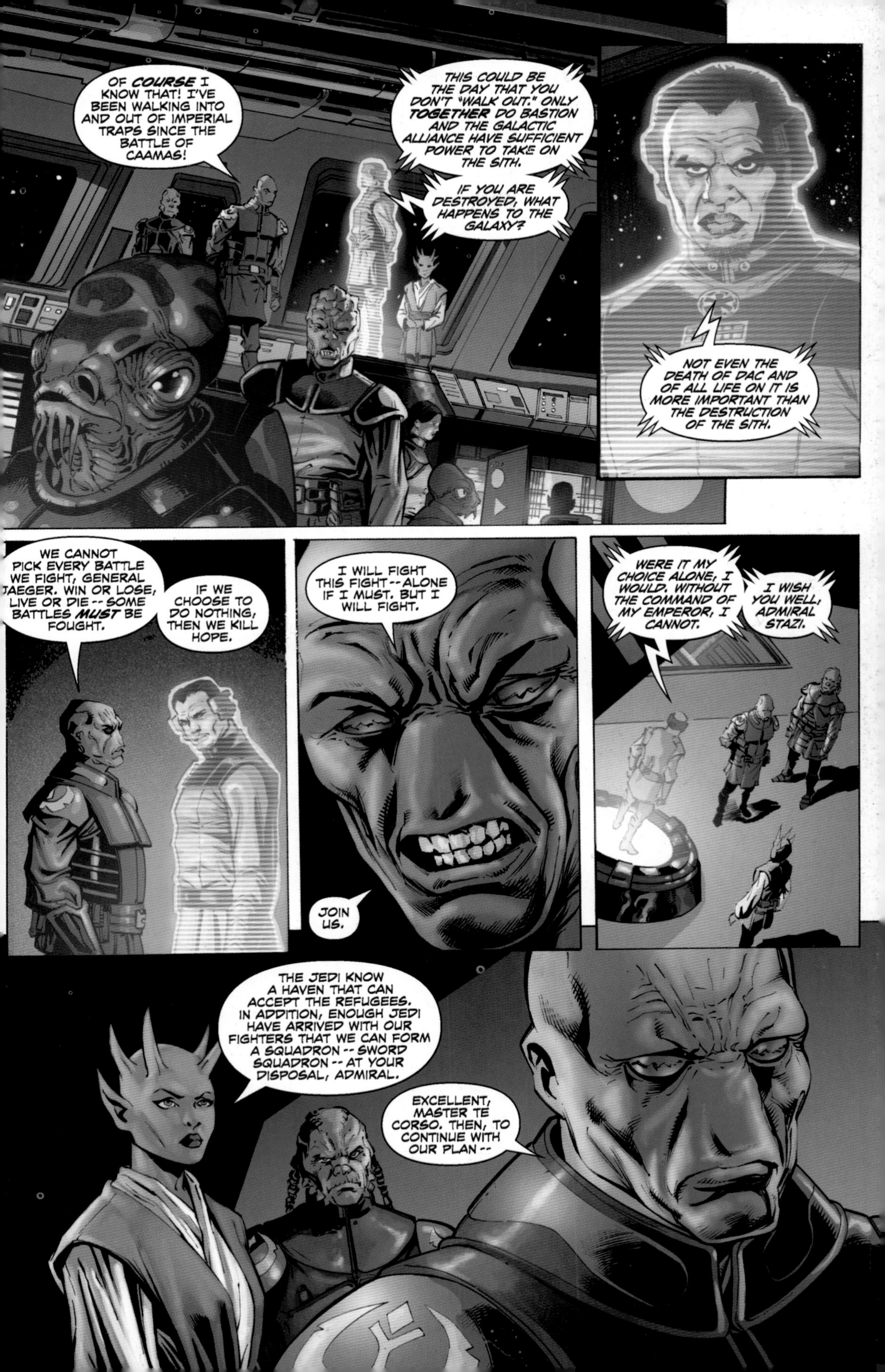
OF COURSE I KNOW THAT! I'VE BEEN WALKING INTO AND OUT OF IMPERIAL TRAPS SINCE THE BATTLE OF CAAMAS!
THIS COULD BE THE DAY THAT YOU DON'T "WALK OUT." ONLY TOGETHER DO BASTION AND THE GALACTIC ALLIANCE HAVE SUFFICIENT POWER TO TAKE ON THE SITH.
IF YOU ARE DESTROYED, WHAT HAPPENS TO THE GALAXY?
NOT EVEN THE DEATH OF DAC AND OF ALL LIFE ON IT IS MORE IMPORTANT THAN THE DESTRUCTION OF THE SITH.
WE CANNOT PICK EVERY BATTLE WE FIGHT, GENERAL JAEGER. WIN OR LOSE, LIVE OR DIE -- SOME BATTLES MUST BE FOUGHT.
IF WE CHOOSE TO DO NOTHING, THEN WE KILL HOPE.
I WILL FIGHT THIS FIGHT -- ALONE IF I MUST. BUT I WILL FIGHT.
JOIN US.
WERE IT MY CHOICE ALONE, I WOULD. WITHOUT THE COMMAND OF MY EMPEROR, I CANNOT.
I WISH YOU WELL, ADMIRAL STAZI.
THE JEDI KNOW A HAVEN THAT CAN ACCEPT THE REFUGEES. IN ADDITION, ENOUGH JEDI HAVE ARRIVED WITH OUR FIGHTERS THAT WE CAN FORM A SQUADRON -- SWORD SQUADRON -- AT YOUR DISPOSAL, ADMIRAL.
EXCELLENT, MASTER TE CORSO. THEN, TO CONTINUE WITH OUR PLAN --

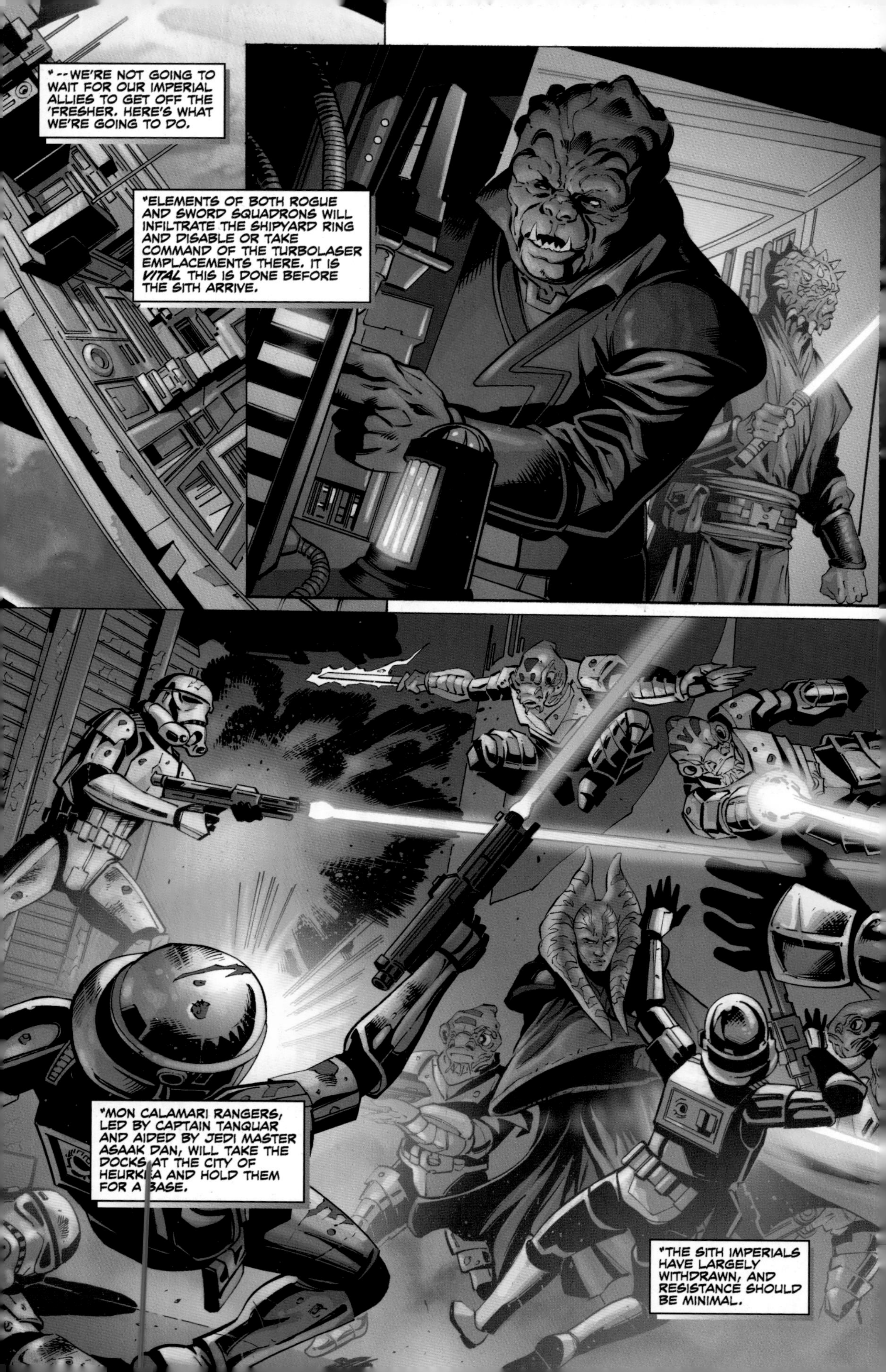
"--WE'RE NOT GOING TO WAIT FOR OUR IMPERIAL ALLIES TO GET OFF THE 'FRESHER. HERE'S WHAT WE'RE GOING TO DO.
"ELEMENTS OF BOTH ROGUE AND SWORD SQUADRONS WILL INFILTRATE THE SHIPYARD RING AND DISABLE OR TAKE COMMAND OF THE TURBOLASER EMPLACEMENTS THERE. IT IS VITAL THIS IS DONE BEFORE THE SITH ARRIVE.
"MON CALAMARI RANGERS, LED BY CAPTAIN TANQUAR AND AIDED BY JEDI MASTER ASAAK DAN, WILL TAKE THE DOCKS AT THE CITY OF HEURKEA AND HOLD THEM FOR A BASE.
"THE SITH IMPERIALS HAVE LARGELY WITHDRAWN, AND RESISTANCE SHOULD BE MINIMAL.

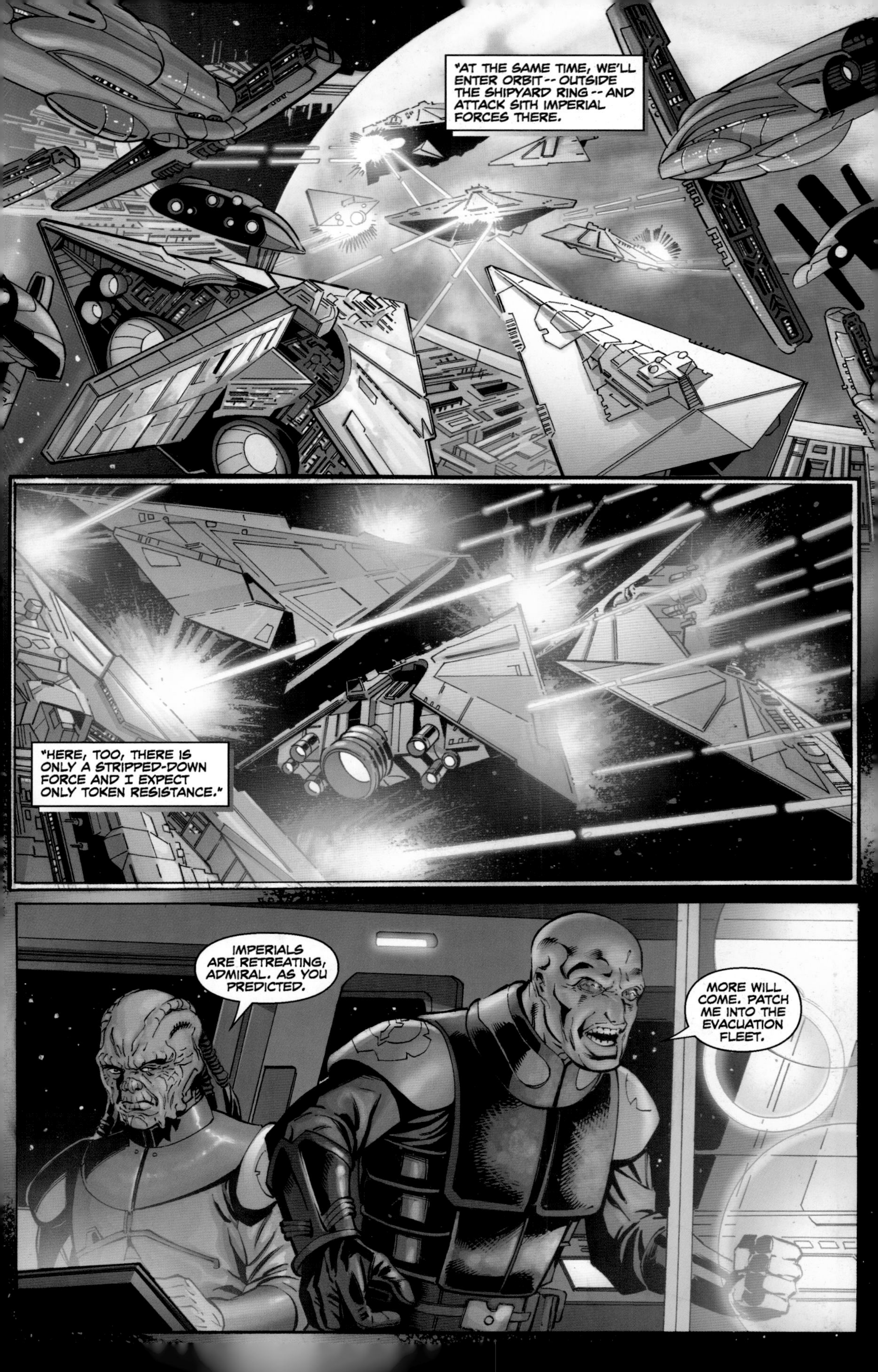
"AT THE SAME TIME, WE'LL ENTER ORBIT -- OUTSIDE THE SHIPYARD RING -- AND ATTACK SITH IMPERIAL FORCES THERE.
"HERE, TOO, THERE IS ONLY A STRIPPED-DOWN FORCE AND I EXPECT ONLY TOKEN RESISTANCE."
IMPERIALS ARE RETREATING, ADMIRAL. AS YOU PREDICTED.
MORE WILL COME. PATCH ME INTO THE EVACUATION FLEET.

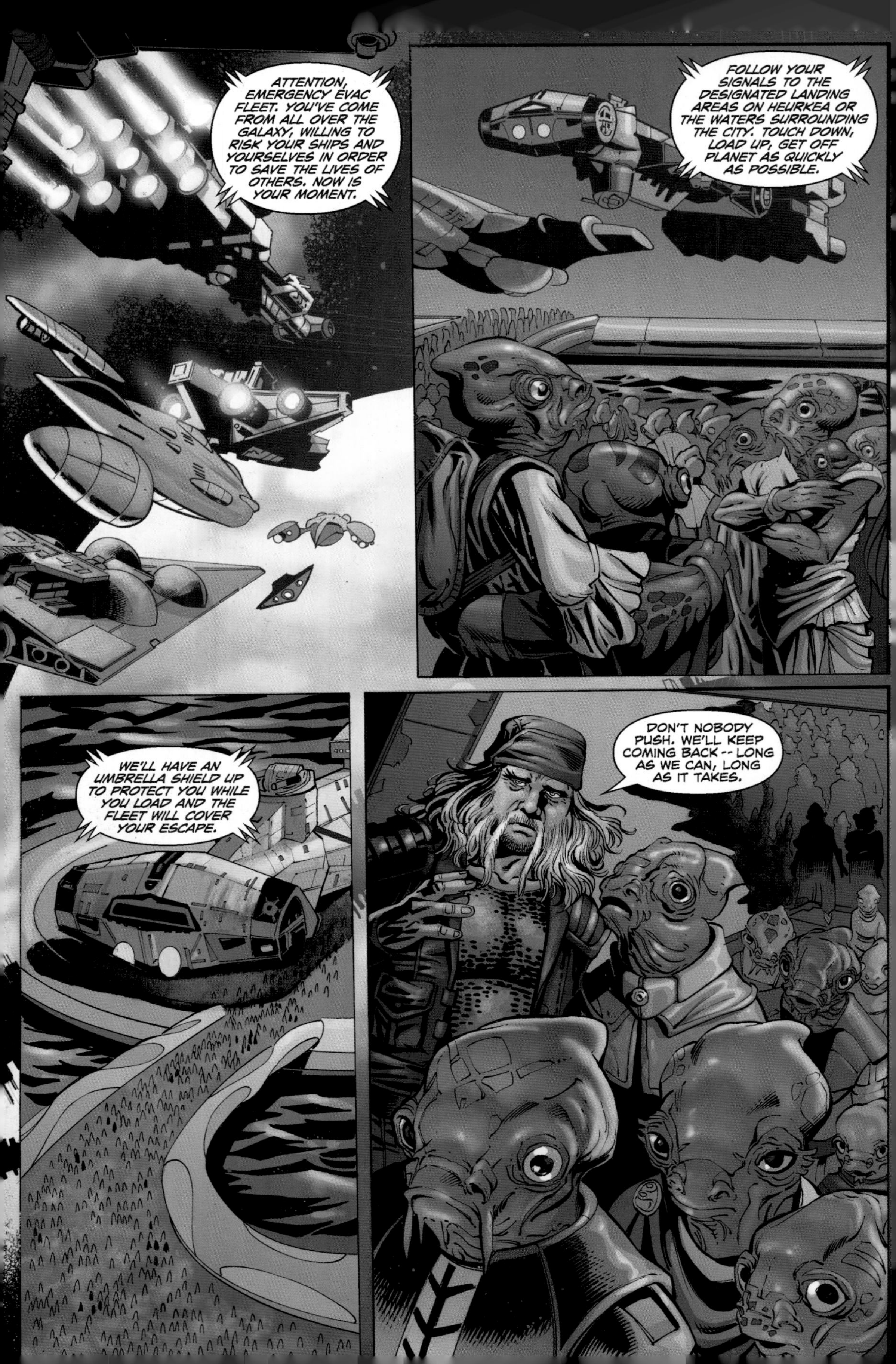
ATTENTION, EMERGENCY EVAC FLEET. YOU'VE COME FROM ALL OVER THE GALAXY, WILLING TO RISK YOUR SHIPS AND YOURSELVES IN ORDER TO SAVE THE LIVES OF OTHERS. NOW IS YOUR MOMENT.
FOLLOW YOUR SIGNALS TO THE DESIGNATED LANDING AREAS ON HEURKEA OR THE WATERS SURROUNDING THE CITY. TOUCH DOWN, LOAD UP, GET OFF PLANET AS QUICKLY AS POSSIBLE.
WE'LL HAVE AN UMBRELLA SHIELD UP TO PROTECT YOU WHILE YOU LOAD AND THE FLEET WILL COVER YOUR ESCAPE.
DON'T NOBODY PUSH. WE'LL KEEP COMING BACK -- LONG AS WE CAN, LONG AS IT TAKES.

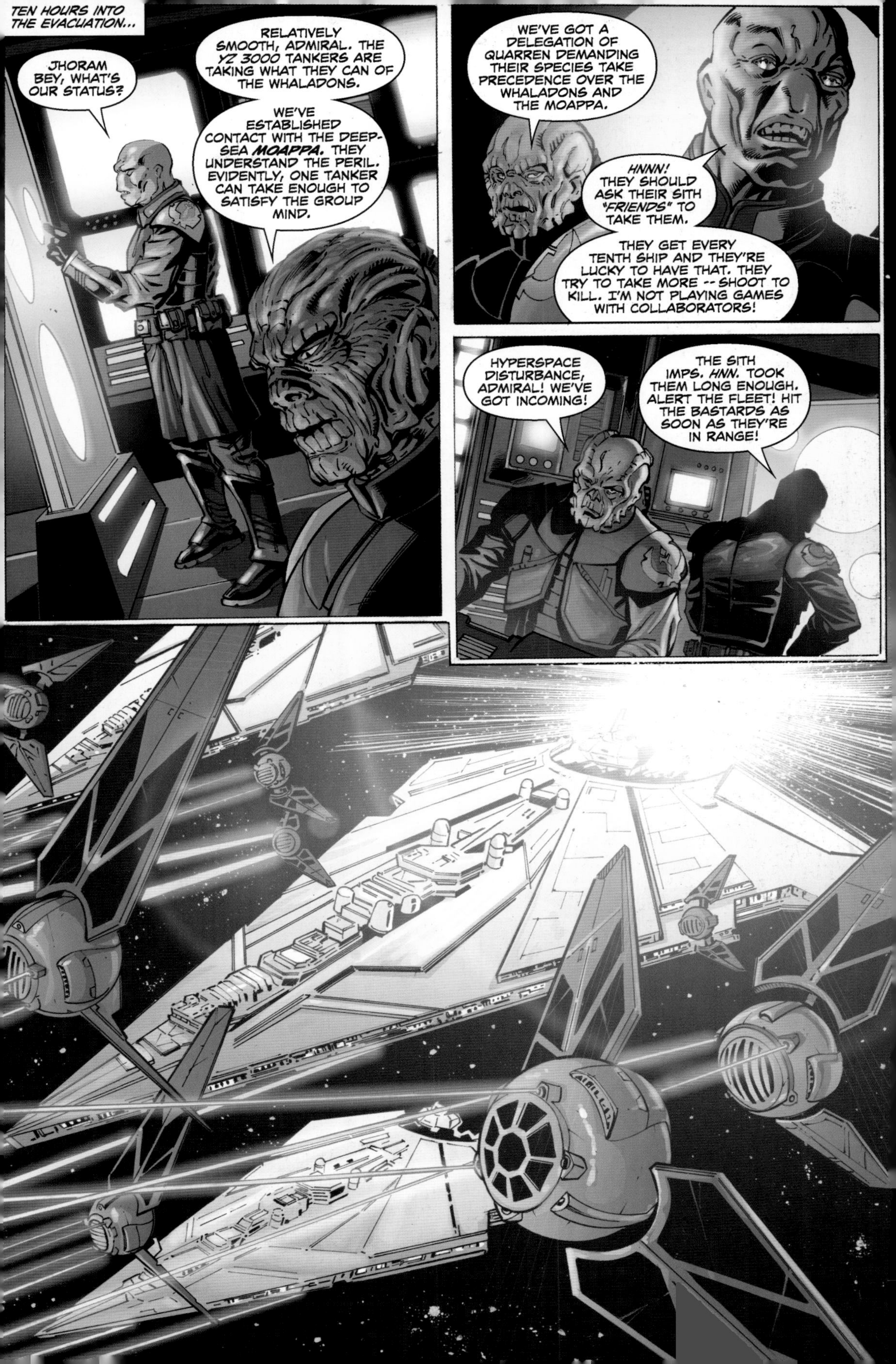
TEN HOURS INTO THE EVACUATION...
JHORAM BEY, WHAT'S OUR STATUS?
RELATIVELY SMOOTH, ADMIRAL. THE YZ 3000 TANKERS ARE TAKING WHAT THEY CAN OF THE WHALADONS.
WE'VE ESTABLISHED CONTACT WITH THE DEEP-SEA MOAPPA. THEY UNDERSTAND THE PERIL. EVIDENTLY, ONE TANKER CAN TAKE ENOUGH TO SATISFY THE GROUP MIND.
WE'VE GOT A DELEGATION OF QUARREN DEMANDING THEIR SPECIES TAKE PRECEDENCE OVER THE WHALADONS AND THE MOAPPA.
HNNN! THEY SHOULD ASK THEIR SITH "FRIENDS" TO TAKE THEM.
THEY GET EVERY TENTH SHIP AND THEY'RE LUCKY TO HAVE THAT. THEY TRY TO TAKE MORE -- SHOOT TO KILL. I'M NOT PLAYING GAMES WITH COLLABORATORS!
HYPERSPACE DISTURBANCE, ADMIRAL! WE'VE GOT INCOMING!
THE SITH IMPS. HNN. TOOK THEM LONG ENOUGH. ALERT THE FLEET! HIT THE BASTARDS AS SOON AS THEY'RE IN RANGE!

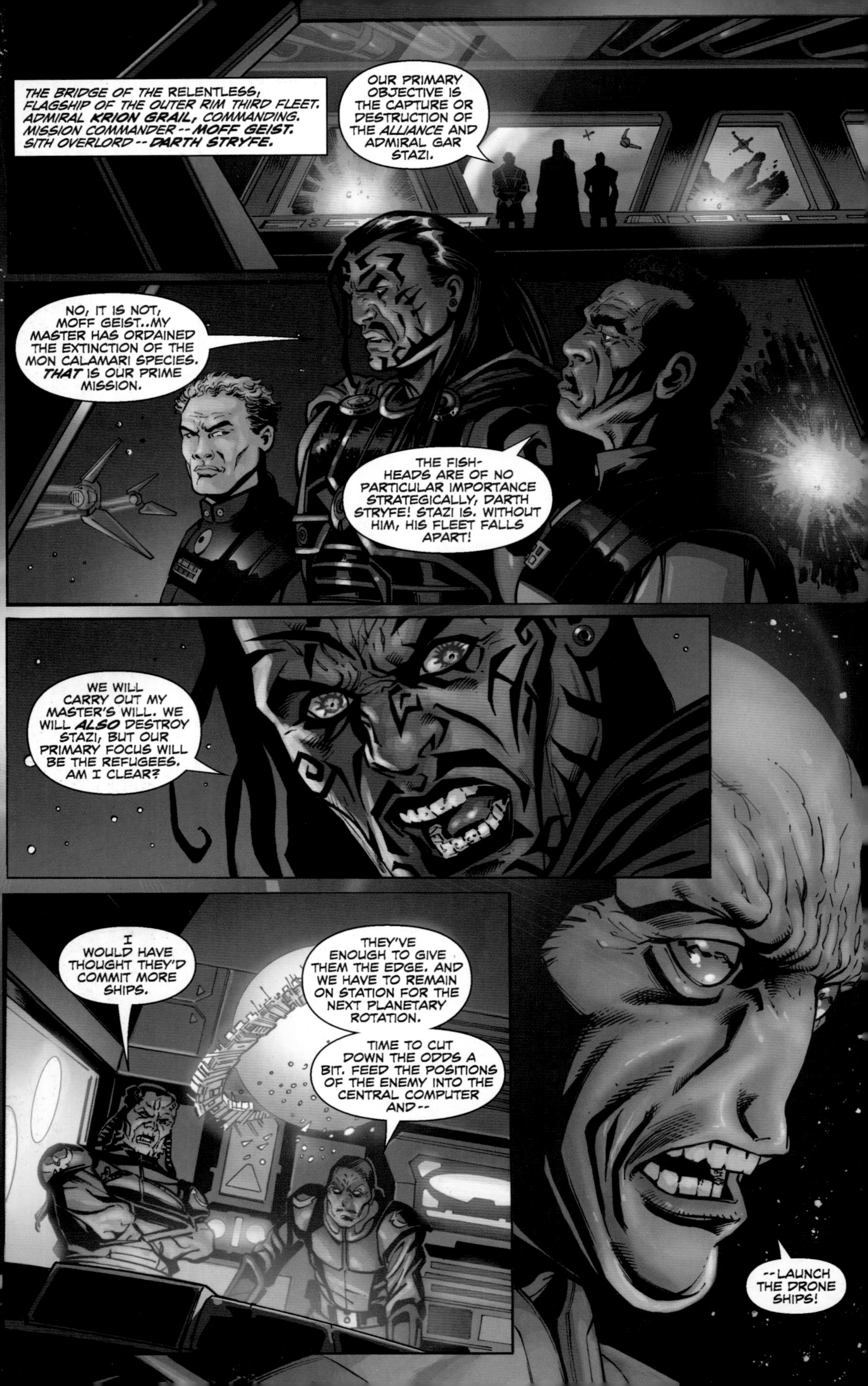
THE BRIDGE OF THE RELENTLESS, FLAGSHIP OF THE OUTER RIM THIRD FLEET. ADMIRAL KRION GRAIL, COMMANDING. MISSION COMMANDER -- MOFF GEIST. SITH OVERLORD -- DARTH STRYFE.
OUR PRIMARY OBJECTIVE IS THE CAPTURE OR DESTRUCTION OF THE ALLIANCE AND ADMIRAL GAR STAZI.
NO, IT IS NOT, MOFF GEIST..MY MASTER HAS ORDAINED THE EXTINCTION OF THE MON CALAMARI SPECIES. THAT IS OUR PRIME MISSION.
THE FISH-HEADS ARE OF NO PARTICULAR IMPORTANCE STRATEGICALLY, DARTH STRYFE! STAZI IS. WITHOUT HIM, HIS FLEET FALLS APART!
WE WILL CARRY OUT MY MASTER'S WILL. WE WILL ALSO DESTROY STAZI, BUT OUR PRIMARY FOCUS WILL BE THE REFUGEES. AM I CLEAR?
I WOULD HAVE THOUGHT THEY'D COMMIT MORE SHIPS.
THEY'VE ENOUGH TO GIVE THEM THE EDGE. AND WE HAVE TO REMAIN ON STATION FOR THE NEXT PLANETARY ROTATION.
TIME TO CUT DOWN THE ODDS A BIT. FEED THE POSITIONS OF THE ENEMY INTO THE CENTRAL COMPUTER AND--
--LAUNCH THE DRONE SHIPS!

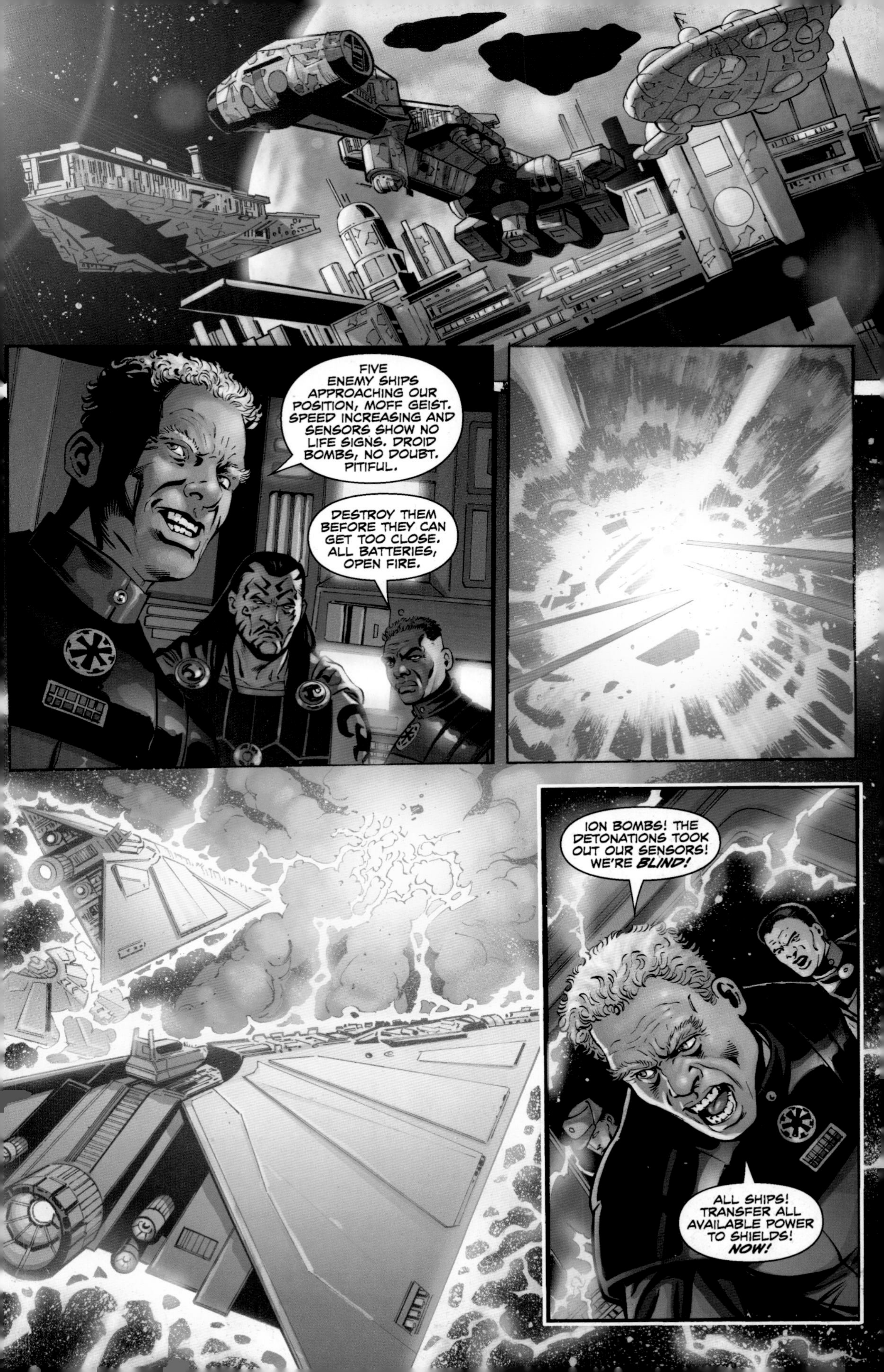
FIVE ENEMY SHIPS APPROACHING OUR POSITION, MOFF GEIST. SPEED INCREASING AND SENSORS SHOW NO LIFE SIGNS. DROID BOMBS, NO DOUBT. PITIFUL.
DESTROY THEM BEFORE THEY CAN GET TOO CLOSE. ALL BATTERIES, OPEN FIRE.
ION BOMBS! THE DETONATIONS TOOK OUT OUR SENSORS! WE'RE *BLIND!*
ALL SHIPS! TRANSFER ALL AVAILABLE POWER TO SHIELDS! *NOW!*

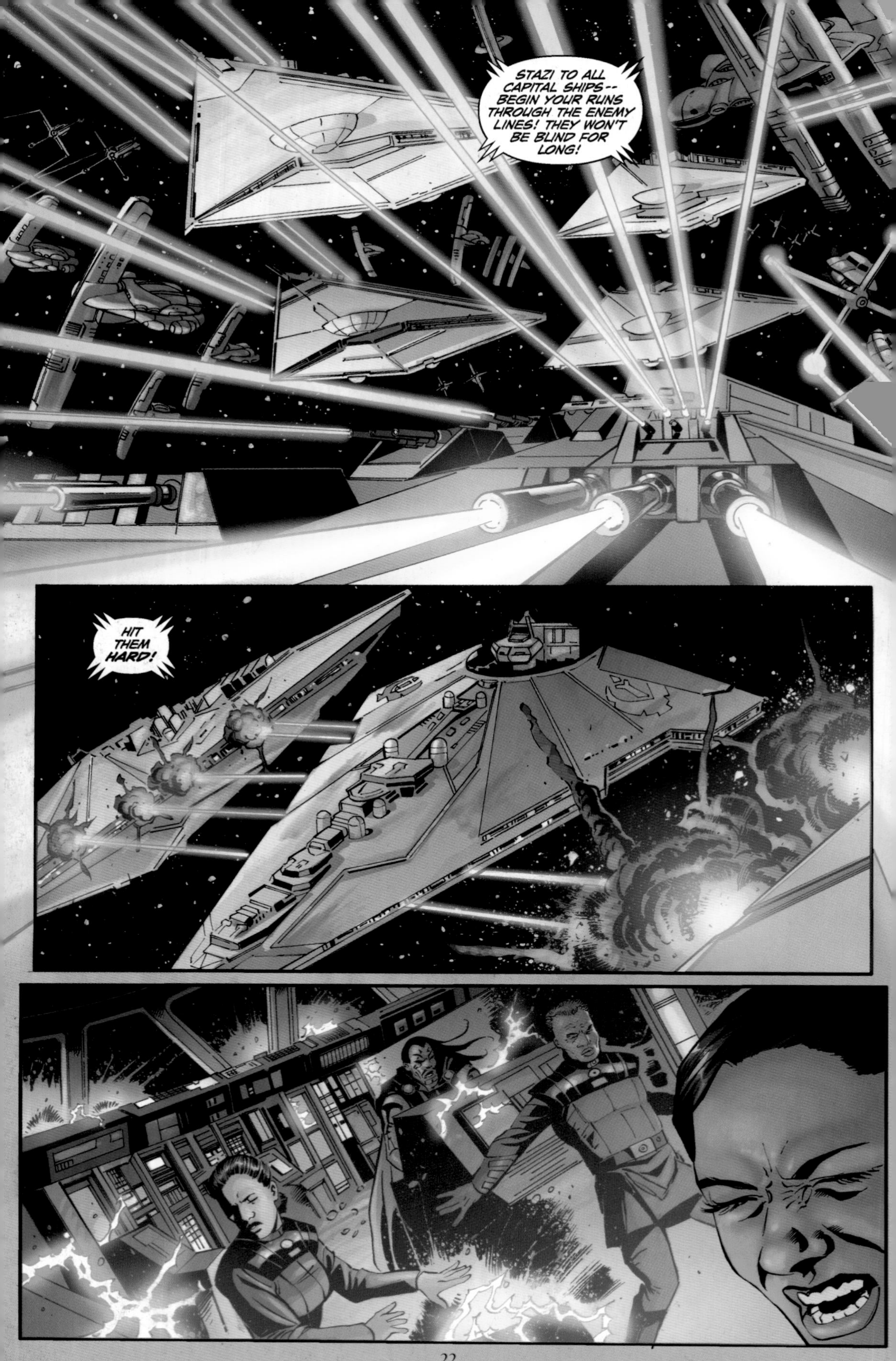
STAZI TO ALL CAPITAL SHIPS-- BEGIN YOUR RUNS THROUGH THE ENEMY LINES! THEY WON'T BE BLIND FOR LONG!
HIT THEM HARD!

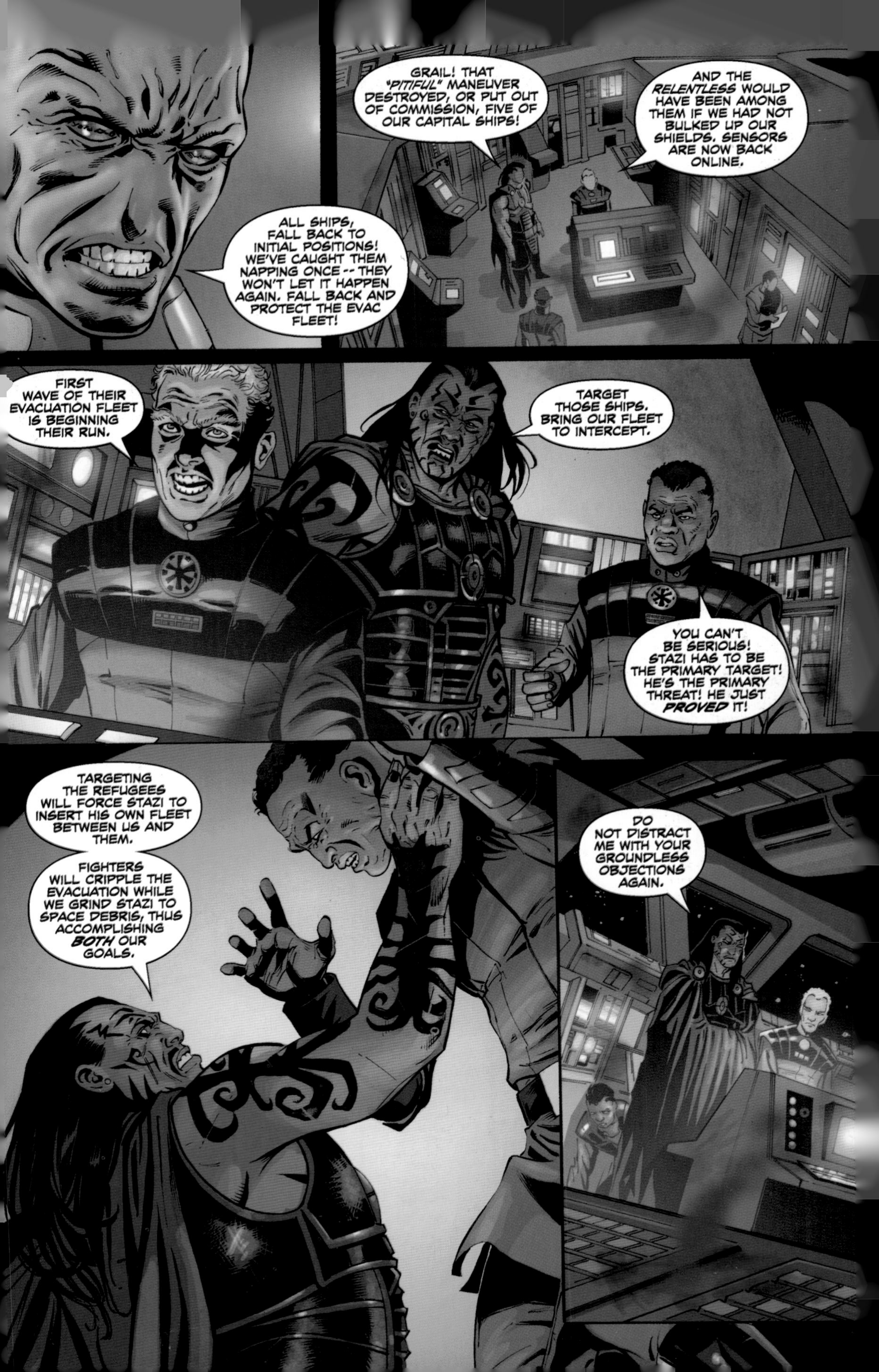
ALL SHIPS, FALL BACK TO INITIAL POSITIONS! WE'VE CAUGHT THEM NAPPING ONCE -- THEY WON'T LET IT HAPPEN AGAIN. FALL BACK AND PROTECT THE EVAC FLEET!
GRAIL! THAT "PITIFUL" MANEUVER DESTROYED, OR PUT OUT OF COMMISSION, FIVE OF OUR CAPITAL SHIPS!
AND THE RELENTLESS WOULD HAVE BEEN AMONG THEM IF WE HAD NOT BULKED UP OUR SHIELDS. SENSORS ARE NOW BACK ONLINE.
FIRST WAVE OF THEIR EVACUATION FLEET IS BEGINNING THEIR RUN.
TARGET THOSE SHIPS. BRING OUR FLEET TO INTERCEPT.
YOU CAN'T BE SERIOUS! STAZI HAS TO BE THE PRIMARY TARGET! HE'S THE PRIMARY THREAT! HE JUST PROVED IT!
TARGETING THE REFUGEES WILL FORCE STAZI TO INSERT HIS OWN FLEET BETWEEN US AND THEM.
FIGHTERS WILL CRIPPLE THE EVACUATION WHILE WE GRIND STAZI TO SPACE DEBRIS, THUS ACCOMPLISHING BOTH OUR GOALS.
DO NOT DISTRACT ME WITH YOUR GROUNDLESS OBJECTIONS AGAIN.

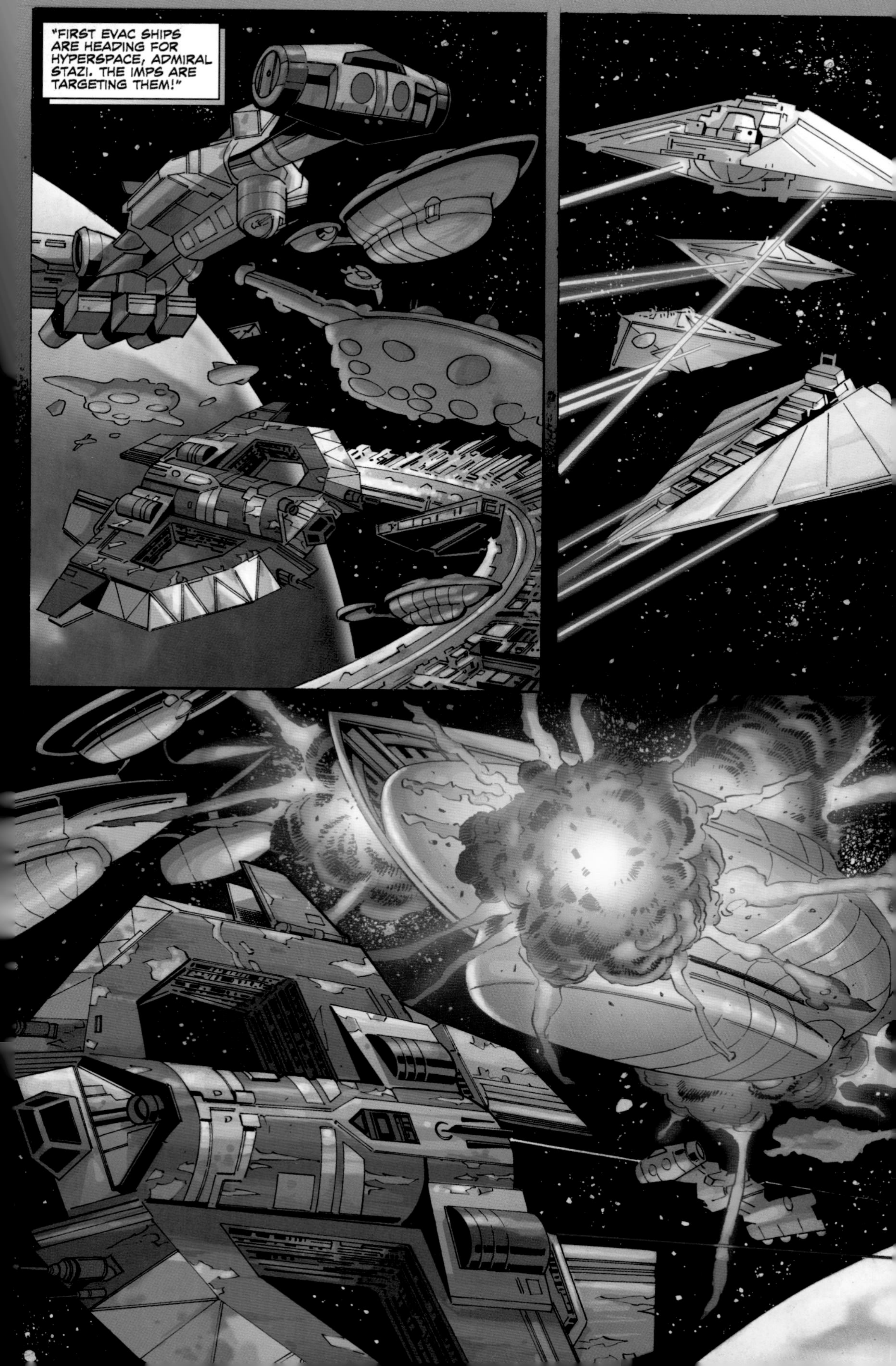
"FIRST EVAC SHIPS ARE HEADING FOR HYPERSPACE, ADMIRAL STAZI. THE IMPS ARE TARGETING THEM!"

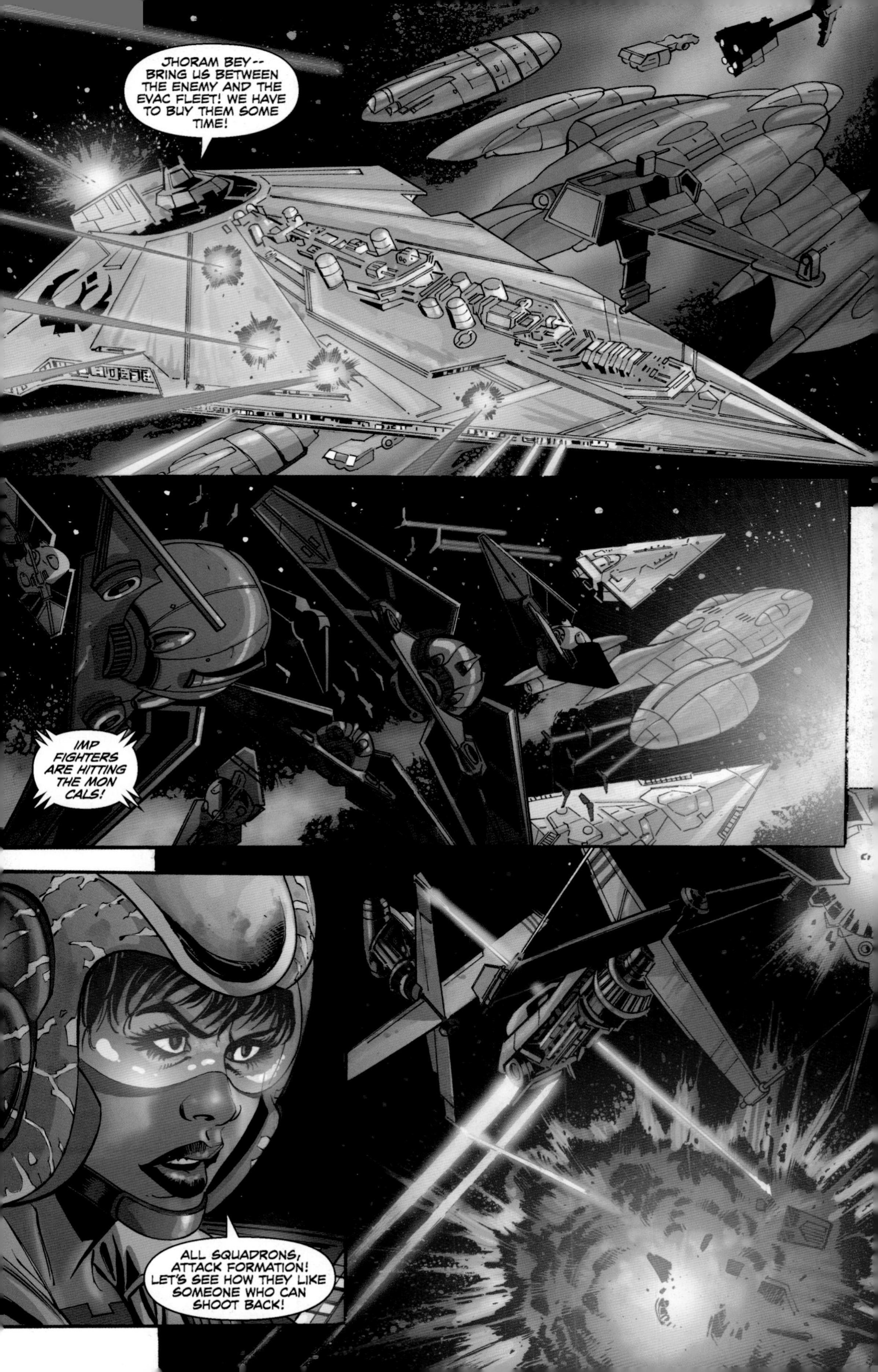
JHORAM BEY-- BRING US BETWEEN THE ENEMY AND THE EVAC FLEET! WE HAVE TO BUY THEM SOME TIME!
IMP FIGHTERS ARE HITTING THE MON CALS!
ALL SQUADRONS, ATTACK FORMATION! LET'S SEE HOW THEY LIKE SOMEONE WHO CAN SHOOT BACK!

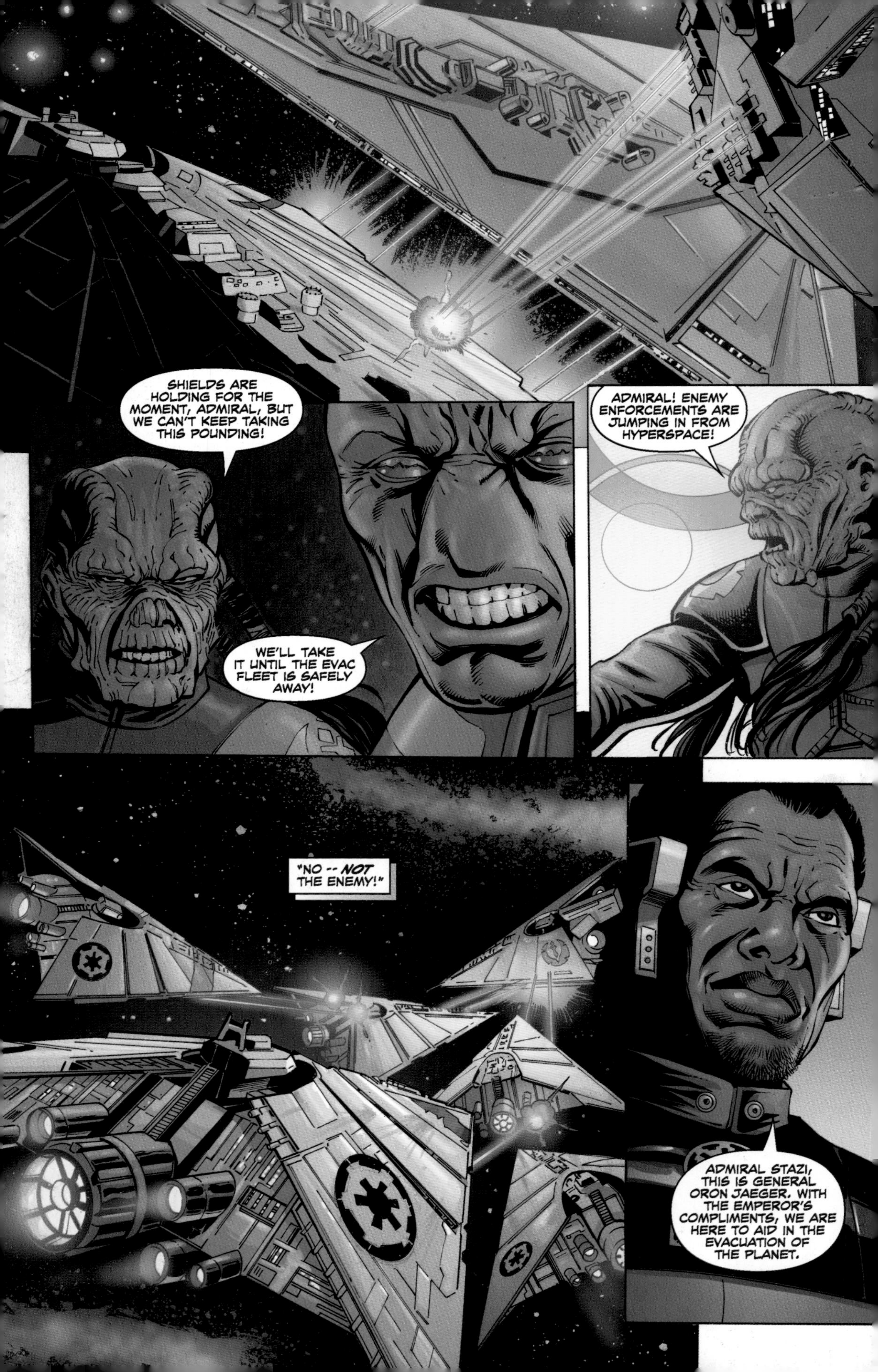
SHIELDS ARE HOLDING FOR THE MOMENT, ADMIRAL, BUT WE CAN'T KEEP TAKING THIS POUNDING!
WE'LL TAKE IT UNTIL THE EVAC FLEET IS SAFELY AWAY!
ADMIRAL! ENEMY ENFORCEMENTS ARE JUMPING IN FROM HYPERSPACE!
"NO -- *NOT* THE ENEMY!"
ADMIRAL STAZI, THIS IS GENERAL ORON JAEGER. WITH THE EMPEROR'S COMPLIMENTS, WE ARE HERE TO AID IN THE EVACUATION OF THE PLANET.

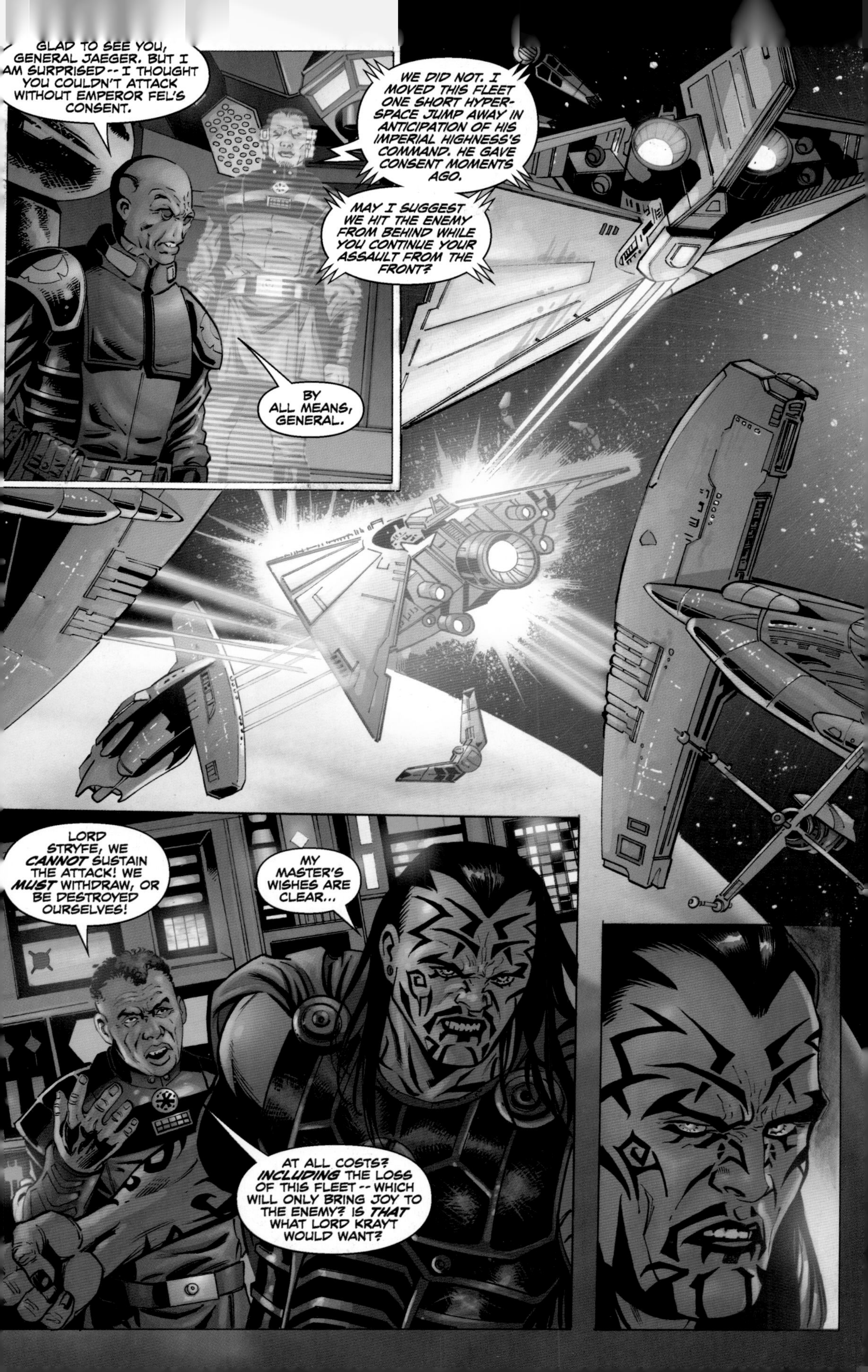
GLAD TO SEE YOU, GENERAL JAEGER. BUT I AM SURPRISED-- I THOUGHT YOU COULDN'T ATTACK WITHOUT EMPEROR FEL'S CONSENT.
WE DID NOT. I MOVED THIS FLEET ONE SHORT HYPER-SPACE JUMP AWAY IN ANTICIPATION OF HIS IMPERIAL HIGHNESS'S COMMAND. HE GAVE CONSENT MOMENTS AGO.
MAY I SUGGEST WE HIT THE ENEMY FROM BEHIND WHILE YOU CONTINUE YOUR ASSAULT FROM THE FRONT?
BY ALL MEANS, GENERAL.
LORD STRYFE, WE *CANNOT* SUSTAIN THE ATTACK! WE *MUST* WITHDRAW, OR BE DESTROYED OURSELVES!
MY MASTER'S WISHES ARE CLEAR...
AT ALL COSTS? *INCLUDING* THE LOSS OF THIS FLEET-- WHICH WILL ONLY BRING JOY TO THE ENEMY? IS *THAT* WHAT LORD KRAYT WOULD WANT?

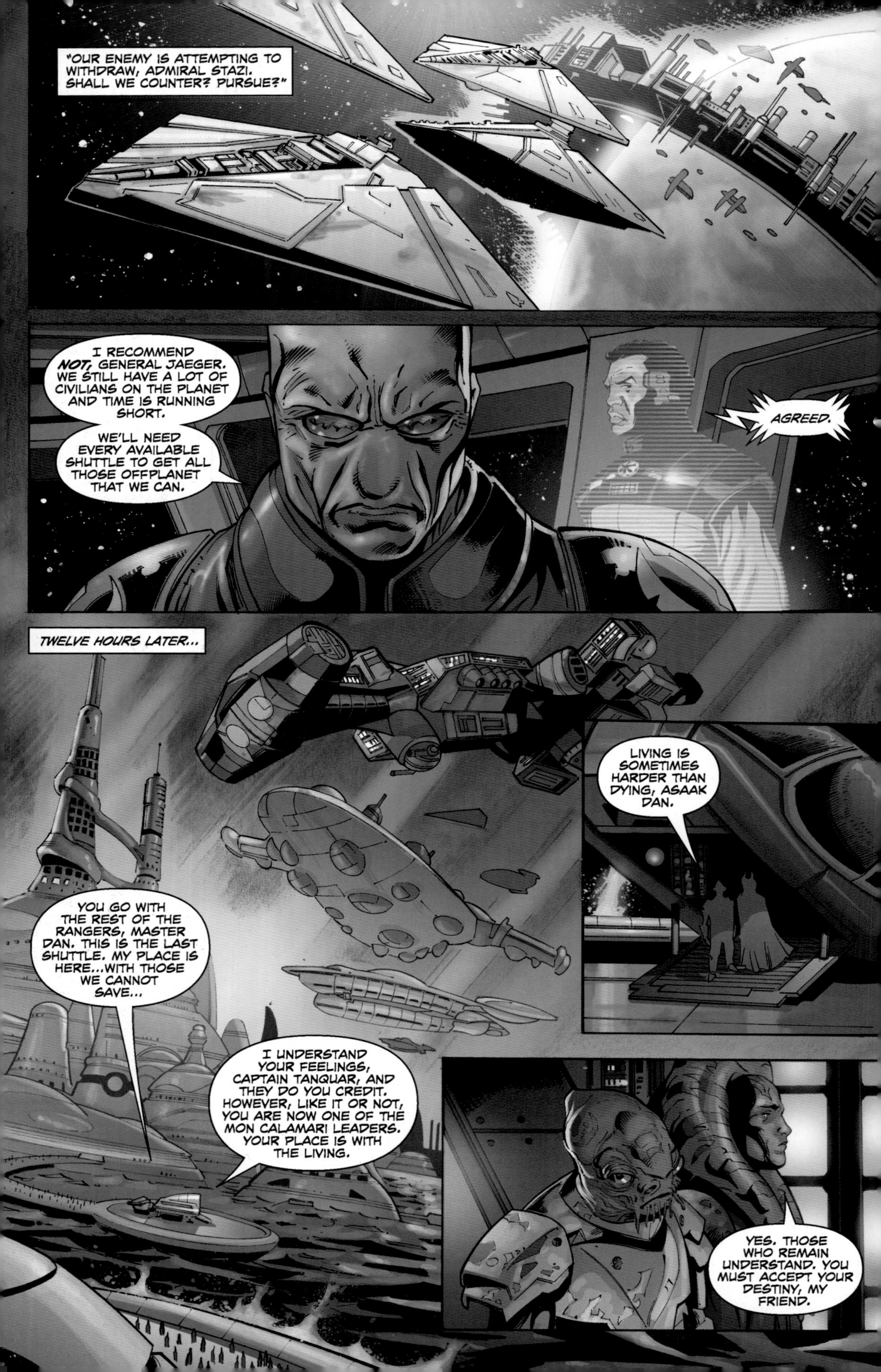
"OUR ENEMY IS ATTEMPTING TO WITHDRAW, ADMIRAL STAZI. SHALL WE COUNTER? PURSUE?"
I RECOMMEND NOT, GENERAL JAEGER. WE STILL HAVE A LOT OF CIVILIANS ON THE PLANET AND TIME IS RUNNING SHORT.
WE'LL NEED EVERY AVAILABLE SHUTTLE TO GET ALL THOSE OFFPLANET THAT WE CAN.
AGREED.
TWELVE HOURS LATER...
YOU GO WITH THE REST OF THE RANGERS, MASTER DAN. THIS IS THE LAST SHUTTLE. MY PLACE IS HERE...WITH THOSE WE CANNOT SAVE...
LIVING IS SOMETIMES HARDER THAN DYING, ASAAK DAN.
I UNDERSTAND YOUR FEELINGS, CAPTAIN TANQUAR, AND THEY DO YOU CREDIT. HOWEVER, LIKE IT OR NOT, YOU ARE NOW ONE OF THE MON CALAMARI LEADERS. YOUR PLACE IS WITH THE LIVING.
YES. THOSE WHO REMAIN UNDERSTAND. YOU MUST ACCEPT YOUR DESTINY, MY FRIEND.

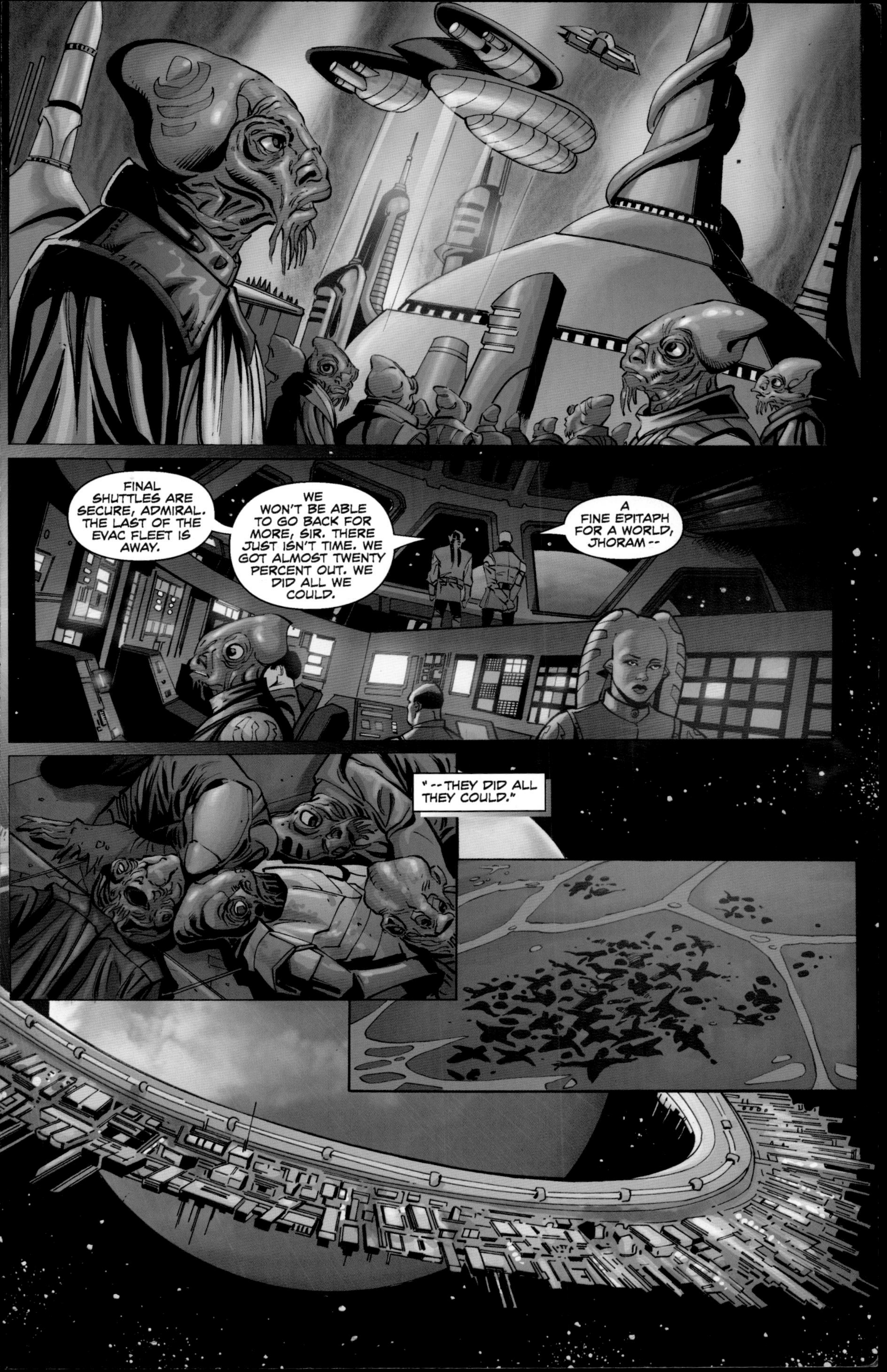
FINAL SHUTTLES ARE SECURE, ADMIRAL. THE LAST OF THE EVAC FLEET IS AWAY.
WE WON'T BE ABLE TO GO BACK FOR MORE, SIR. THERE JUST ISN'T TIME. WE GOT ALMOST TWENTY PERCENT OUT. WE DID ALL WE COULD.
A FINE EPITAPH FOR A WORLD, JHORAM --
"--THEY DID ALL THEY COULD."

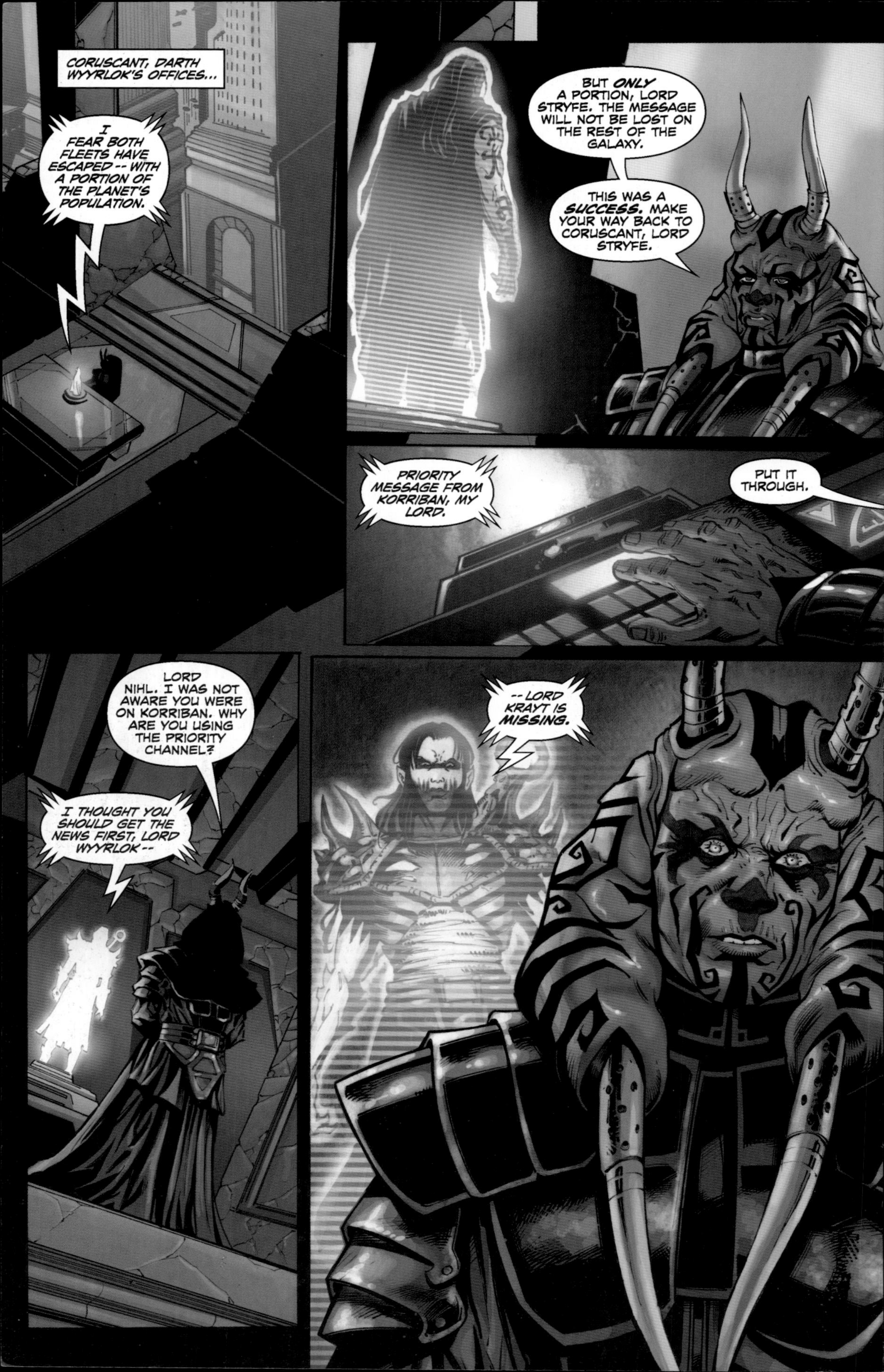
CORUSCANT, DARTH WYYRLOK'S OFFICES...
I FEAR BOTH FLEETS HAVE ESCAPED -- WITH A PORTION OF THE PLANET'S POPULATION.
BUT ONLY A PORTION, LORD STRYFE. THE MESSAGE WILL NOT BE LOST ON THE REST OF THE GALAXY.
THIS WAS A SUCCESS. MAKE YOUR WAY BACK TO CORUSCANT, LORD STRYFE.
PRIORITY MESSAGE FROM KORRIBAN, MY LORD.
PUT IT THROUGH.
LORD NIHL. I WAS NOT AWARE YOU WERE ON KORRIBAN. WHY ARE YOU USING THE PRIORITY CHANNEL?
I THOUGHT YOU SHOULD GET THE NEWS FIRST, LORD WYYRLOK --
-- LORD KRAYT IS MISSING.

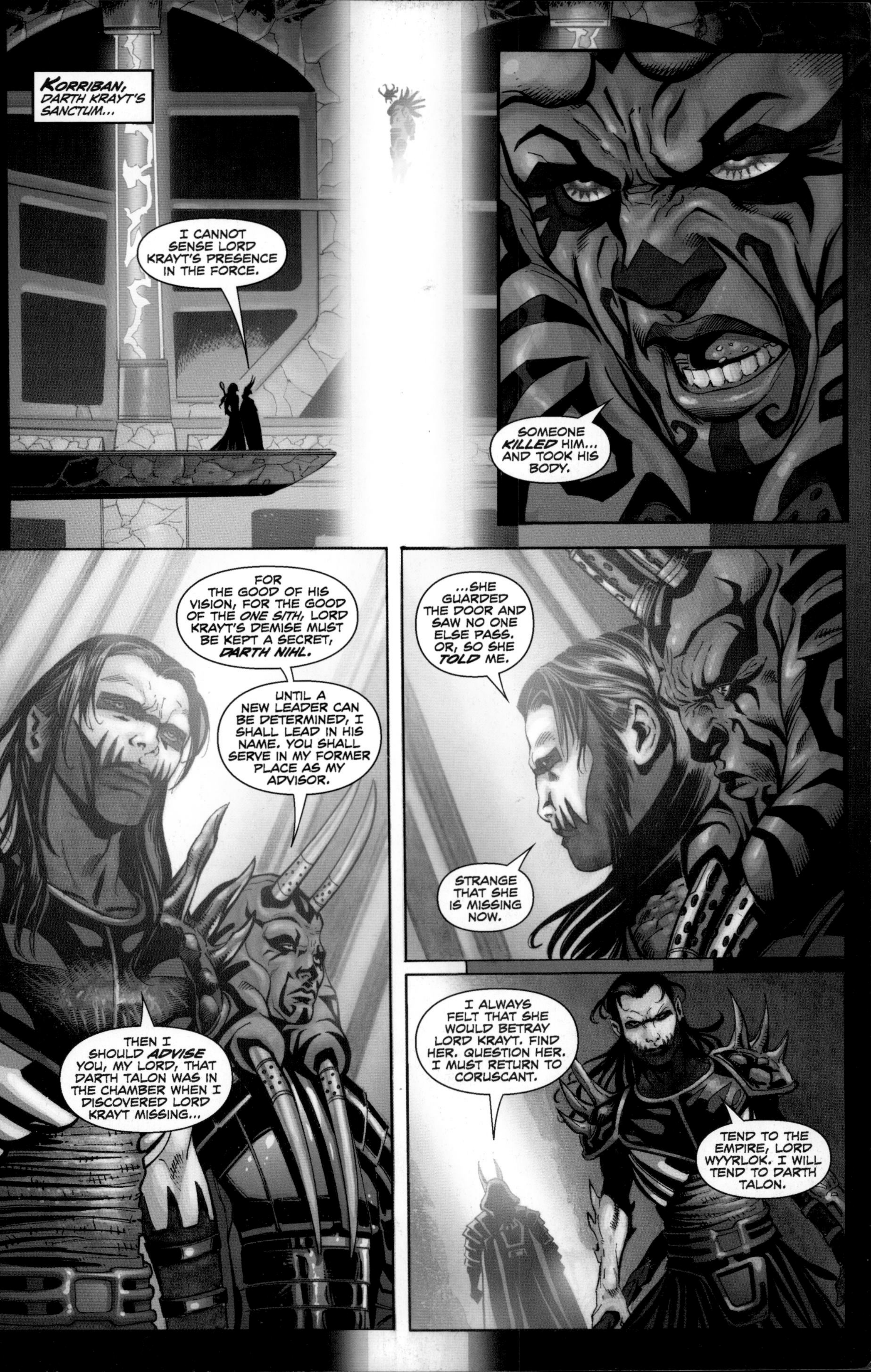
KORRIBAN, DARTH KRAYT'S SANCTUM...
I CANNOT SENSE LORD KRAYT'S PRESENCE IN THE FORCE.
SOMEONE KILLED HIM... AND TOOK HIS BODY.
FOR THE GOOD OF HIS VISION, FOR THE GOOD OF THE ONE SITH, LORD KRAYT'S DEMISE MUST BE KEPT A SECRET, DARTH NIHL.
UNTIL A NEW LEADER CAN BE DETERMINED, I SHALL LEAD IN HIS NAME. YOU SHALL SERVE IN MY FORMER PLACE AS MY ADVISOR.
THEN I SHOULD ADVISE YOU, MY LORD, THAT DARTH TALON WAS IN THE CHAMBER WHEN I DISCOVERED LORD KRAYT MISSING...
...SHE GUARDED THE DOOR AND SAW NO ONE ELSE PASS. OR, SO SHE TOLD ME.
STRANGE THAT SHE IS MISSING NOW.
I ALWAYS FELT THAT SHE WOULD BETRAY LORD KRAYT. FIND HER. QUESTION HER. I MUST RETURN TO CORUSCANT.
TEND TO THE EMPIRE, LORD WYYRLOK. I WILL TEND TO DARTH TALON.

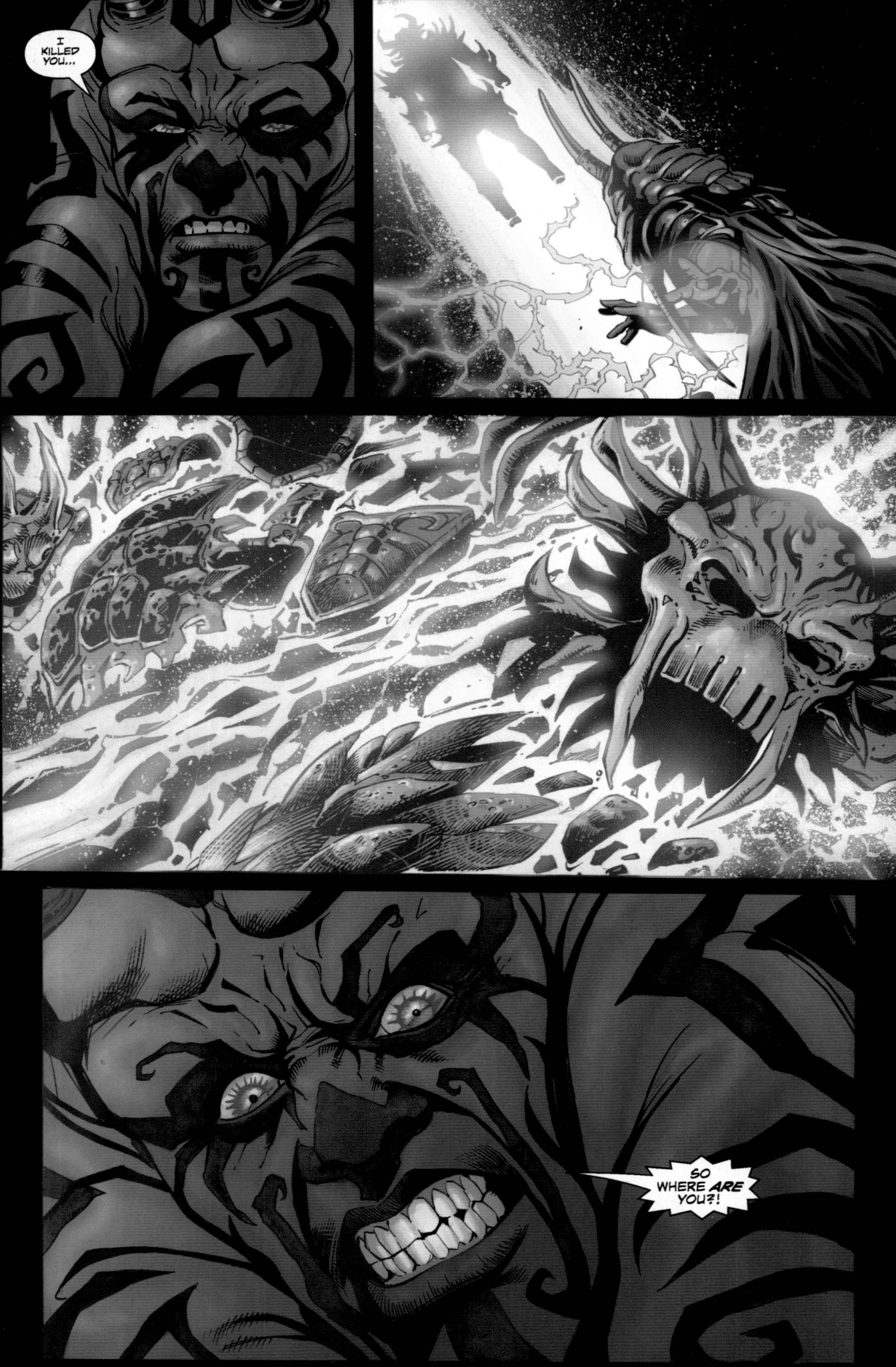
I KILLED YOU...
SO WHERE *ARE* YOU?!

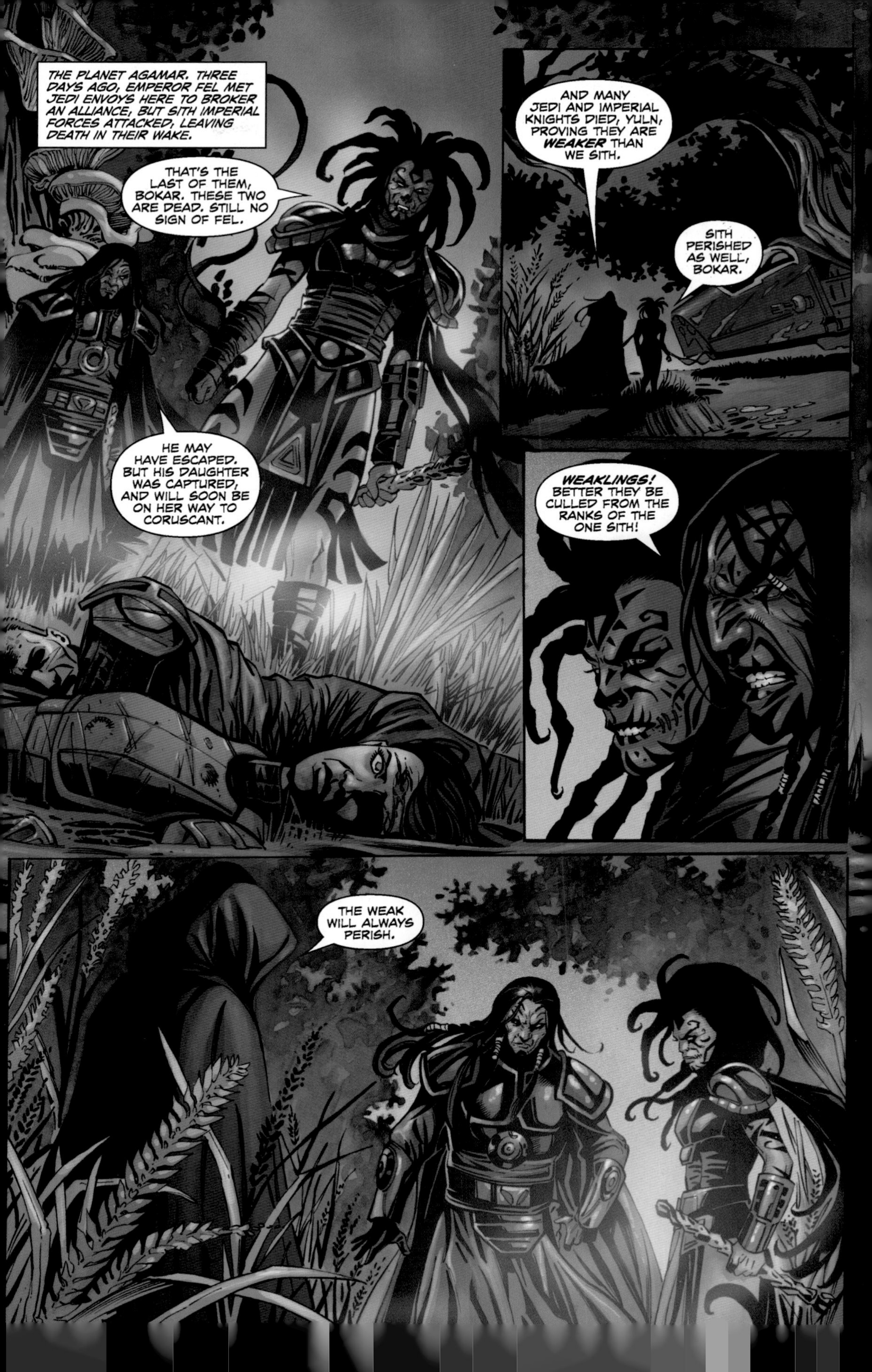
THE PLANET AGAMAR. THREE DAYS AGO, EMPEROR FEL MET JEDI ENVOYS HERE TO BROKER AN ALLIANCE, BUT SITH IMPERIAL FORCES ATTACKED, LEAVING DEATH IN THEIR WAKE.
THAT'S THE LAST OF THEM, BOKAR. THESE TWO ARE DEAD. STILL NO SIGN OF FEL.
HE MAY HAVE ESCAPED. BUT HIS DAUGHTER WAS CAPTURED, AND WILL SOON BE ON HER WAY TO CORUSCANT.
AND MANY JEDI AND IMPERIAL KNIGHTS DIED, YULN, PROVING THEY ARE WEAKER THAN WE SITH.
SITH PERISHED AS WELL, BOKAR.
WEAKLINGS! BETTER THEY BE CULLED FROM THE RANKS OF THE ONE SITH!
THE WEAK WILL ALWAYS PERISH.

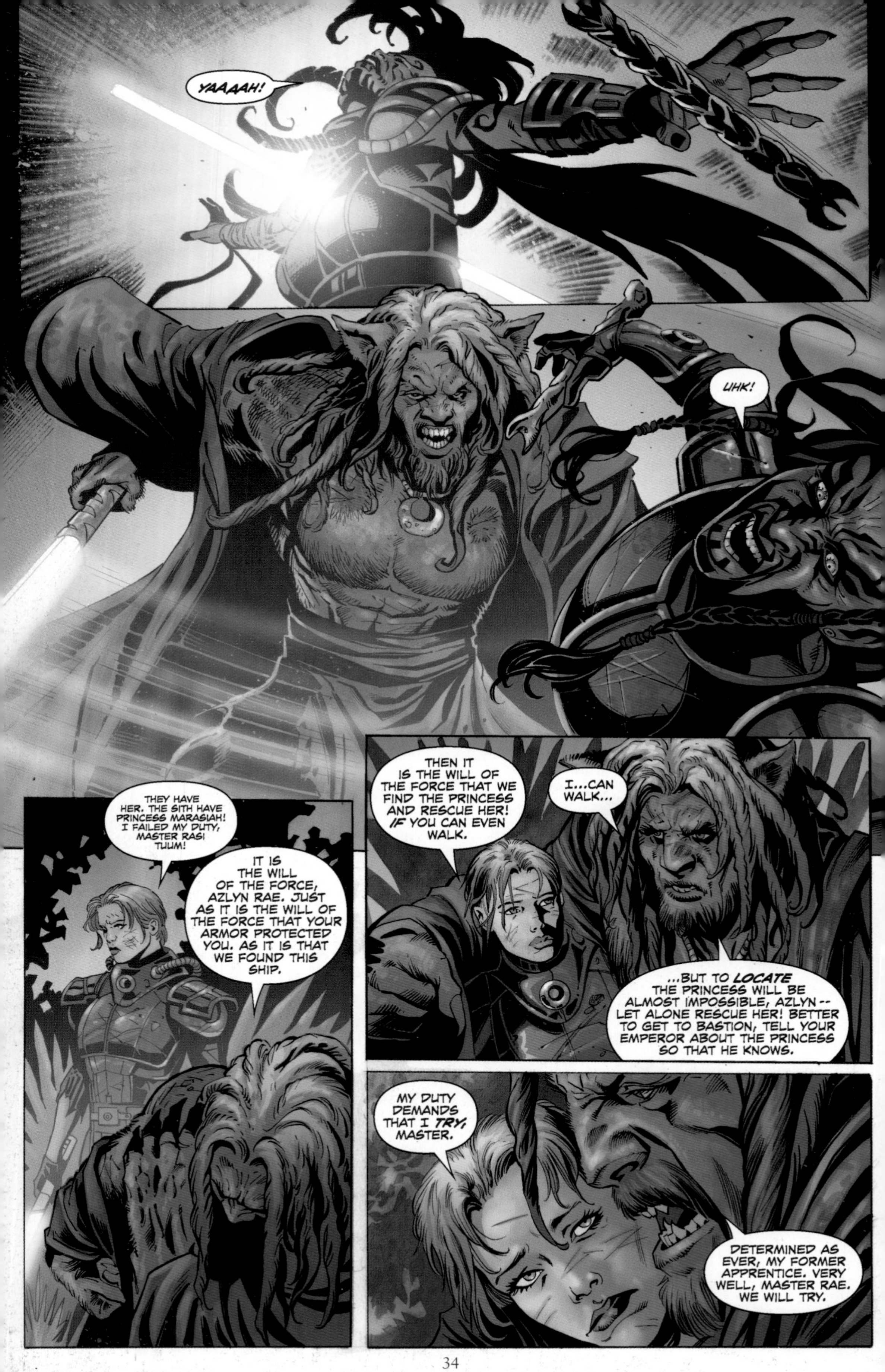
YAAAAH!
UHK!
THEY HAVE HER. THE SITH HAVE PRINCESS MARASIAH! I FAILED MY DUTY, MASTER RASI TUUM!
IT IS THE WILL OF THE FORCE, AZLYN RAE. JUST AS IT IS THE WILL OF THE FORCE THAT YOUR ARMOR PROTECTED YOU. AS IT IS THAT WE FOUND THIS SHIP.
THEN IT IS THE WILL OF THE FORCE THAT WE FIND THE PRINCESS AND RESCUE HER! IF YOU CAN EVEN WALK.
I...CAN WALK...
...BUT TO LOCATE THE PRINCESS WILL BE ALMOST IMPOSSIBLE, AZLYN -- LET ALONE RESCUE HER! BETTER TO GET TO BASTION, TELL YOUR EMPEROR ABOUT THE PRINCESS SO THAT HE KNOWS.
MY DUTY DEMANDS THAT I TRY, MASTER.
DETERMINED AS EVER, MY FORMER APPRENTICE. VERY WELL, MASTER RAE. WE WILL TRY.

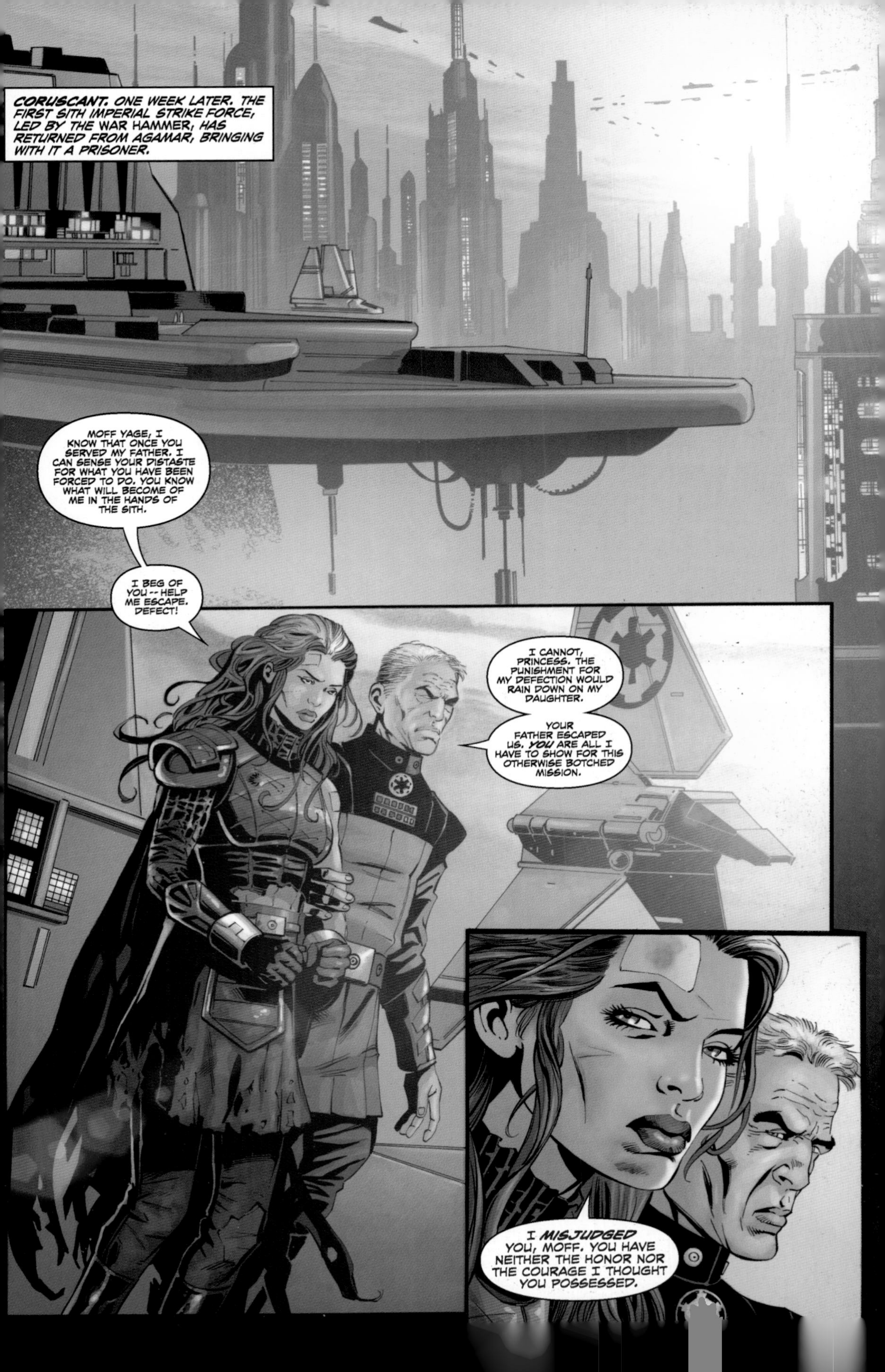
CORUSCANT. ONE WEEK LATER. THE FIRST SITH IMPERIAL STRIKE FORCE, LED BY THE WAR HAMMER, HAS RETURNED FROM AGAMAR, BRINGING WITH IT A PRISONER.
MOFF YAGE, I KNOW THAT ONCE YOU SERVED MY FATHER. I CAN SENSE YOUR DISTASTE FOR WHAT YOU HAVE BEEN FORCED TO DO. YOU KNOW WHAT WILL BECOME OF ME IN THE HANDS OF THE SITH.
I BEG OF YOU -- HELP ME ESCAPE. DEFECT!
I CANNOT, PRINCESS. THE PUNISHMENT FOR MY DEFECTION WOULD RAIN DOWN ON MY DAUGHTER.
YOUR FATHER ESCAPED US. YOU ARE ALL I HAVE TO SHOW FOR THIS OTHERWISE BOTCHED MISSION.
I MISJUDGED YOU, MOFF. YOU HAVE NEITHER THE HONOR NOR THE COURAGE I THOUGHT YOU POSSESSED.

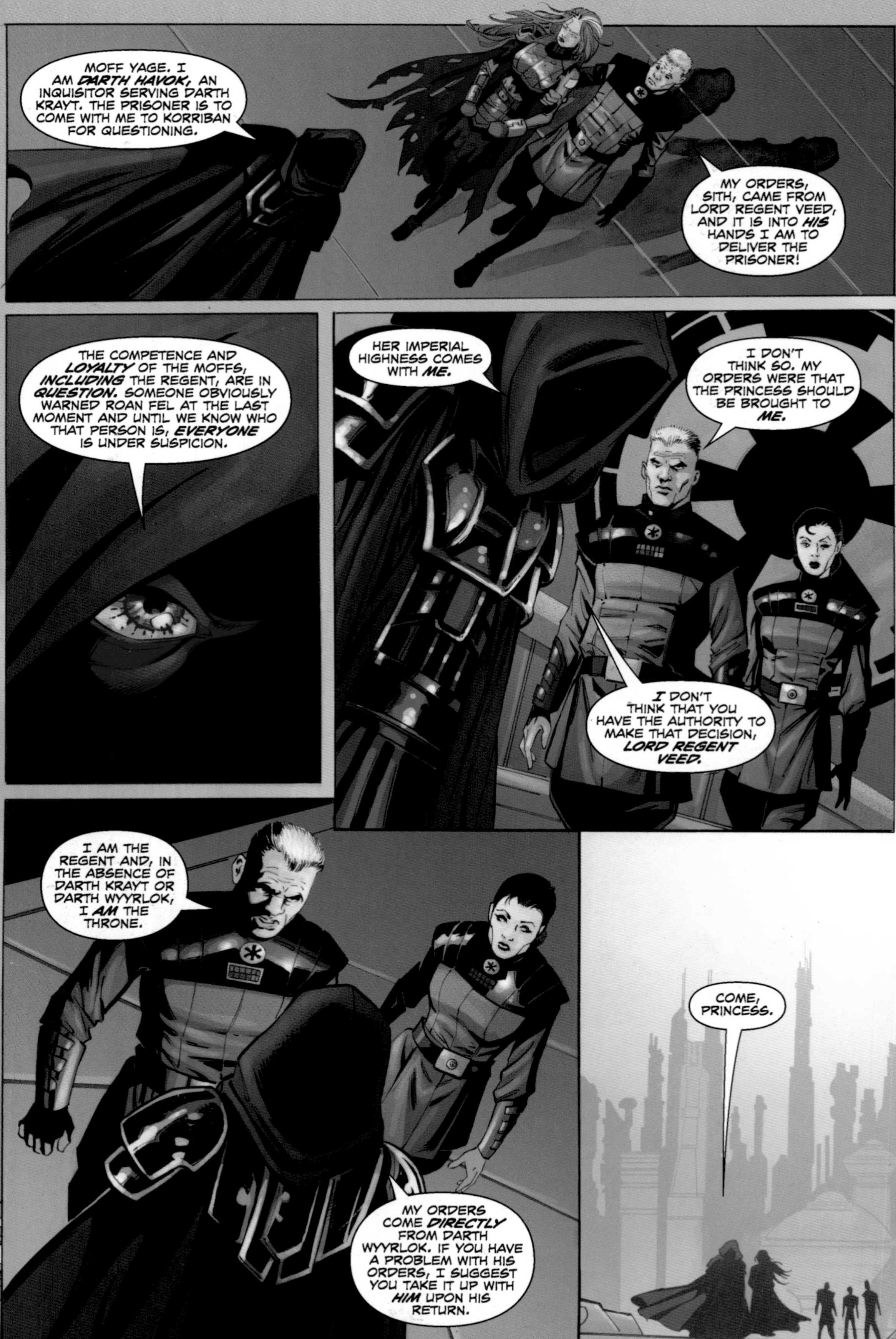
MOFF YAGE. I AM DARTH HAVOK, AN INQUISITOR SERVING DARTH KRAYT. THE PRISONER IS TO COME WITH ME TO KORRIBAN FOR QUESTIONING.
MY ORDERS, SITH, CAME FROM LORD REGENT VEED, AND IT IS INTO HIS HANDS I AM TO DELIVER THE PRISONER!
THE COMPETENCE AND LOYALTY OF THE MOFFS, INCLUDING THE REGENT, ARE IN QUESTION. SOMEONE OBVIOUSLY WARNED ROAN FEL AT THE LAST MOMENT AND UNTIL WE KNOW WHO THAT PERSON IS, EVERYONE IS UNDER SUSPICION.
HER IMPERIAL HIGHNESS COMES WITH ME.
I DON'T THINK SO. MY ORDERS WERE THAT THE PRINCESS SHOULD BE BROUGHT TO ME.
I DON'T THINK THAT YOU HAVE THE AUTHORITY TO MAKE THAT DECISION, LORD REGENT VEED.
I AM THE REGENT AND, IN THE ABSENCE OF DARTH KRAYT OR DARTH WYYRLOK, I AM THE THRONE.
MY ORDERS COME DIRECTLY FROM DARTH WYYRLOK. IF YOU HAVE A PROBLEM WITH HIS ORDERS, I SUGGEST YOU TAKE IT UP WITH HIM UPON HIS RETURN.
COME, PRINCESS.

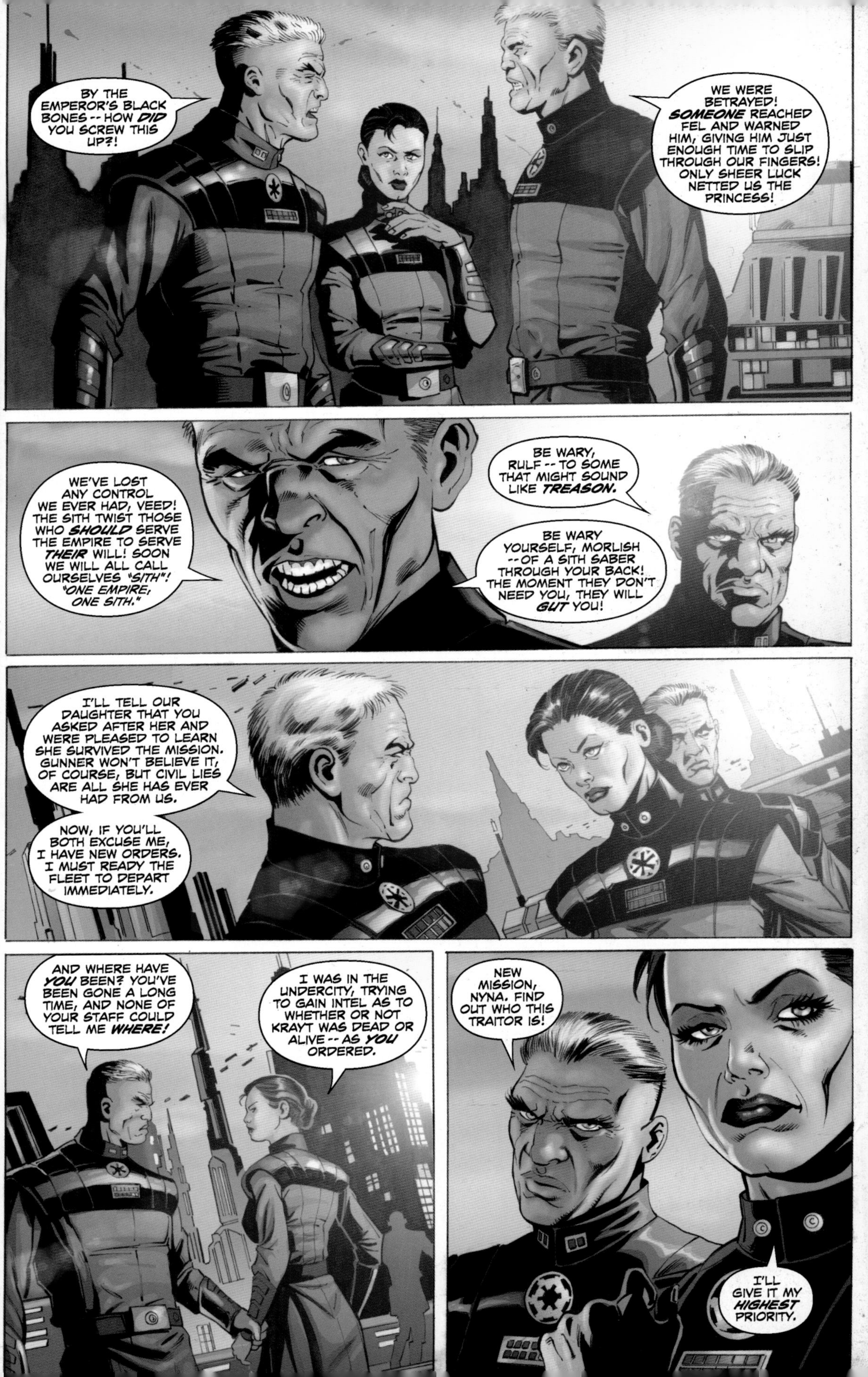
BY THE EMPEROR'S BLACK BONES -- HOW *DID* YOU SCREW THIS UP?!
WE WERE BETRAYED! *SOMEONE* REACHED FEL AND WARNED HIM, GIVING HIM JUST ENOUGH TIME TO SLIP THROUGH OUR FINGERS! ONLY SHEER LUCK NETTED US THE PRINCESS!
WE'VE LOST ANY CONTROL WE EVER HAD, VEED! THE SITH TWIST THOSE WHO *SHOULD* SERVE THE EMPIRE TO SERVE *THEIR* WILL! SOON WE WILL ALL CALL OURSELVES *"SITH"*! *"ONE EMPIRE, ONE SITH."*
BE WARY, RULF -- TO SOME THAT MIGHT SOUND LIKE *TREASON.*
BE WARY YOURSELF, MORLISH -- OF A SITH SABER THROUGH YOUR BACK! THE MOMENT THEY DON'T NEED YOU, THEY WILL *GUT* YOU!
I'LL TELL OUR DAUGHTER THAT YOU ASKED AFTER HER AND WERE PLEASED TO LEARN SHE SURVIVED THE MISSION. GUNNER WON'T BELIEVE IT, OF COURSE, BUT CIVIL LIES ARE ALL SHE HAS EVER HAD FROM US.
NOW, IF YOU'LL BOTH EXCUSE ME, I HAVE NEW ORDERS. I MUST READY THE FLEET TO DEPART IMMEDIATELY.
AND WHERE HAVE *YOU* BEEN? YOU'VE BEEN GONE A LONG TIME, AND NONE OF YOUR STAFF COULD TELL ME *WHERE!*
I WAS IN THE UNDERCITY, TRYING TO GAIN INTEL AS TO WHETHER OR NOT KRAYT WAS DEAD OR ALIVE -- AS *YOU* ORDERED.
NEW MISSION, NYNA. FIND OUT WHO THIS TRAITOR IS!
I'LL GIVE IT MY *HIGHEST* PRIORITY.

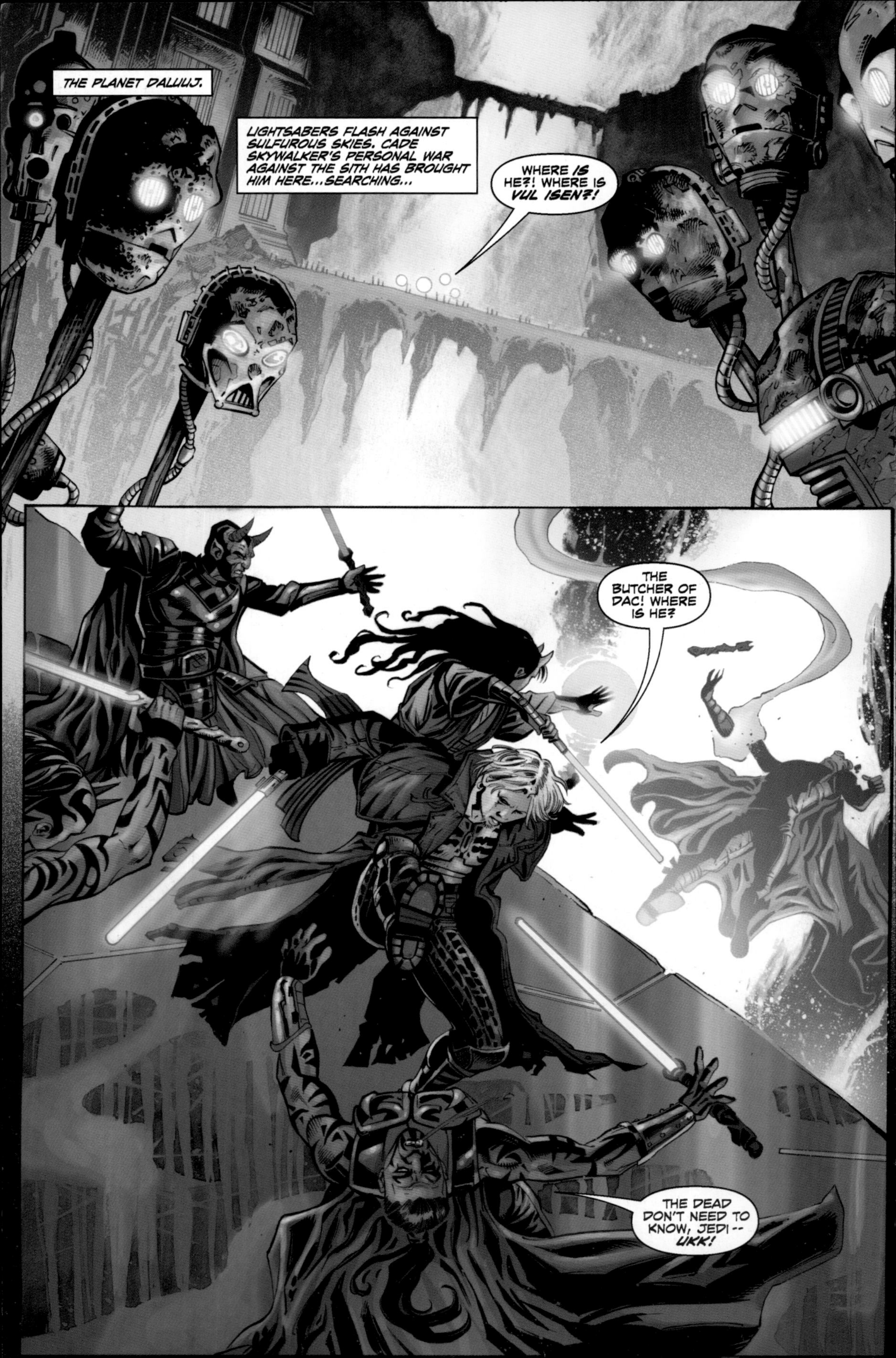
THE PLANET DALUUJ.
LIGHTSABERS FLASH AGAINST SULFUROUS SKIES. CADE SKYWALKER'S PERSONAL WAR AGAINST THE SITH HAS BROUGHT HIM HERE...SEARCHING...
WHERE IS HE?! WHERE IS VUL ISEN?!
THE BUTCHER OF DAC! WHERE IS HE?
THE DEAD DON'T NEED TO KNOW, JEDI -- UKK!

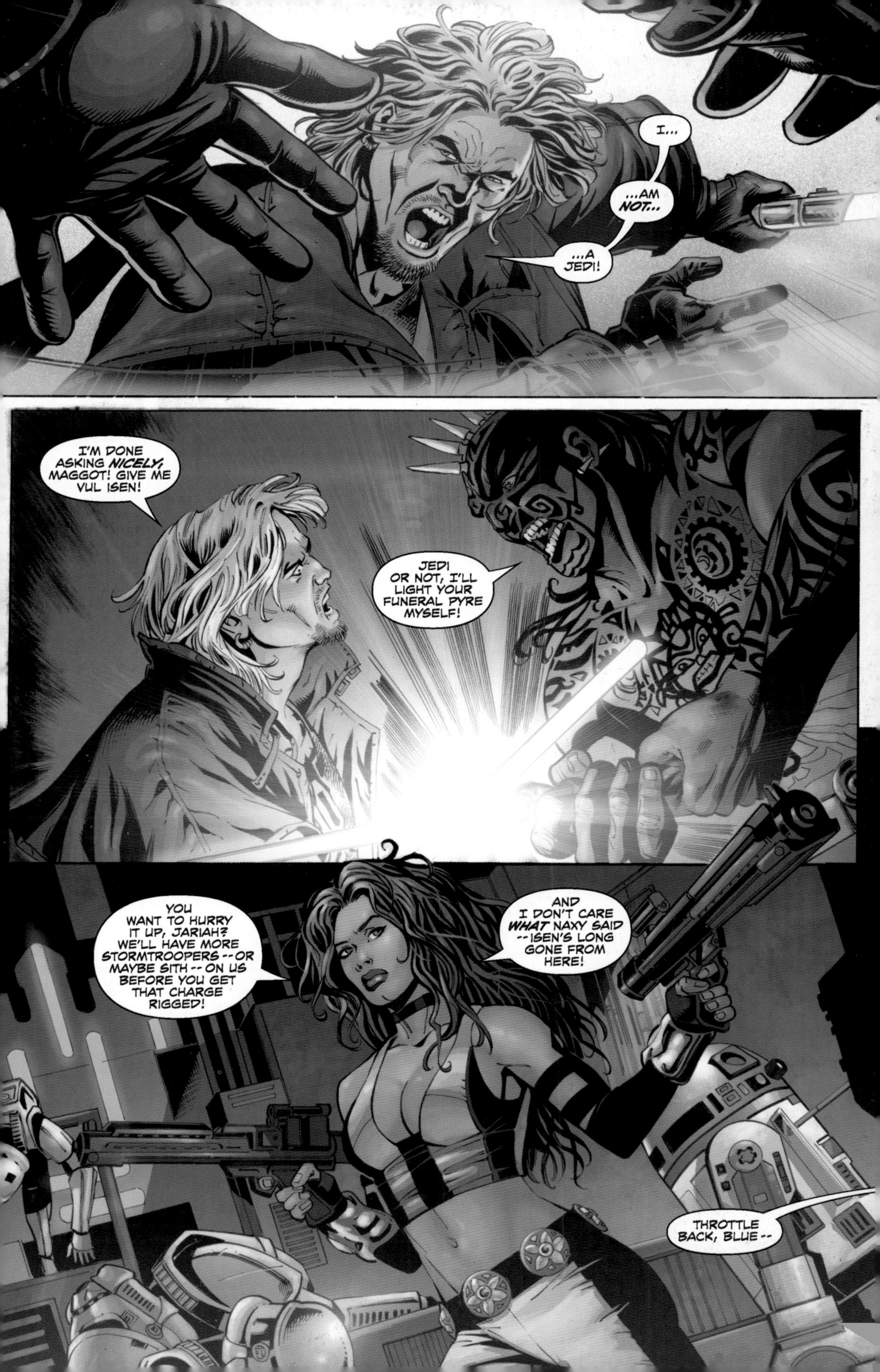
I...
...AM NOT...
...A JEDI!
I'M DONE ASKING NICELY, MAGGOT! GIVE ME VUL ISEN!
JEDI OR NOT, I'LL LIGHT YOUR FUNERAL PYRE MYSELF!
YOU WANT TO HURRY IT UP, JARIAH? WE'LL HAVE MORE STORMTROOPERS --OR MAYBE SITH-- ON US BEFORE YOU GET THAT CHARGE RIGGED!
AND I DON'T CARE WHAT NAXY SAID --ISEN'S LONG GONE FROM HERE!
THROTTLE BACK, BLUE--

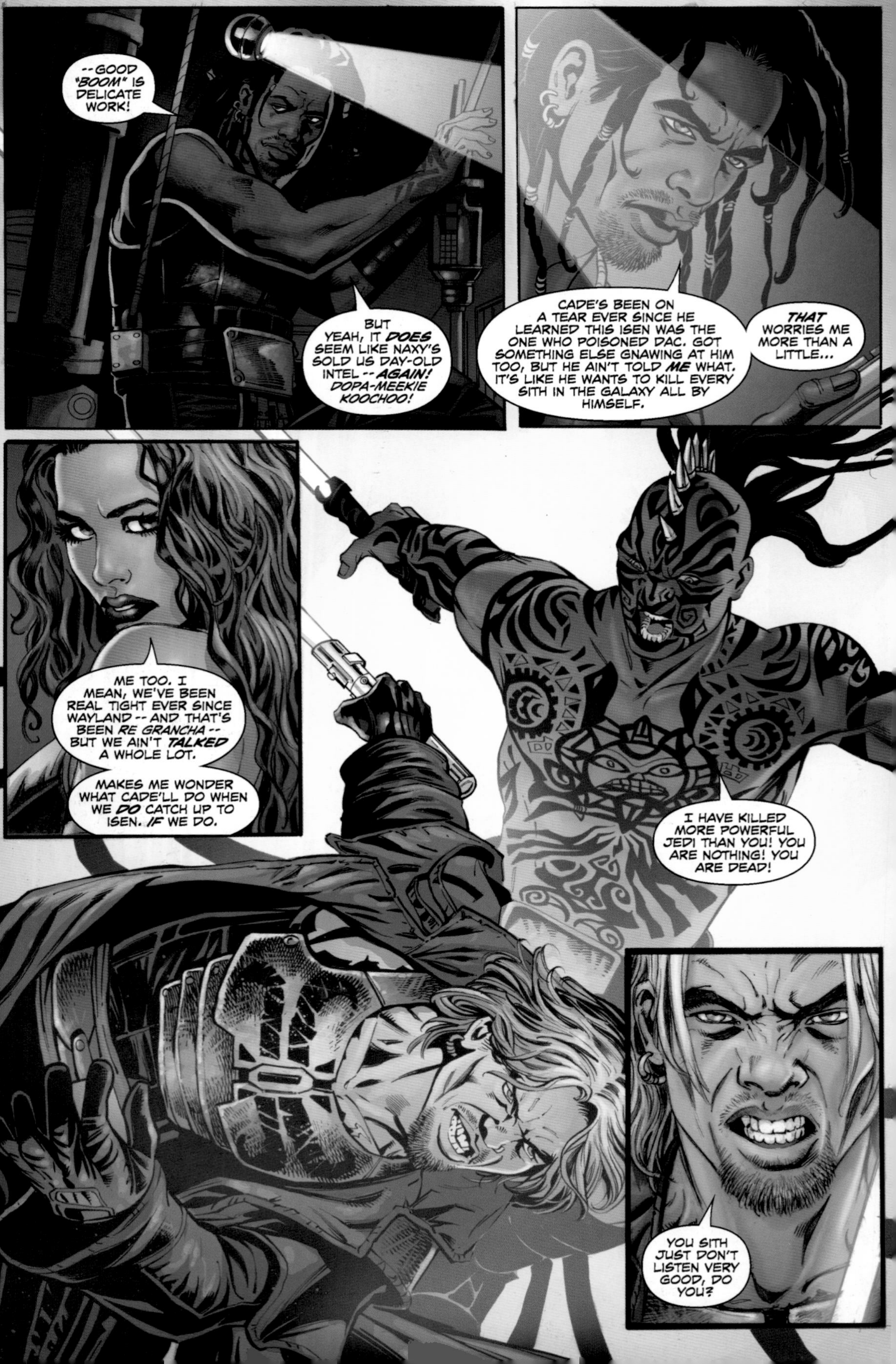
--GOOD "BOOM" IS DELICATE WORK!
BUT YEAH, IT DOES SEEM LIKE NAXY'S SOLD US DAY-OLD INTEL --AGAIN! DOPA-MEEKIE KOOCHOO!
CADE'S BEEN ON A TEAR EVER SINCE HE LEARNED THIS ISEN WAS THE ONE WHO POISONED DAC. GOT SOMETHING ELSE GNAWING AT HIM TOO, BUT HE AIN'T TOLD ME WHAT. IT'S LIKE HE WANTS TO KILL EVERY SITH IN THE GALAXY ALL BY HIMSELF.
THAT WORRIES ME MORE THAN A LITTLE...
ME TOO. I MEAN, WE'VE BEEN REAL TIGHT EVER SINCE WAYLAND -- AND THAT'S BEEN RE GRANCHA -- BUT WE AIN'T TALKED A WHOLE LOT.
MAKES ME WONDER WHAT CADE'LL DO WHEN WE DO CATCH UP TO ISEN. IF WE DO.
I HAVE KILLED MORE POWERFUL JEDI THAN YOU! YOU ARE NOTHING! YOU ARE DEAD!
YOU SITH JUST DON'T LISTEN VERY GOOD, DO YOU?

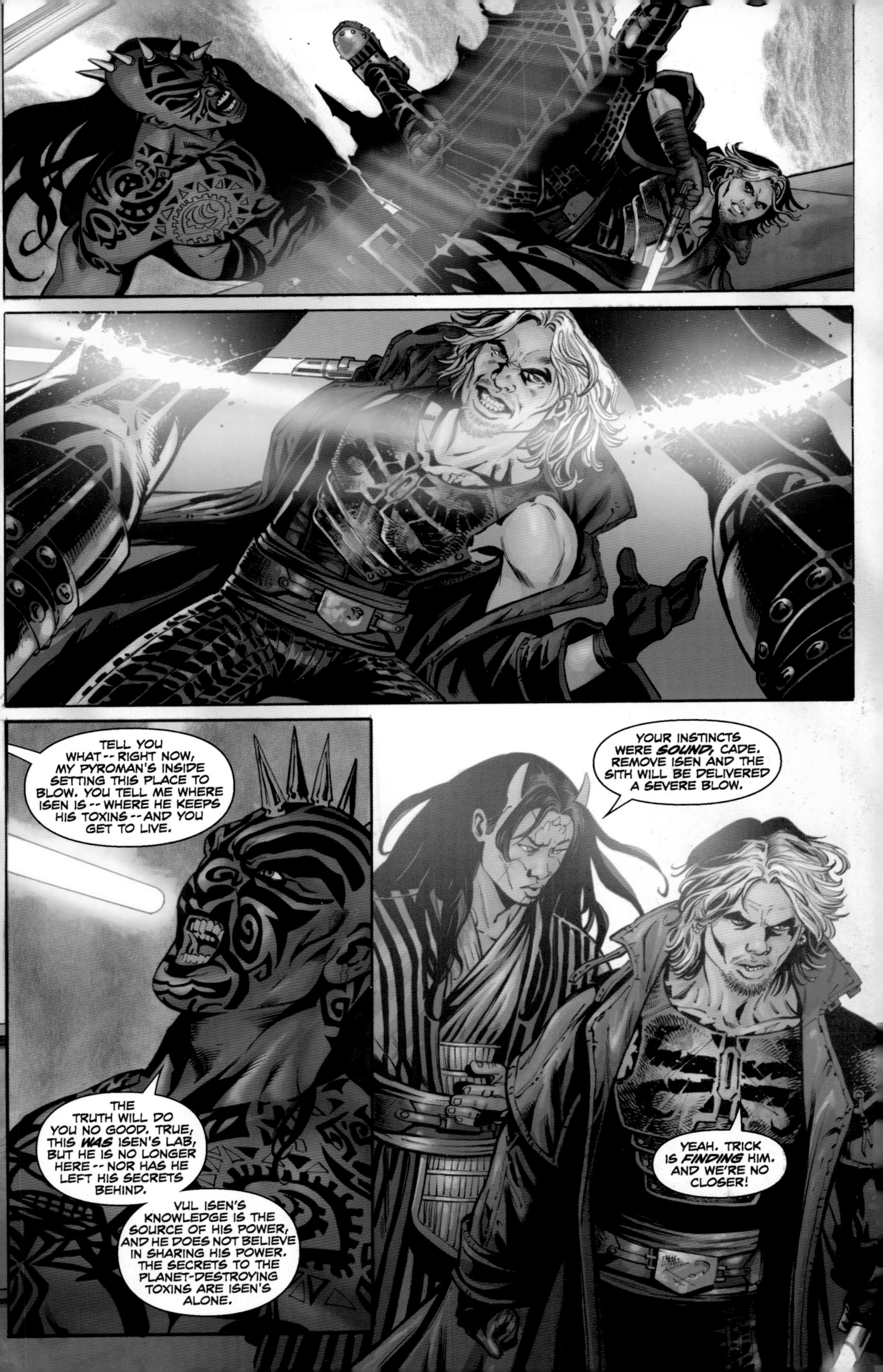
TELL YOU WHAT -- RIGHT NOW, MY PYROMAN'S INSIDE SETTING THIS PLACE TO BLOW. YOU TELL ME WHERE ISEN IS -- WHERE HE KEEPS HIS TOXINS -- AND YOU GET TO LIVE.
YOUR INSTINCTS WERE SOUND, CADE. REMOVE ISEN AND THE SITH WILL BE DELIVERED A SEVERE BLOW.
THE TRUTH WILL DO YOU NO GOOD. TRUE, THIS WAS ISEN'S LAB, BUT HE IS NO LONGER HERE -- NOR HAS HE LEFT HIS SECRETS BEHIND.
VUL ISEN'S KNOWLEDGE IS THE SOURCE OF HIS POWER, AND HE DOES NOT BELIEVE IN SHARING HIS POWER. THE SECRETS TO THE PLANET-DESTROYING TOXINS ARE ISEN'S ALONE.
YEAH. TRICK IS FINDING HIM. AND WE'RE NO CLOSER!

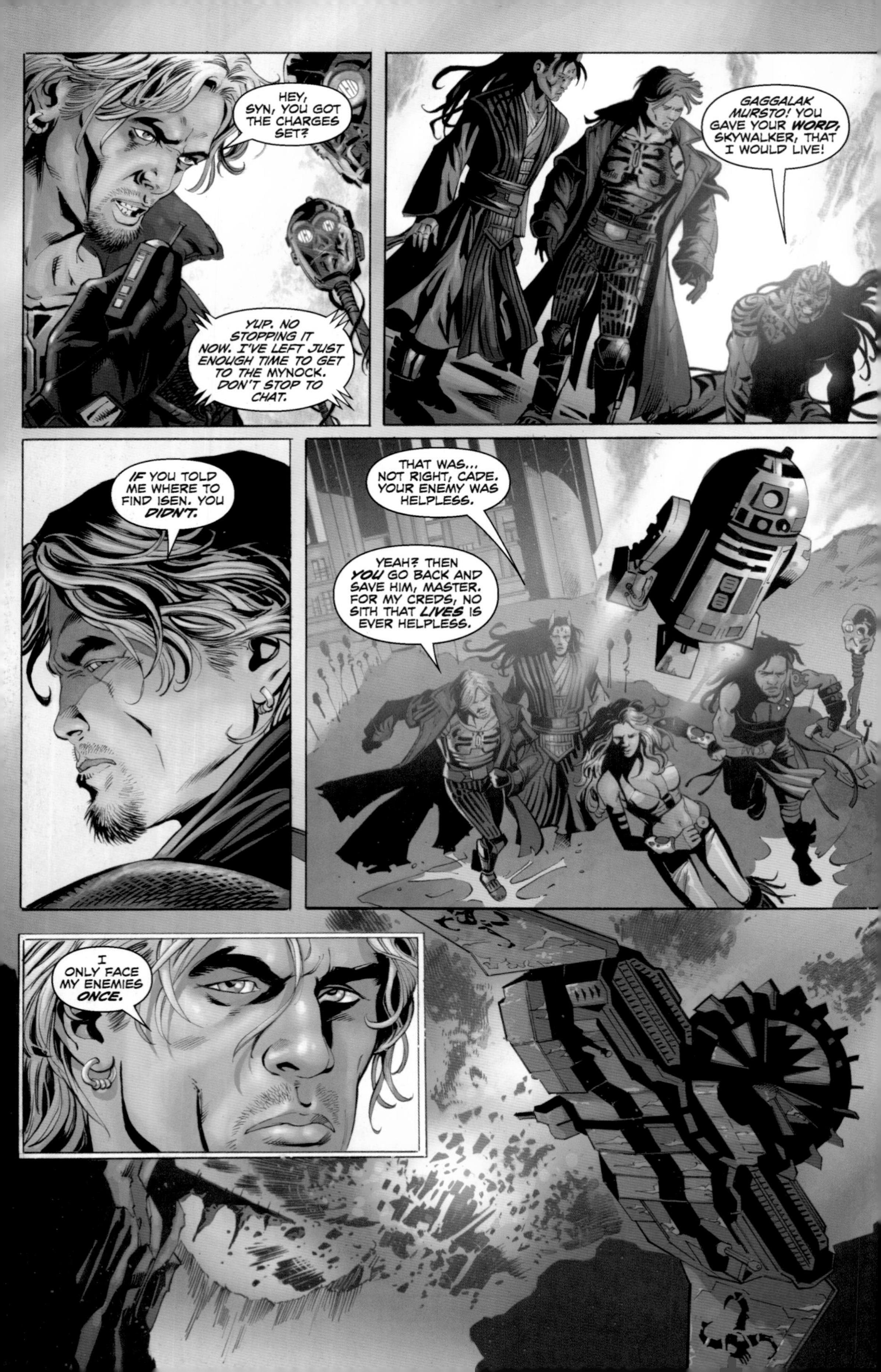
HEY, SYN, YOU GOT THE CHARGES SET?
YUP. NO STOPPING IT NOW. I'VE LEFT JUST ENOUGH TIME TO GET TO THE MYNOCK. DON'T STOP TO CHAT.
GAGGALAK MURSTO! YOU GAVE YOUR WORD, SKYWALKER, THAT I WOULD LIVE!
IF YOU TOLD ME WHERE TO FIND ISEN. YOU DIDN'T.
THAT WAS... NOT RIGHT, CADE. YOUR ENEMY WAS HELPLESS.
YEAH? THEN YOU GO BACK AND SAVE HIM, MASTER. FOR MY CREDS, NO SITH THAT LIVES IS EVER HELPLESS.
I ONLY FACE MY ENEMIES ONCE.

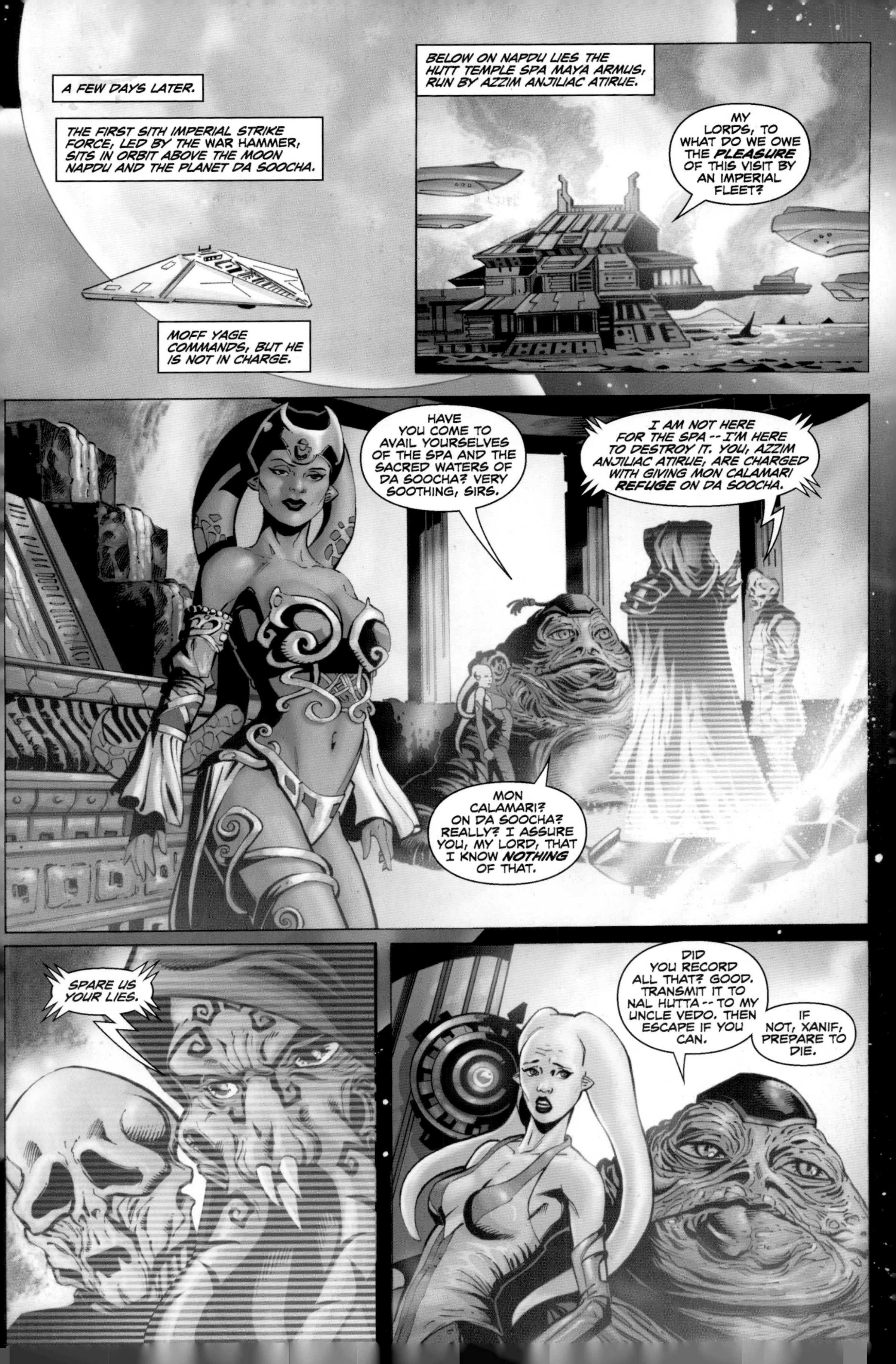
A FEW DAYS LATER.
THE FIRST SITH IMPERIAL STRIKE FORCE, LED BY THE WAR HAMMER, SITS IN ORBIT ABOVE THE MOON NAPDU AND THE PLANET DA SOOCHA.
MOFF YAGE COMMANDS, BUT HE IS NOT IN CHARGE.
BELOW ON NAPDU LIES THE HUTT TEMPLE SPA MAYA ARMUS, RUN BY AZZIM ANJILIAC ATIRUE.
MY LORDS, TO WHAT DO WE OWE THE PLEASURE OF THIS VISIT BY AN IMPERIAL FLEET?
HAVE YOU COME TO AVAIL YOURSELVES OF THE SPA AND THE SACRED WATERS OF DA SOOCHA? VERY SOOTHING, SIRS.
I AM NOT HERE FOR THE SPA -- I'M HERE TO DESTROY IT. YOU, AZZIM ANJILIAC ATIRUE, ARE CHARGED WITH GIVING MON CALAMARI REFUGE ON DA SOOCHA.
MON CALAMARI? ON DA SOOCHA? REALLY? I ASSURE YOU, MY LORD, THAT I KNOW NOTHING OF THAT.
SPARE US YOUR LIES.
DID YOU RECORD ALL THAT? GOOD. TRANSMIT IT TO NAL HUTTA -- TO MY UNCLE VEDO. THEN ESCAPE IF YOU CAN.
IF NOT, XANIF, PREPARE TO DIE.

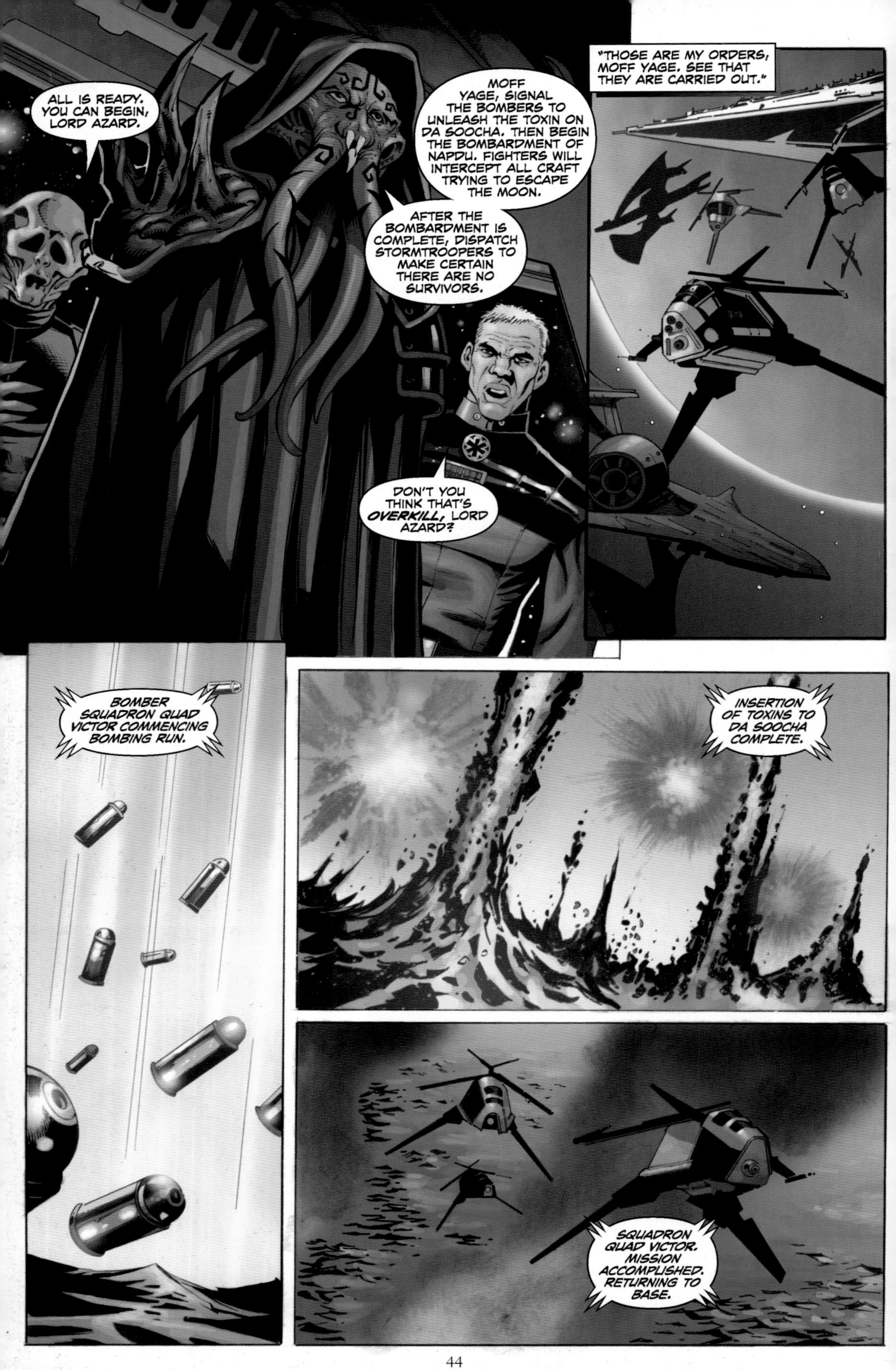
ALL IS READY. YOU CAN BEGIN, LORD AZARD.
MOFF YAGE, SIGNAL THE BOMBERS TO UNLEASH THE TOXIN ON DA SOOCHA. THEN BEGIN THE BOMBARDMENT OF NAPDU. FIGHTERS WILL INTERCEPT ALL CRAFT TRYING TO ESCAPE THE MOON.
AFTER THE BOMBARDMENT IS COMPLETE, DISPATCH STORMTROOPERS TO MAKE CERTAIN THERE ARE NO SURVIVORS.
DON'T YOU THINK THAT'S OVERKILL, LORD AZARD?
"THOSE ARE MY ORDERS, MOFF YAGE. SEE THAT THEY ARE CARRIED OUT."
BOMBER SQUADRON QUAD VICTOR COMMENCING BOMBING RUN.
INSERTION OF TOXINS TO DA SOOCHA COMPLETE.
SQUADRON QUAD VICTOR. MISSION ACCOMPLISHED. RETURNING TO BASE.

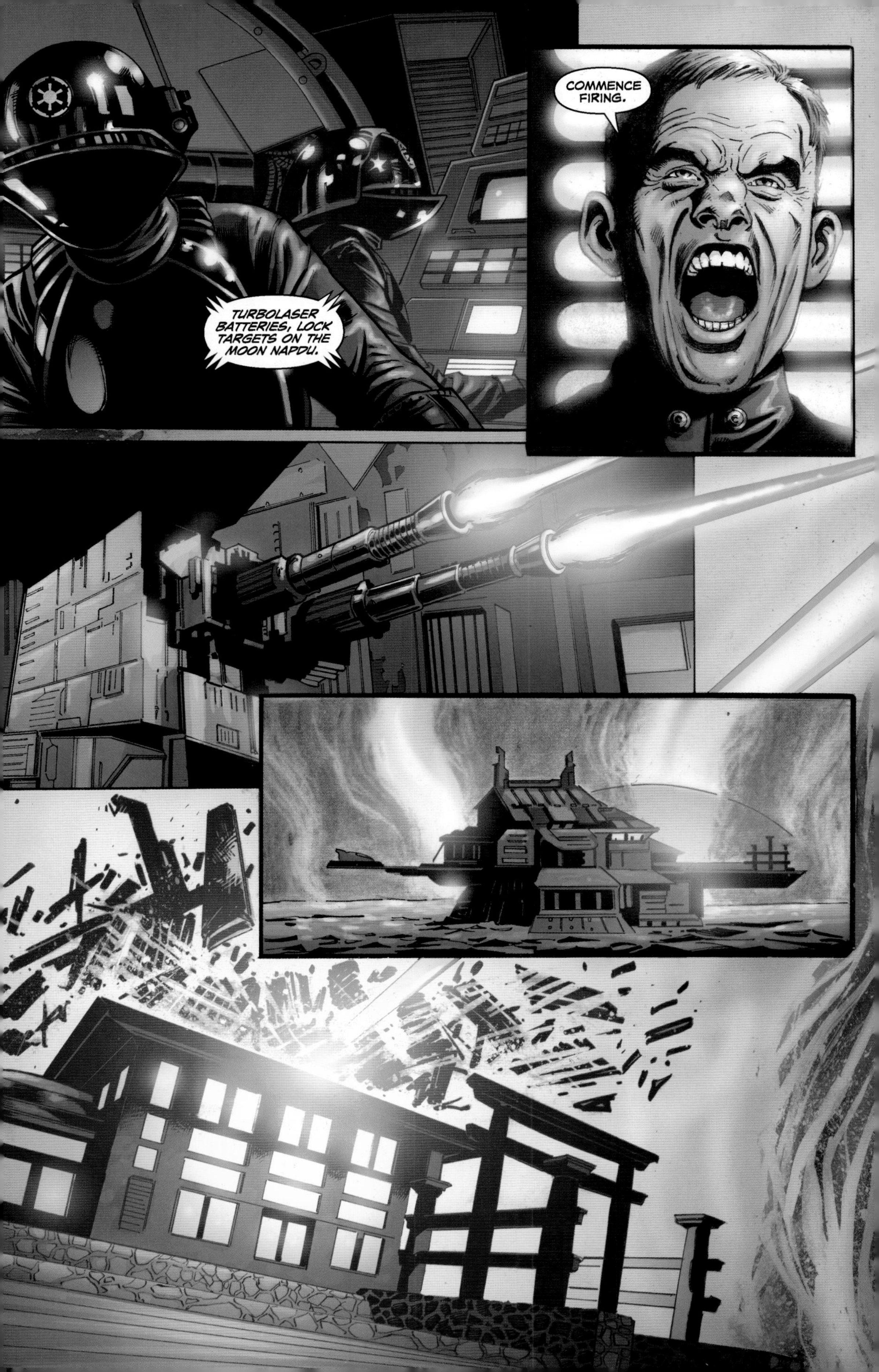
TURBOLASER BATTERIES, LOCK TARGETS ON THE MOON NAPDU.
COMMENCE FIRING.

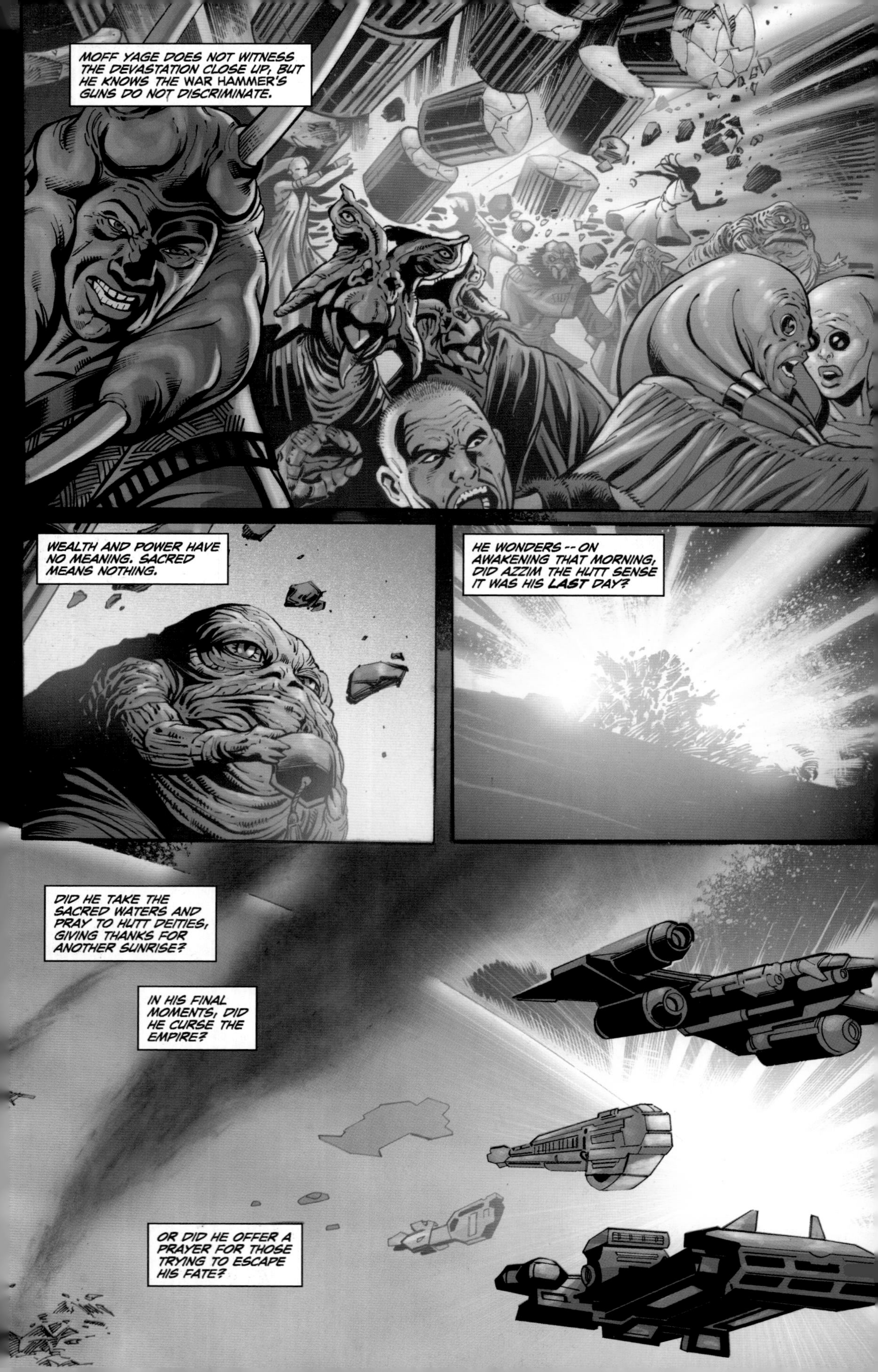
MOFF YAGE DOES NOT WITNESS THE DEVASTATION CLOSE UP, BUT HE KNOWS THE WAR HAMMER'S GUNS DO NOT DISCRIMINATE.
WEALTH AND POWER HAVE NO MEANING. SACRED MEANS NOTHING.
HE WONDERS -- ON AWAKENING THAT MORNING, DID AZZIM THE HUTT SENSE IT WAS HIS LAST DAY?
DID HE TAKE THE SACRED WATERS AND PRAY TO HUTT DEITIES, GIVING THANKS FOR ANOTHER SUNRISE?
IN HIS FINAL MOMENTS, DID HE CURSE THE EMPIRE?
OR DID HE OFFER A PRAYER FOR THOSE TRYING TO ESCAPE HIS FATE?

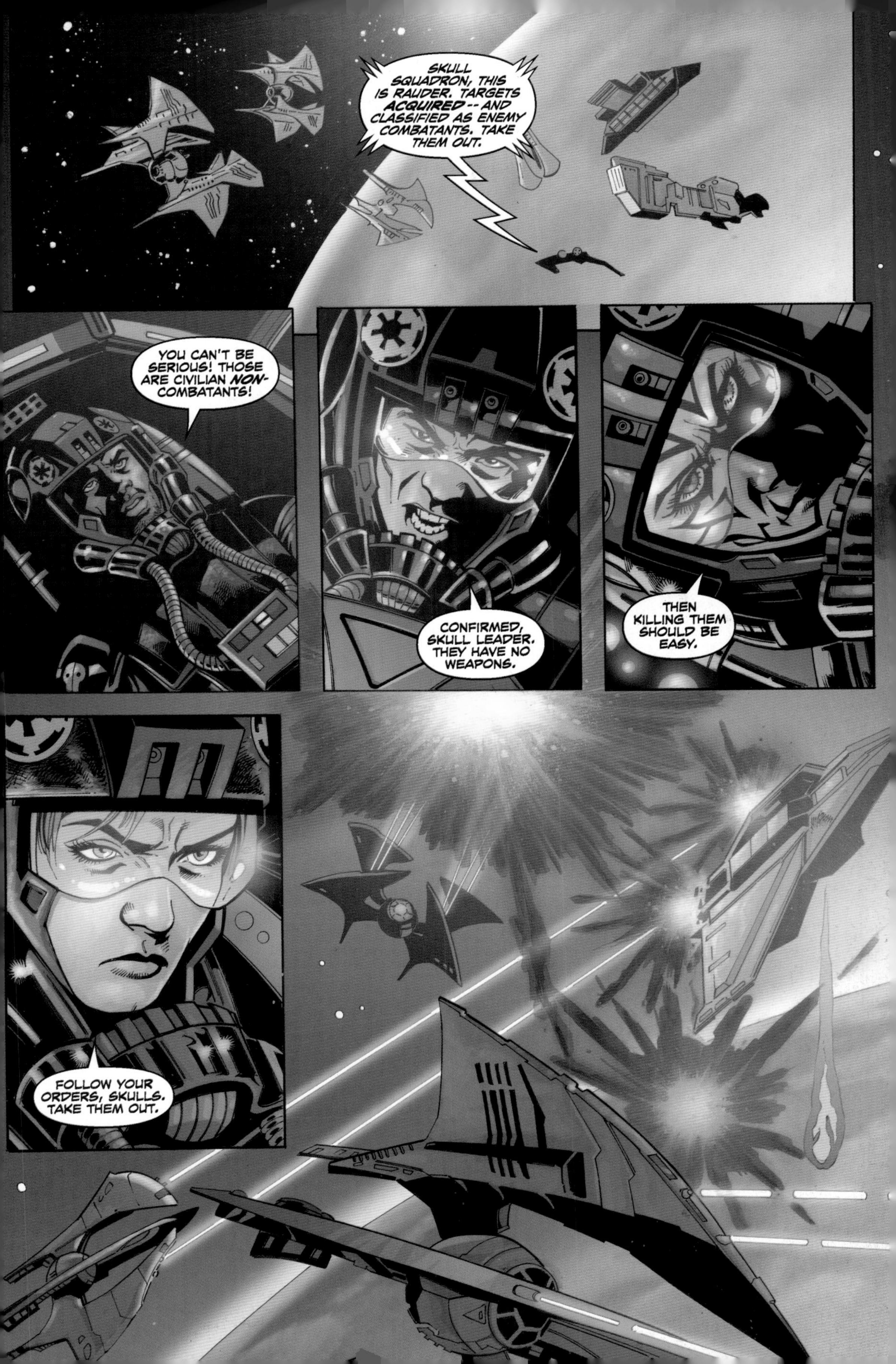
SKULL SQUADRON, THIS IS RAUDER. TARGETS ACQUIRED -- AND CLASSIFIED AS ENEMY COMBATANTS. TAKE THEM OUT.
YOU CAN'T BE SERIOUS! THOSE ARE CIVILIAN NON-COMBATANTS!
CONFIRMED, SKULL LEADER. THEY HAVE NO WEAPONS.
THEN KILLING THEM SHOULD BE EASY.
FOLLOW YOUR ORDERS, SKULLS. TAKE THEM OUT.

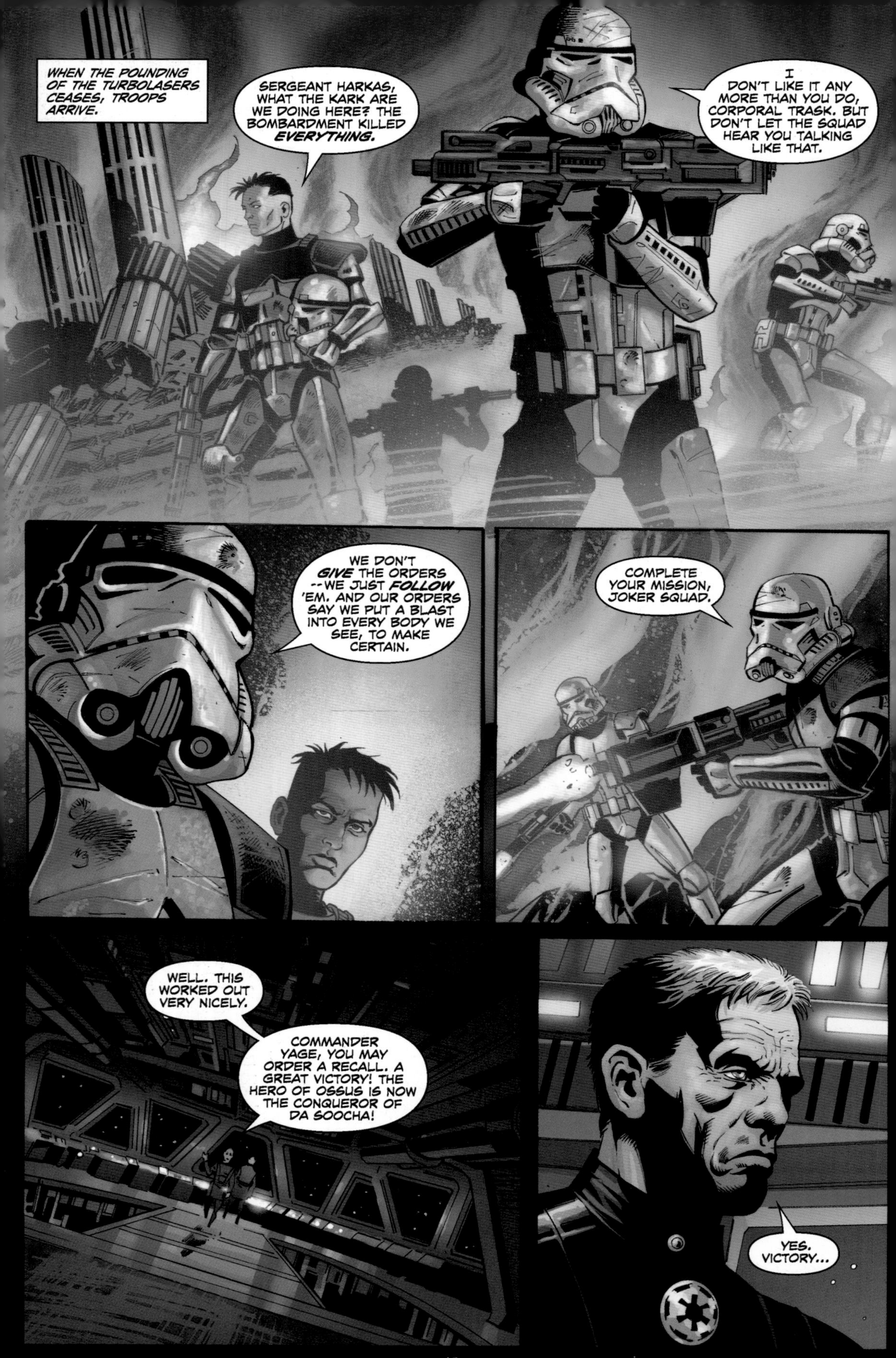
WHEN THE POUNDING OF THE TURBOLASERS CEASES, TROOPS ARRIVE.
SERGEANT HARKAS, WHAT THE KARK ARE WE DOING HERE? THE BOMBARDMENT KILLED EVERYTHING.
I DON'T LIKE IT ANY MORE THAN YOU DO, CORPORAL TRASK. BUT DON'T LET THE SQUAD HEAR YOU TALKING LIKE THAT.
WE DON'T GIVE THE ORDERS --WE JUST FOLLOW 'EM. AND OUR ORDERS SAY WE PUT A BLAST INTO EVERY BODY WE SEE, TO MAKE CERTAIN.
COMPLETE YOUR MISSION, JOKER SQUAD.
WELL. THIS WORKED OUT VERY NICELY.
COMMANDER YAGE, YOU MAY ORDER A RECALL. A GREAT VICTORY! THE HERO OF OSSUS IS NOW THE CONQUEROR OF DA SOOCHA!
YES. VICTORY...

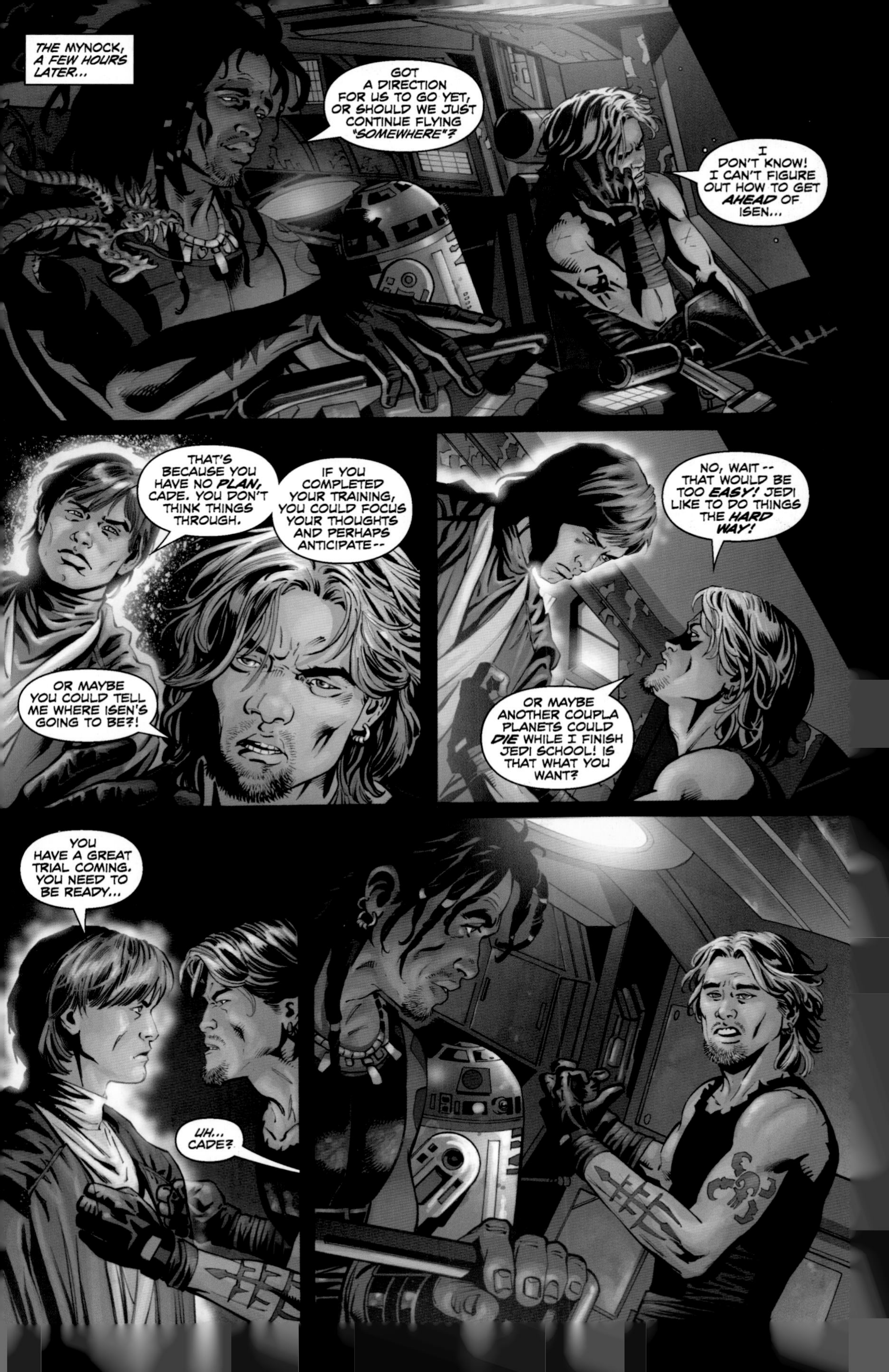
THE MYNOCK, A FEW HOURS LATER...
GOT A DIRECTION FOR US TO GO YET, OR SHOULD WE JUST CONTINUE FLYING "SOMEWHERE"?
I DON'T KNOW! I CAN'T FIGURE OUT HOW TO GET AHEAD OF ISEN...
THAT'S BECAUSE YOU HAVE NO PLAN, CADE. YOU DON'T THINK THINGS THROUGH.
IF YOU COMPLETED YOUR TRAINING, YOU COULD FOCUS YOUR THOUGHTS AND PERHAPS ANTICIPATE--
OR MAYBE YOU COULD TELL ME WHERE ISEN'S GOING TO BE?!
NO, WAIT -- THAT WOULD BE TOO EASY! JEDI LIKE TO DO THINGS THE HARD WAY!
OR MAYBE ANOTHER COUPLA PLANETS COULD DIE WHILE I FINISH JEDI SCHOOL! IS THAT WHAT YOU WANT?
YOU HAVE A GREAT TRIAL COMING. YOU NEED TO BE READY...
UH... CADE?

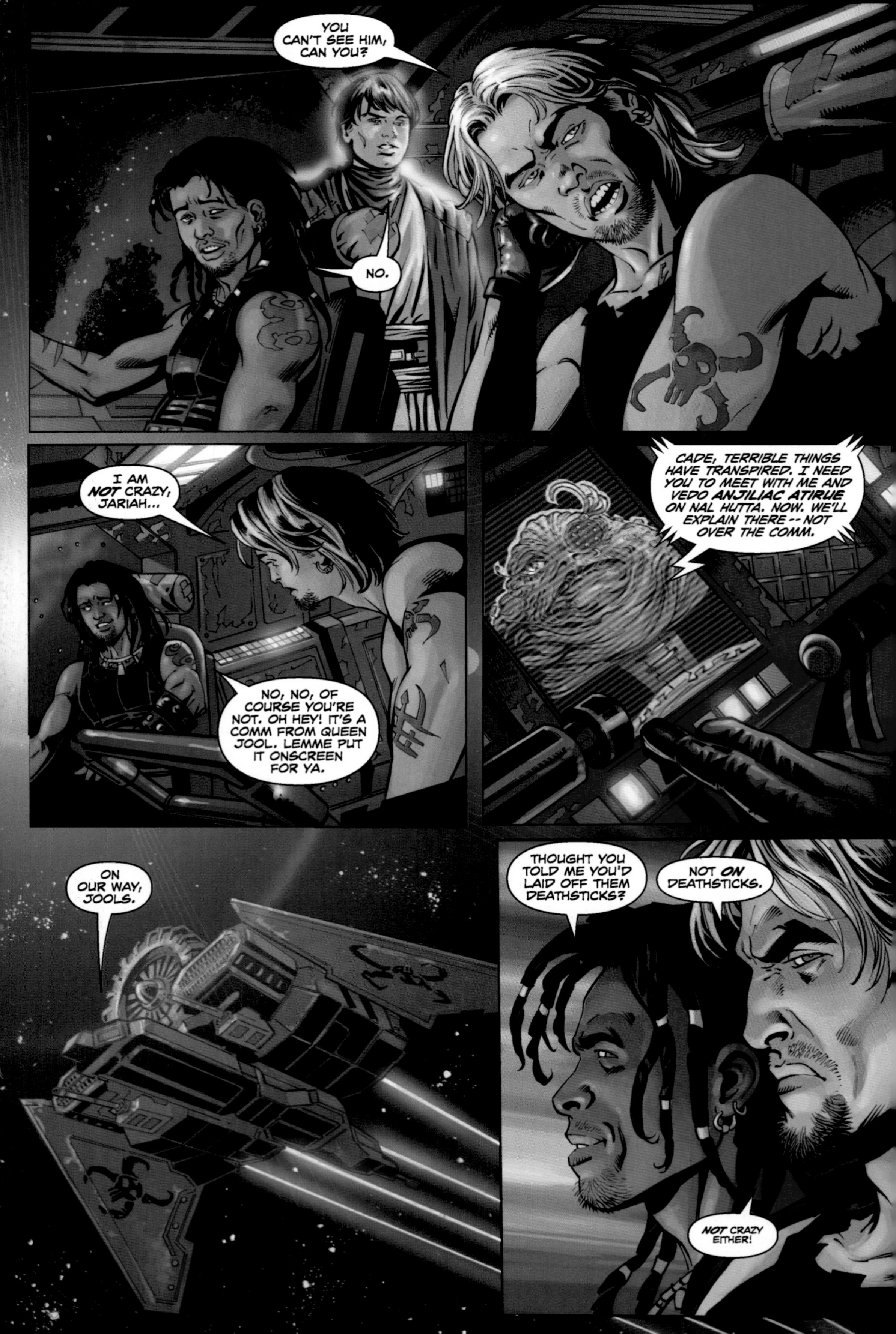
YOU CAN'T SEE HIM, CAN YOU?
NO.
I AM NOT CRAZY, JARIAH...
NO, NO, OF COURSE YOU'RE NOT. OH HEY! IT'S A COMM FROM QUEEN JOOL. LEMME PUT IT ONSCREEN FOR YA.
CADE, TERRIBLE THINGS HAVE TRANSPIRED. I NEED YOU TO MEET WITH ME AND VEDO ANJILIAC ATIRUE ON NAL HUTTA. NOW. WE'LL EXPLAIN THERE -- NOT OVER THE COMM.
ON OUR WAY, JOOLS.
THOUGHT YOU TOLD ME YOU'D LAID OFF THEM DEATHSTICKS?
NOT ON DEATHSTICKS.
NOT CRAZY EITHER!

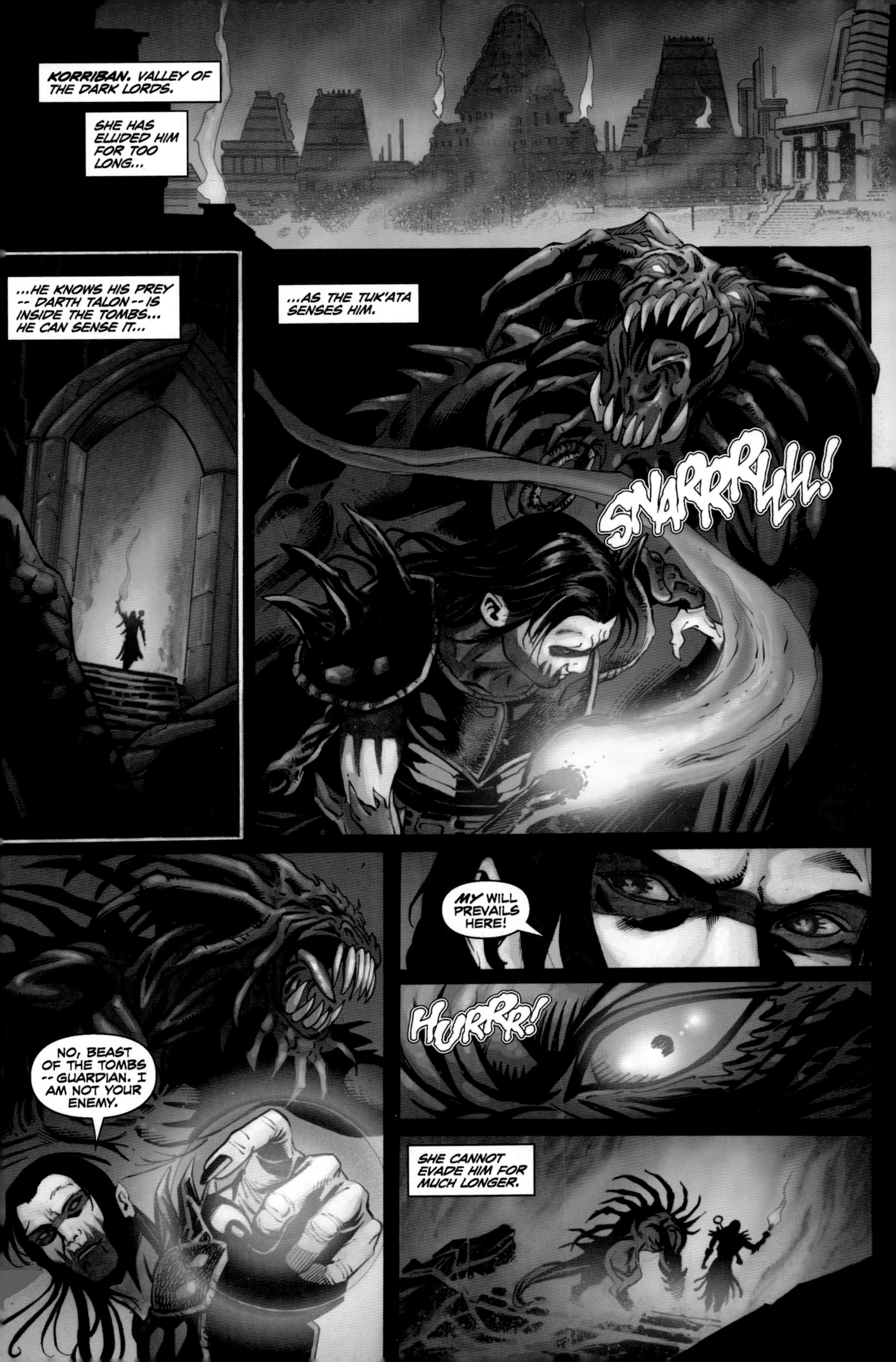
KORRIBAN. VALLEY OF THE DARK LORDS.
SHE HAS ELUDED HIM FOR TOO LONG...
...HE KNOWS HIS PREY -- DARTH TALON -- IS INSIDE THE TOMBS... HE CAN SENSE IT...
...AS THE TUK'ATA SENSES HIM.
SNARRRLLL!
NO, BEAST OF THE TOMBS -- GUARDIAN. I AM NOT YOUR ENEMY.
MY WILL PREVAILS HERE!
HURRR!
SHE CANNOT EVADE HIM FOR MUCH LONGER.

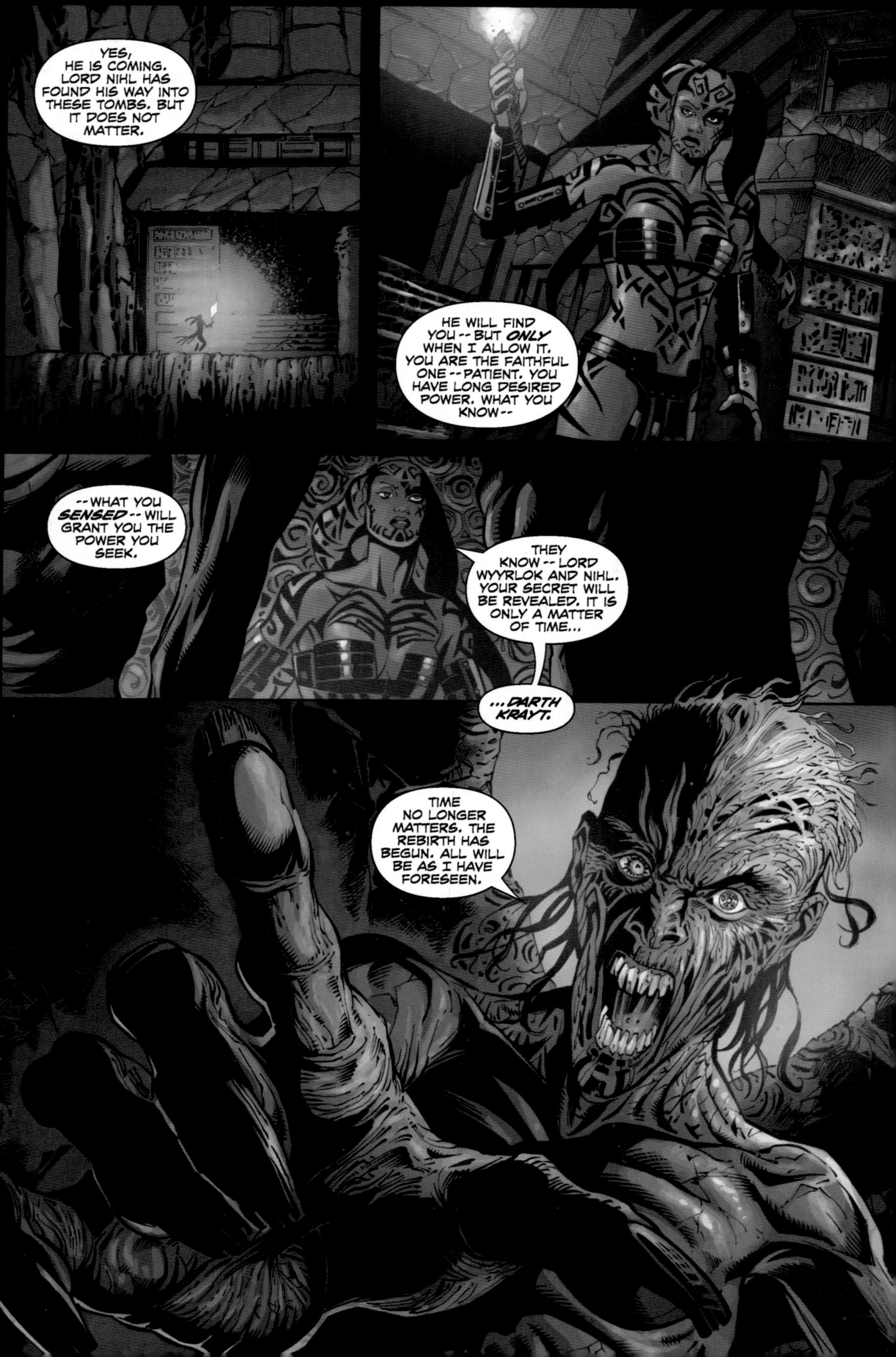
YES, HE IS COMING. LORD NIHL HAS FOUND HIS WAY INTO THESE TOMBS. BUT IT DOES NOT MATTER.
HE WILL FIND YOU--BUT ONLY WHEN I ALLOW IT. YOU ARE THE FAITHFUL ONE--PATIENT. YOU HAVE LONG DESIRED POWER. WHAT YOU KNOW--
--WHAT YOU SENSED--WILL GRANT YOU THE POWER YOU SEEK.
THEY KNOW--LORD WYYRLOK AND NIHL. YOUR SECRET WILL BE REVEALED. IT IS ONLY A MATTER OF TIME...
...DARTH KRAYT.
TIME NO LONGER MATTERS. THE REBIRTH HAS BEGUN. ALL WILL BE AS I HAVE FORESEEN.

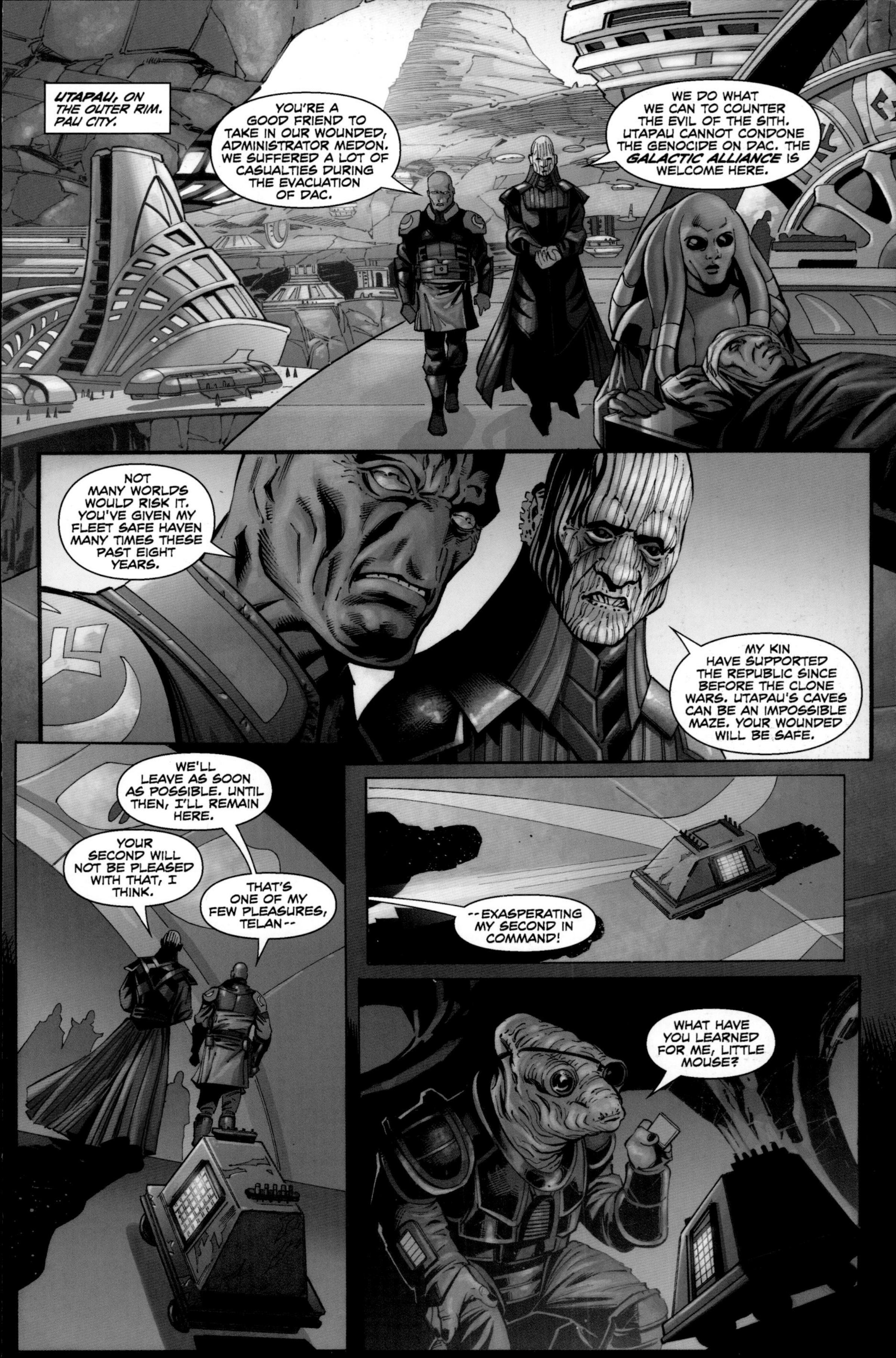
UTAPAU, ON THE OUTER RIM. PAU CITY.
YOU'RE A GOOD FRIEND TO TAKE IN OUR WOUNDED, ADMINISTRATOR MEDON. WE SUFFERED A LOT OF CASUALTIES DURING THE EVACUATION OF DAC.
WE DO WHAT WE CAN TO COUNTER THE EVIL OF THE SITH. UTAPAU CANNOT CONDONE THE GENOCIDE ON DAC. THE GALACTIC ALLIANCE IS WELCOME HERE.
NOT MANY WORLDS WOULD RISK IT. YOU'VE GIVEN MY FLEET SAFE HAVEN MANY TIMES THESE PAST EIGHT YEARS.
MY KIN HAVE SUPPORTED THE REPUBLIC SINCE BEFORE THE CLONE WARS. UTAPAU'S CAVES CAN BE AN IMPOSSIBLE MAZE. YOUR WOUNDED WILL BE SAFE.
WE'LL LEAVE AS SOON AS POSSIBLE. UNTIL THEN, I'LL REMAIN HERE.
YOUR SECOND WILL NOT BE PLEASED WITH THAT, I THINK.
THAT'S ONE OF MY FEW PLEASURES, TELAN--
--EXASPERATING MY SECOND IN COMMAND!
WHAT HAVE YOU LEARNED FOR ME, LITTLE MOUSE?

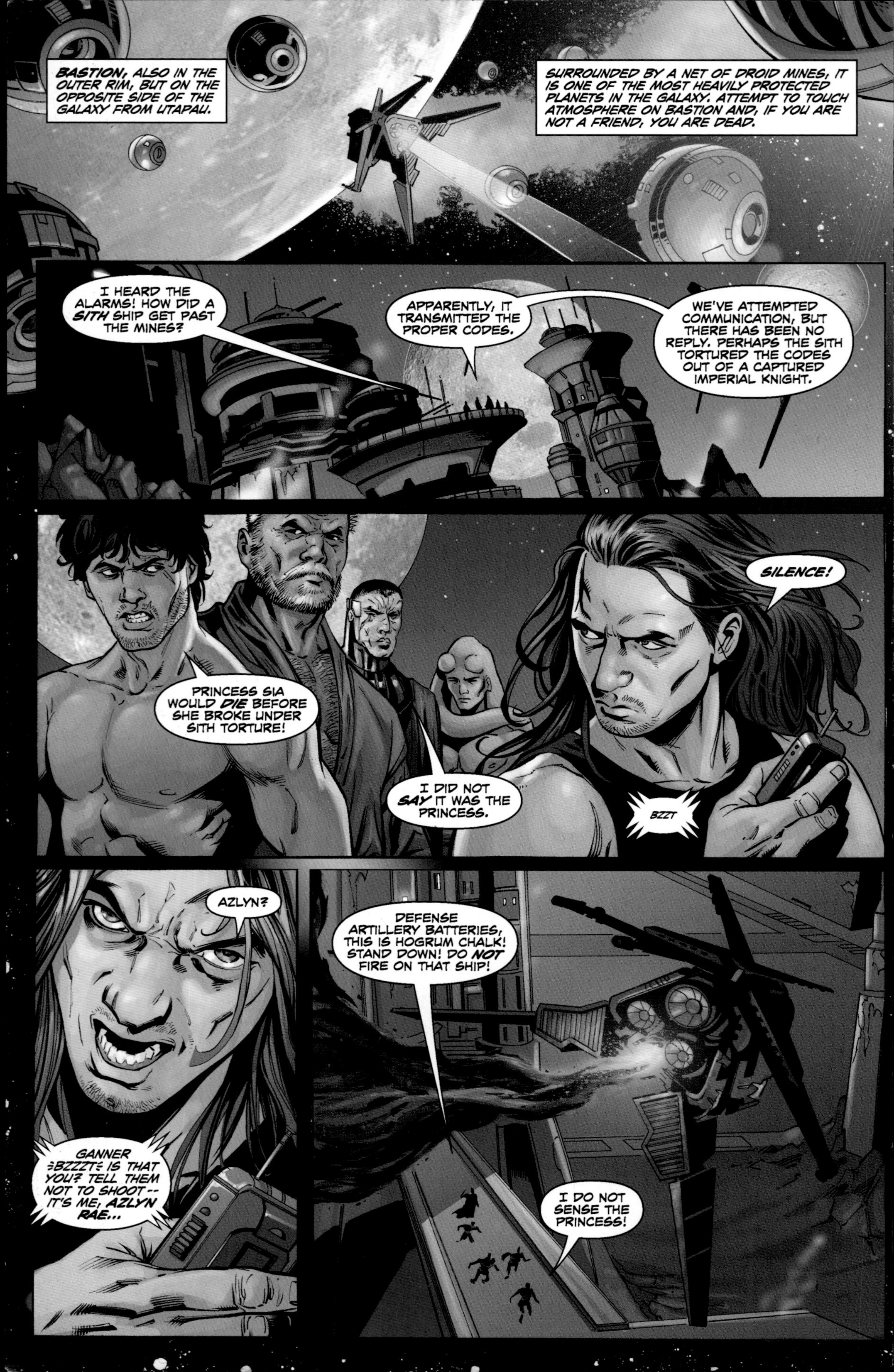
BASTION, ALSO IN THE OUTER RIM, BUT ON THE OPPOSITE SIDE OF THE GALAXY FROM UTAPAU.
SURROUNDED BY A NET OF DROID MINES, IT IS ONE OF THE MOST HEAVILY PROTECTED PLANETS IN THE GALAXY. ATTEMPT TO TOUCH ATMOSPHERE ON BASTION AND, IF YOU ARE NOT A FRIEND, YOU ARE DEAD.
I HEARD THE ALARMS! HOW DID A SITH SHIP GET PAST THE MINES?
APPARENTLY, IT TRANSMITTED THE PROPER CODES.
WE'VE ATTEMPTED COMMUNICATION, BUT THERE HAS BEEN NO REPLY. PERHAPS THE SITH TORTURED THE CODES OUT OF A CAPTURED IMPERIAL KNIGHT.
PRINCESS SIA WOULD DIE BEFORE SHE BROKE UNDER SITH TORTURE!
SILENCE!
I DID NOT SAY IT WAS THE PRINCESS.
BZZT
AZLYN?
GANNER =BZZZT= IS THAT YOU? TELL THEM NOT TO SHOOT-- IT'S ME, AZLYN RAE...
DEFENSE ARTILLERY BATTERIES, THIS IS HOGRUM CHALK! STAND DOWN! DO NOT FIRE ON THAT SHIP!
I DO NOT SENSE THE PRINCESS!

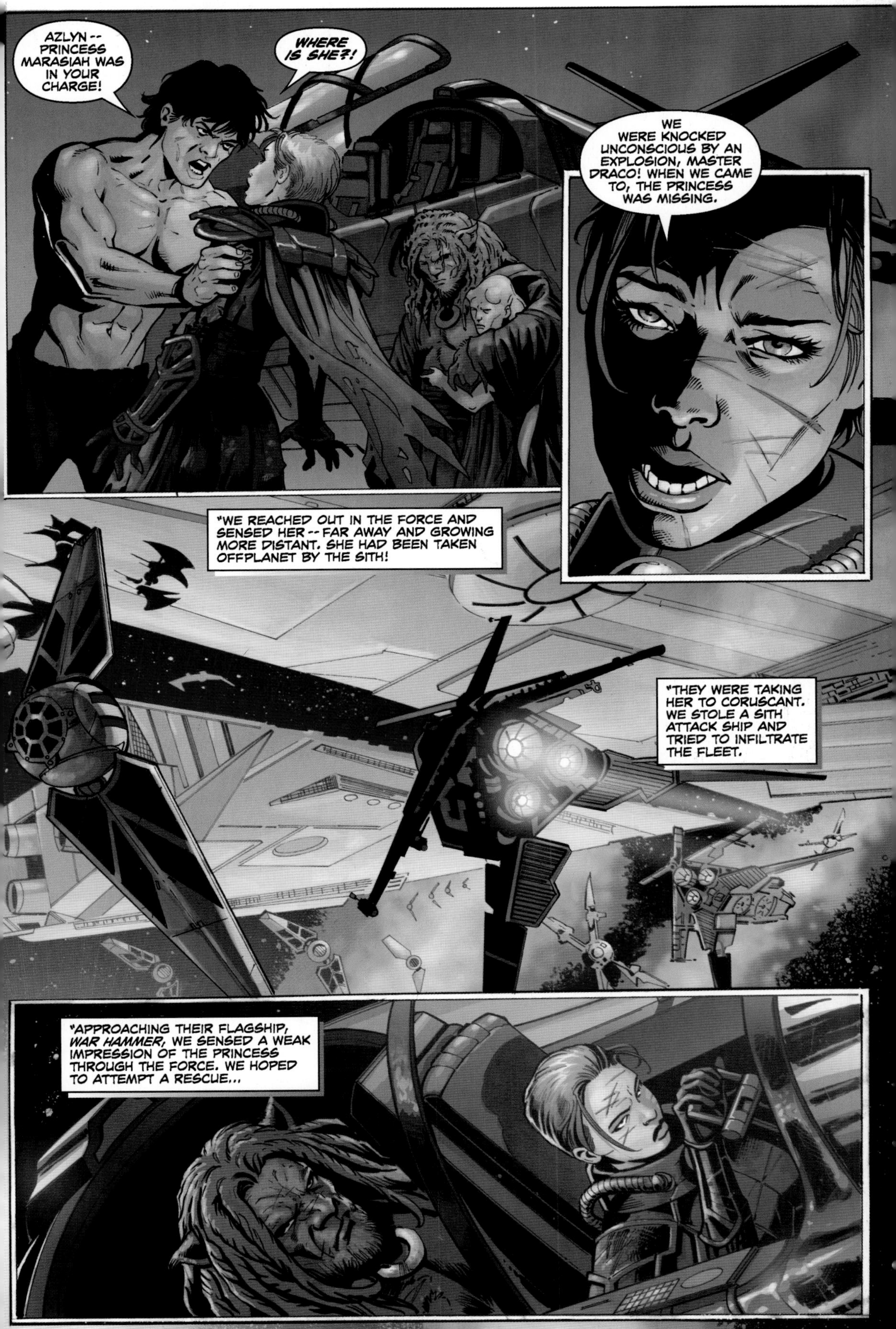
AZLYN -- PRINCESS MARASIAH WAS IN YOUR CHARGE!
WHERE IS SHE?!
WE WERE KNOCKED UNCONSCIOUS BY AN EXPLOSION, MASTER DRACO! WHEN WE CAME TO, THE PRINCESS WAS MISSING.
"WE REACHED OUT IN THE FORCE AND SENSED HER -- FAR AWAY AND GROWING MORE DISTANT. SHE HAD BEEN TAKEN OFFPLANET BY THE SITH!
"THEY WERE TAKING HER TO CORUSCANT. WE STOLE A SITH ATTACK SHIP AND TRIED TO INFILTRATE THE FLEET.
"APPROACHING THEIR FLAGSHIP, WAR HAMMER, WE SENSED A WEAK IMPRESSION OF THE PRINCESS THROUGH THE FORCE. WE HOPED TO ATTEMPT A RESCUE...

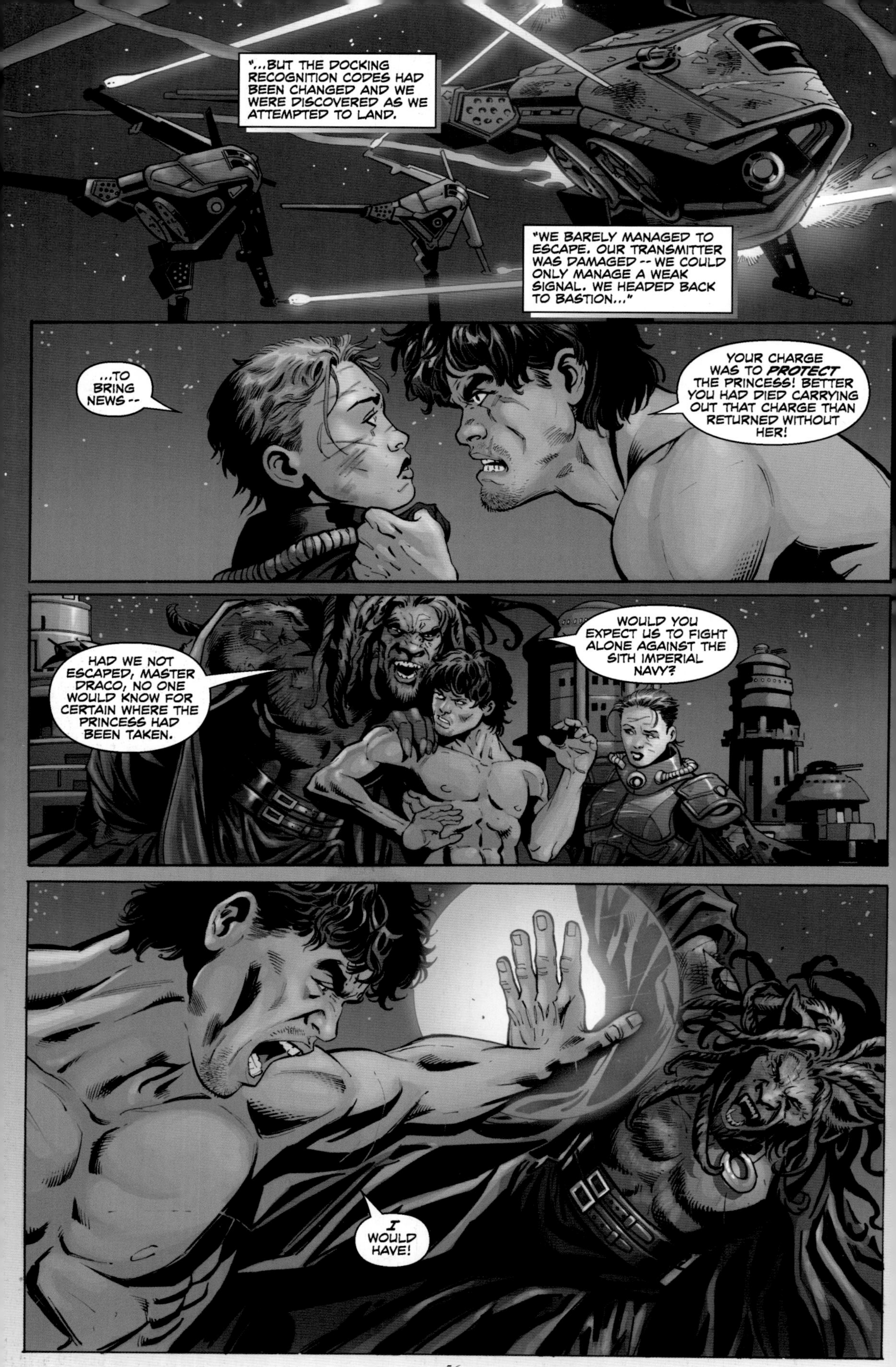
"...BUT THE DOCKING RECOGNITION CODES HAD BEEN CHANGED AND WE WERE DISCOVERED AS WE ATTEMPTED TO LAND.
"WE BARELY MANAGED TO ESCAPE. OUR TRANSMITTER WAS DAMAGED -- WE COULD ONLY MANAGE A WEAK SIGNAL. WE HEADED BACK TO BASTION..."
...TO BRING NEWS --
YOUR CHARGE WAS TO *PROTECT* THE PRINCESS! BETTER YOU HAD DIED CARRYING OUT THAT CHARGE THAN RETURNED WITHOUT HER!
HAD WE NOT ESCAPED, MASTER DRACO, NO ONE WOULD KNOW FOR CERTAIN WHERE THE PRINCESS HAD BEEN TAKEN.
WOULD YOU EXPECT US TO FIGHT ALONE AGAINST THE SITH IMPERIAL NAVY?
I WOULD HAVE!

WE ARE, PURPORTEDLY, ALLIES, MASTER ANTARES. BUT, PLEASE, DO NOT ASSUME FOR A MOMENT THAT I WILL LET YOU HARM A FELLOW JEDI.

MASTER YOURSELF. YOU DO YOUR EMPEROR NO CREDIT.

FINISH YOUR POSTURING LATER, YOUNG MASTERS. HIS IMPERIAL MAJESTY REQUIRES HIS KNIGHTS IN HIS QUARTERS. *IMMEDIATELY.*

SHORTLY, IN ROAN FEL'S QUARTERS...

THE NEWS, BLUNTLY PUT, IS DISASTROUS. MY CONTACT ON CORUSCANT HAS JUST INFORMED ME THAT THE PRINCESS MARASIAH HAS BEEN TAKEN TO KORRIBAN.

WE COULD NOT RESCUE HER FROM THERE IF WE HAD A *THOUSAND* SHIPS!

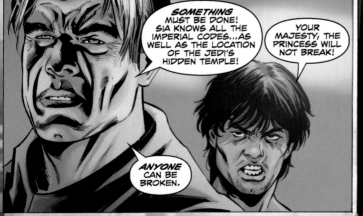

SOMETHING MUST BE DONE! SIA KNOWS ALL THE IMPERIAL CODES...AS WELL AS THE LOCATION OF THE JEDI'S HIDDEN TEMPLE!

YOUR MAJESTY, THE PRINCESS WILL NOT BREAK!

ANYONE CAN BE BROKEN.

YOU HAVE THREE HOURS TO FORM A PLAN FOR RESCUE. IF SIA CANNOT BE SAVED, SHE MUST BE STILLED.

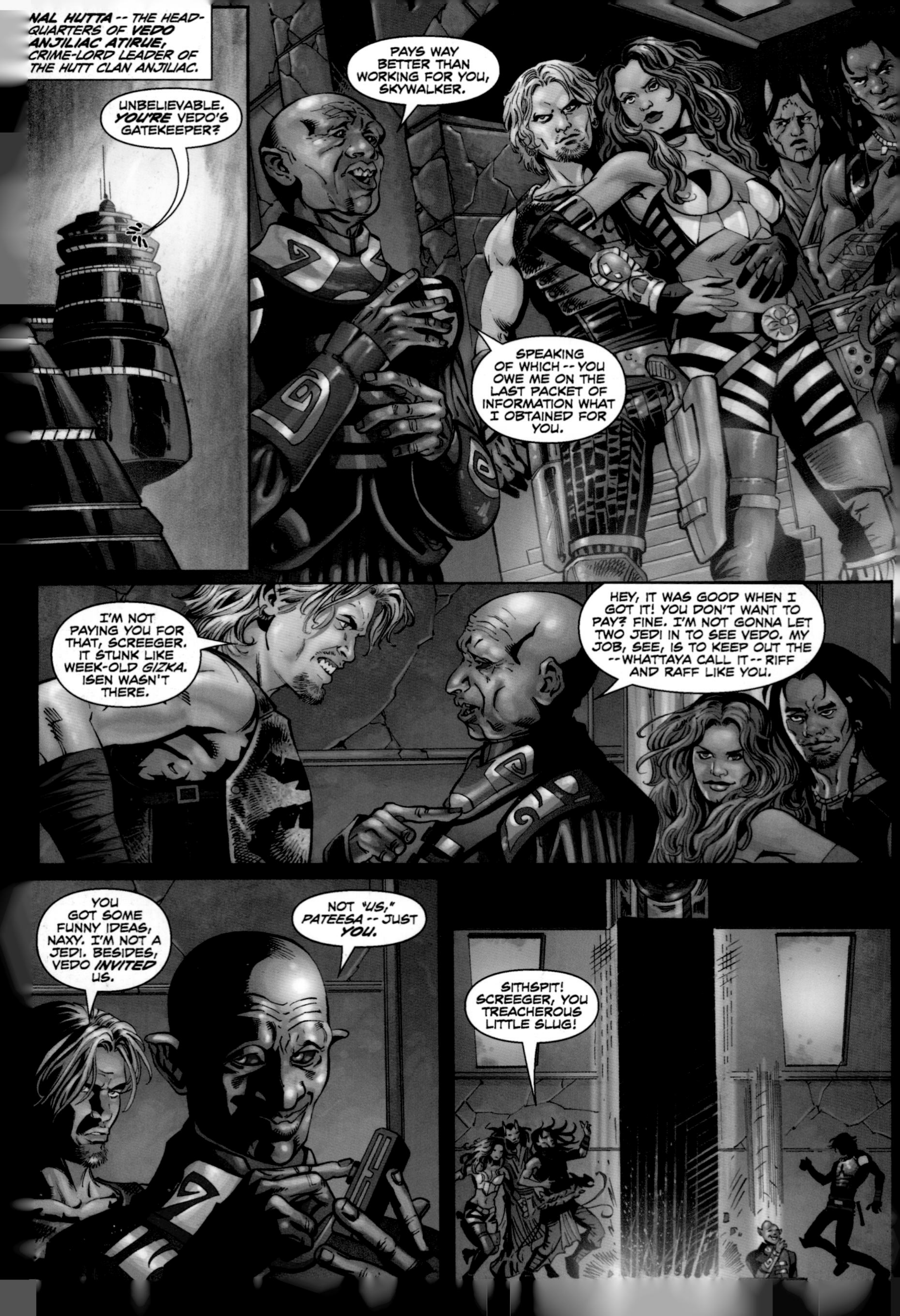
NAL HUTTA -- THE HEADQUARTERS OF VEDO ANJILIAC ATIRUE, CRIME-LORD LEADER OF THE HUTT CLAN ANJILIAC.
UNBELIEVABLE. YOU'RE VEDO'S GATEKEEPER?
PAYS WAY BETTER THAN WORKING FOR YOU, SKYWALKER.
SPEAKING OF WHICH -- YOU OWE ME ON THE LAST PACKET OF INFORMATION WHAT I OBTAINED FOR YOU.
I'M NOT PAYING YOU FOR THAT, SCREEGER. IT STUNK LIKE WEEK-OLD GIZKA. ISEN WASN'T THERE.
HEY, IT WAS GOOD WHEN I GOT IT! YOU DON'T WANT TO PAY? FINE. I'M NOT GONNA LET TWO JEDI IN TO SEE VEDO. MY JOB, SEE, IS TO KEEP OUT THE -- WHATTAYA CALL IT -- RIFF AND RAFF LIKE YOU.
YOU GOT SOME FUNNY IDEAS, NAXY. I'M NOT A JEDI. BESIDES, VEDO INVITED US.
NOT "US," PATEESA -- JUST YOU.
SITHSPIT! SCREEGER, YOU TREACHEROUS LITTLE SLUG!

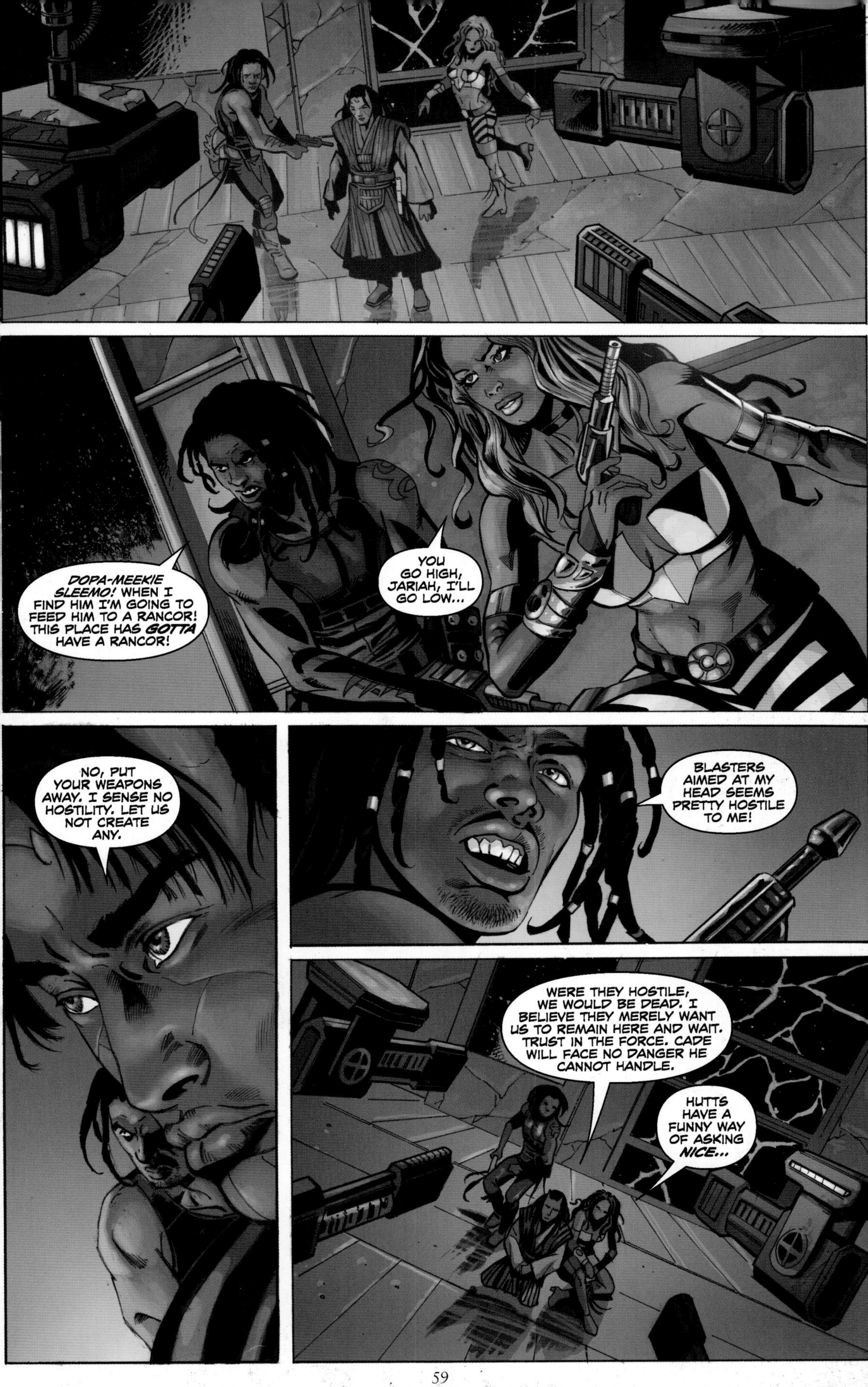
DOPA-MEEKIE SLEEMO! WHEN I FIND HIM I'M GOING TO FEED HIM TO A RANCOR! THIS PLACE HAS GOTTA HAVE A RANCOR!
YOU GO HIGH, JARIAH, I'LL GO LOW...
NO, PUT YOUR WEAPONS AWAY. I SENSE NO HOSTILITY. LET US NOT CREATE ANY.
BLASTERS AIMED AT MY HEAD SEEMS PRETTY HOSTILE TO ME!
WERE THEY HOSTILE, WE WOULD BE DEAD. I BELIEVE THEY MERELY WANT US TO REMAIN HERE AND WAIT. TRUST IN THE FORCE. CADE WILL FACE NO DANGER HE CANNOT HANDLE.
HUTTS HAVE A FUNNY WAY OF ASKING NICE...

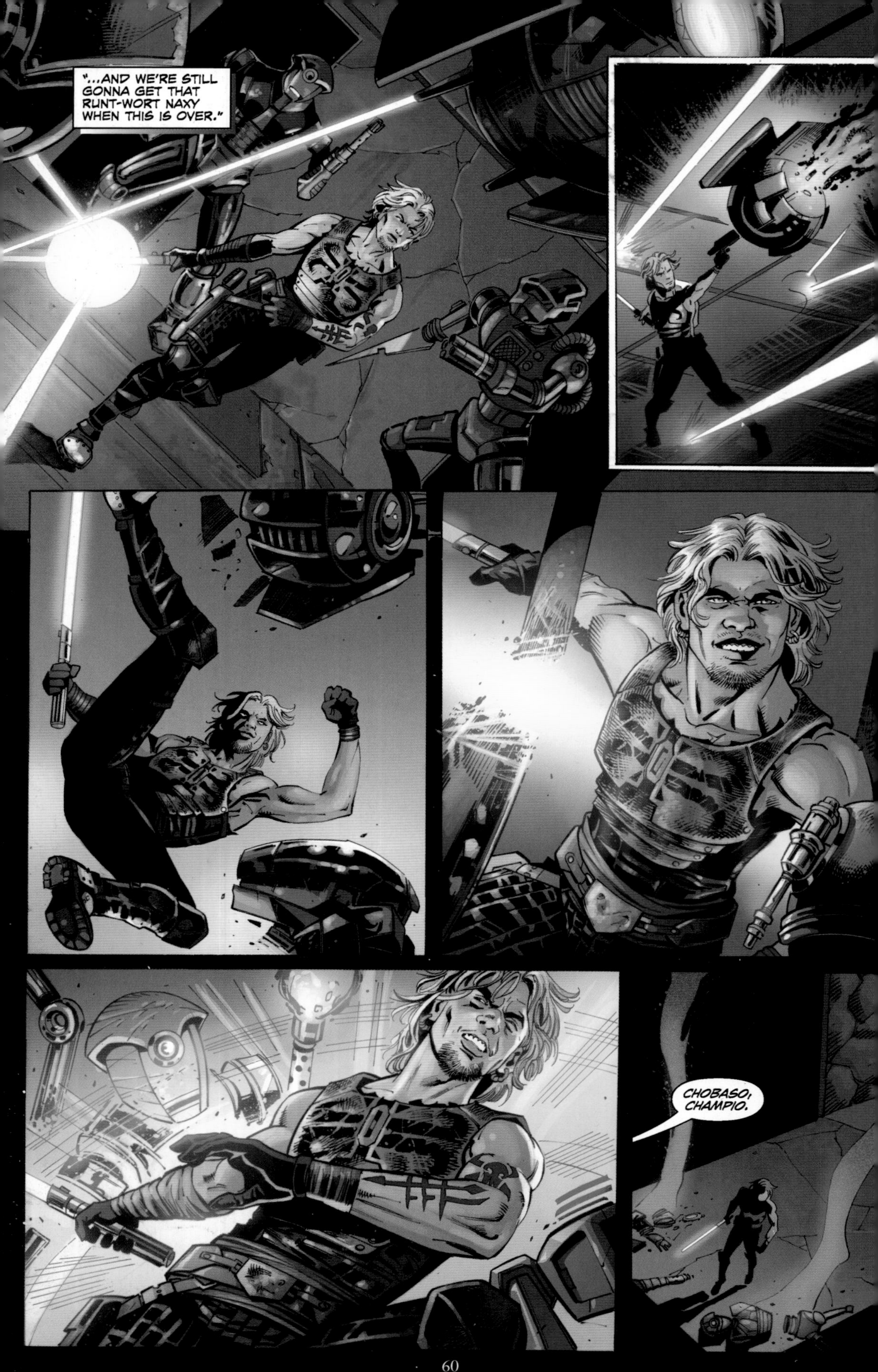
"...AND WE'RE STILL GONNA GET THAT RUNT-WORT NAXY WHEN THIS IS OVER."
CHOBASO, CHAMPIO.

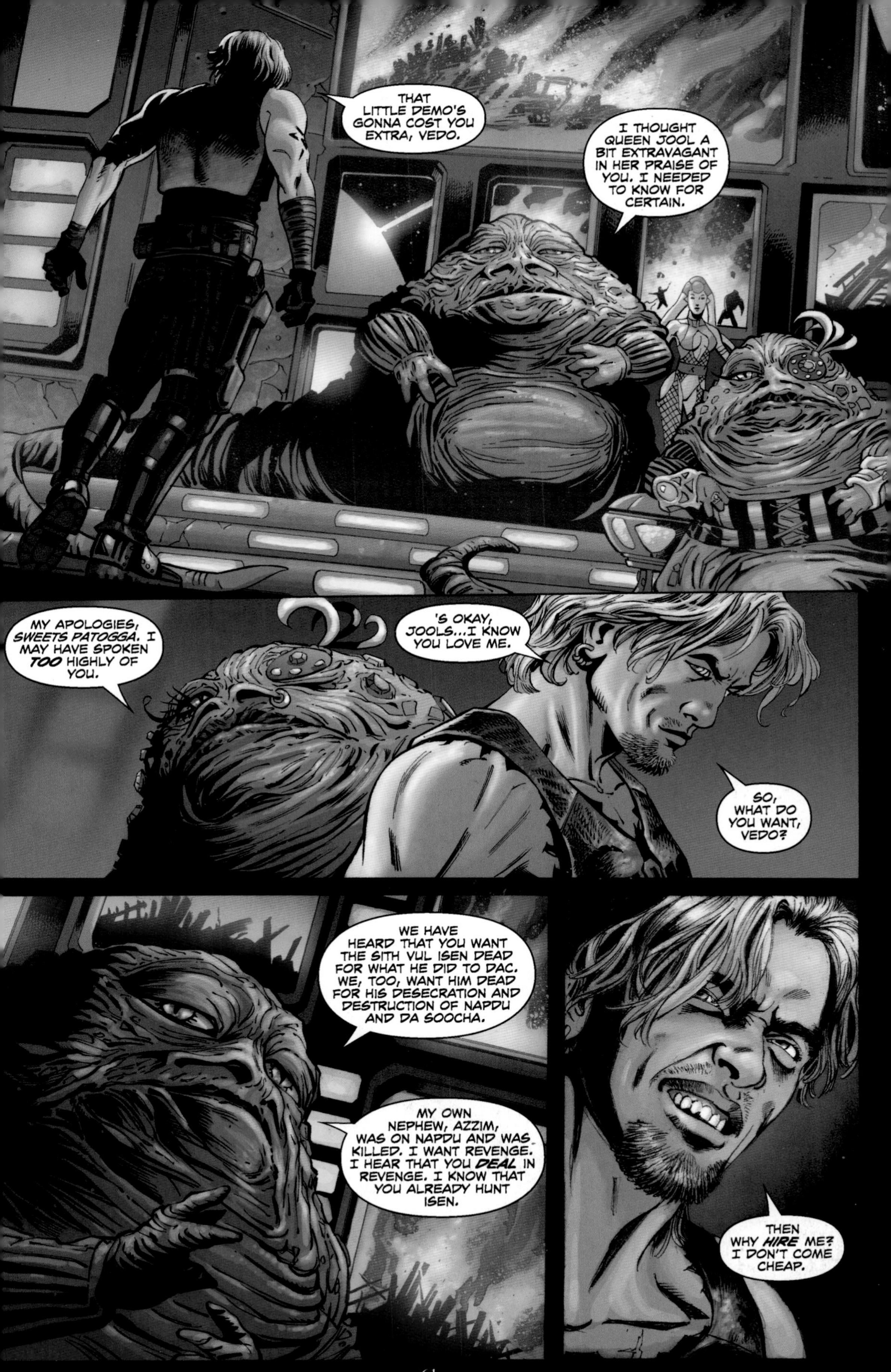
THAT LITTLE DEMO'S GONNA COST YOU EXTRA, VEDO.
I THOUGHT QUEEN JOOL A BIT EXTRAVAGANT IN HER PRAISE OF YOU. I NEEDED TO KNOW FOR CERTAIN.
MY APOLOGIES, SWEETS PATOGGA. I MAY HAVE SPOKEN TOO HIGHLY OF YOU.
'S OKAY, JOOLS...I KNOW YOU LOVE ME.
SO, WHAT DO YOU WANT, VEDO?
WE HAVE HEARD THAT YOU WANT THE SITH VUL ISEN DEAD FOR WHAT HE DID TO DAC. WE, TOO, WANT HIM DEAD FOR HIS DESECRATION AND DESTRUCTION OF NAPDU AND DA SOOCHA.
MY OWN NEPHEW, AZZIM, WAS ON NAPDU AND WAS KILLED. I WANT REVENGE. I HEAR THAT YOU DEAL IN REVENGE. I KNOW THAT YOU ALREADY HUNT ISEN.
THEN WHY HIRE ME? I DON'T COME CHEAP.

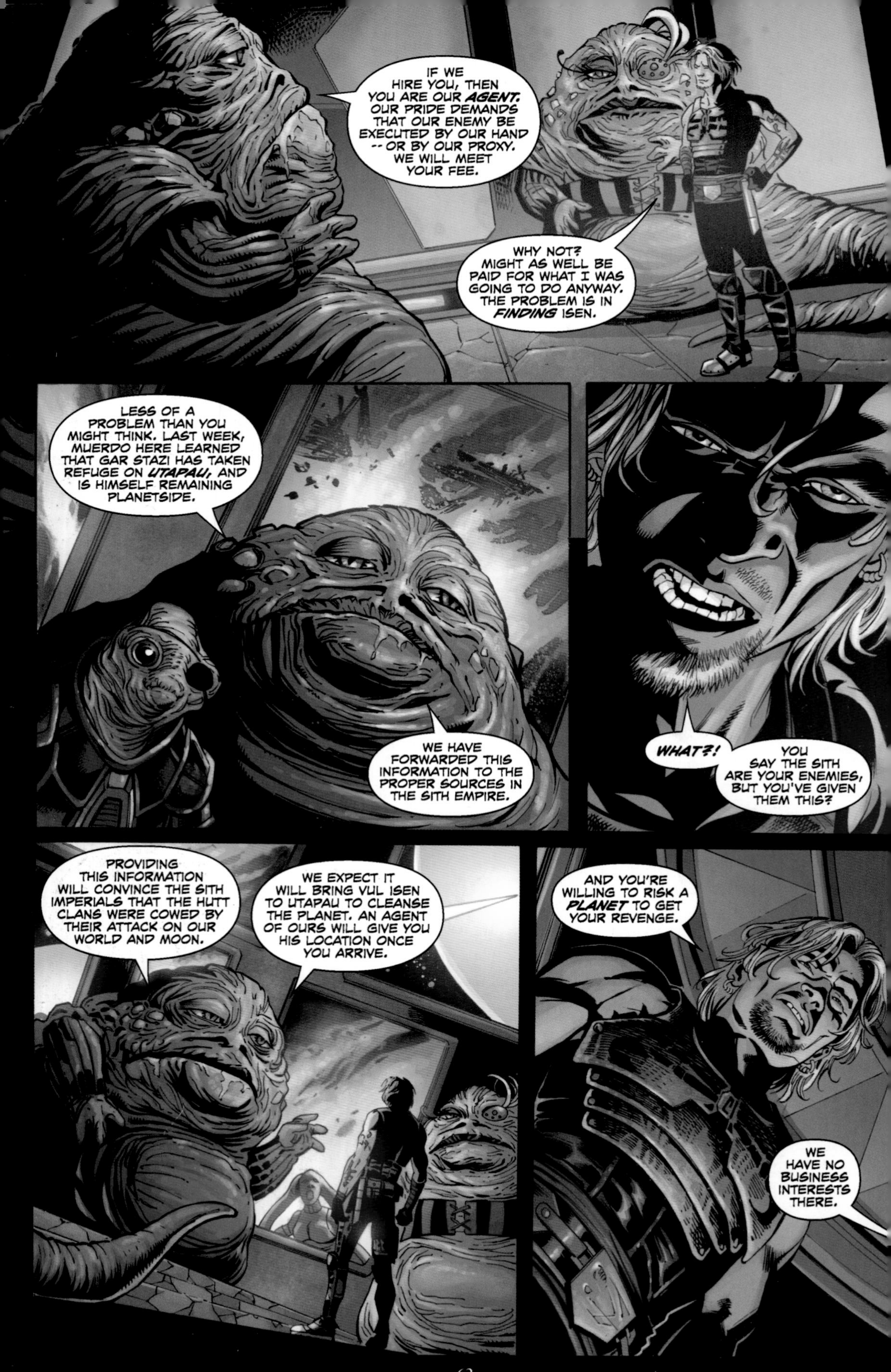
IF WE HIRE YOU, THEN YOU ARE OUR AGENT. OUR PRIDE DEMANDS THAT OUR ENEMY BE EXECUTED BY OUR HAND -- OR BY OUR PROXY. WE WILL MEET YOUR FEE.
WHY NOT? MIGHT AS WELL BE PAID FOR WHAT I WAS GOING TO DO ANYWAY. THE PROBLEM IS IN FINDING ISEN.
LESS OF A PROBLEM THAN YOU MIGHT THINK. LAST WEEK, MUERDO HERE LEARNED THAT GAR STAZI HAS TAKEN REFUGE ON UTAPAU, AND IS HIMSELF REMAINING PLANETSIDE.
WE HAVE FORWARDED THIS INFORMATION TO THE PROPER SOURCES IN THE SITH EMPIRE.
WHAT?!
YOU SAY THE SITH ARE YOUR ENEMIES, BUT YOU'VE GIVEN THEM THIS?
PROVIDING THIS INFORMATION WILL CONVINCE THE SITH IMPERIALS THAT THE HUTT CLANS WERE COWED BY THEIR ATTACK ON OUR WORLD AND MOON.
WE EXPECT IT WILL BRING VUL ISEN TO UTAPAU TO CLEANSE THE PLANET. AN AGENT OF OURS WILL GIVE YOU HIS LOCATION ONCE YOU ARRIVE.
AND YOU'RE WILLING TO RISK A PLANET TO GET YOUR REVENGE.
WE HAVE NO BUSINESS INTERESTS THERE.

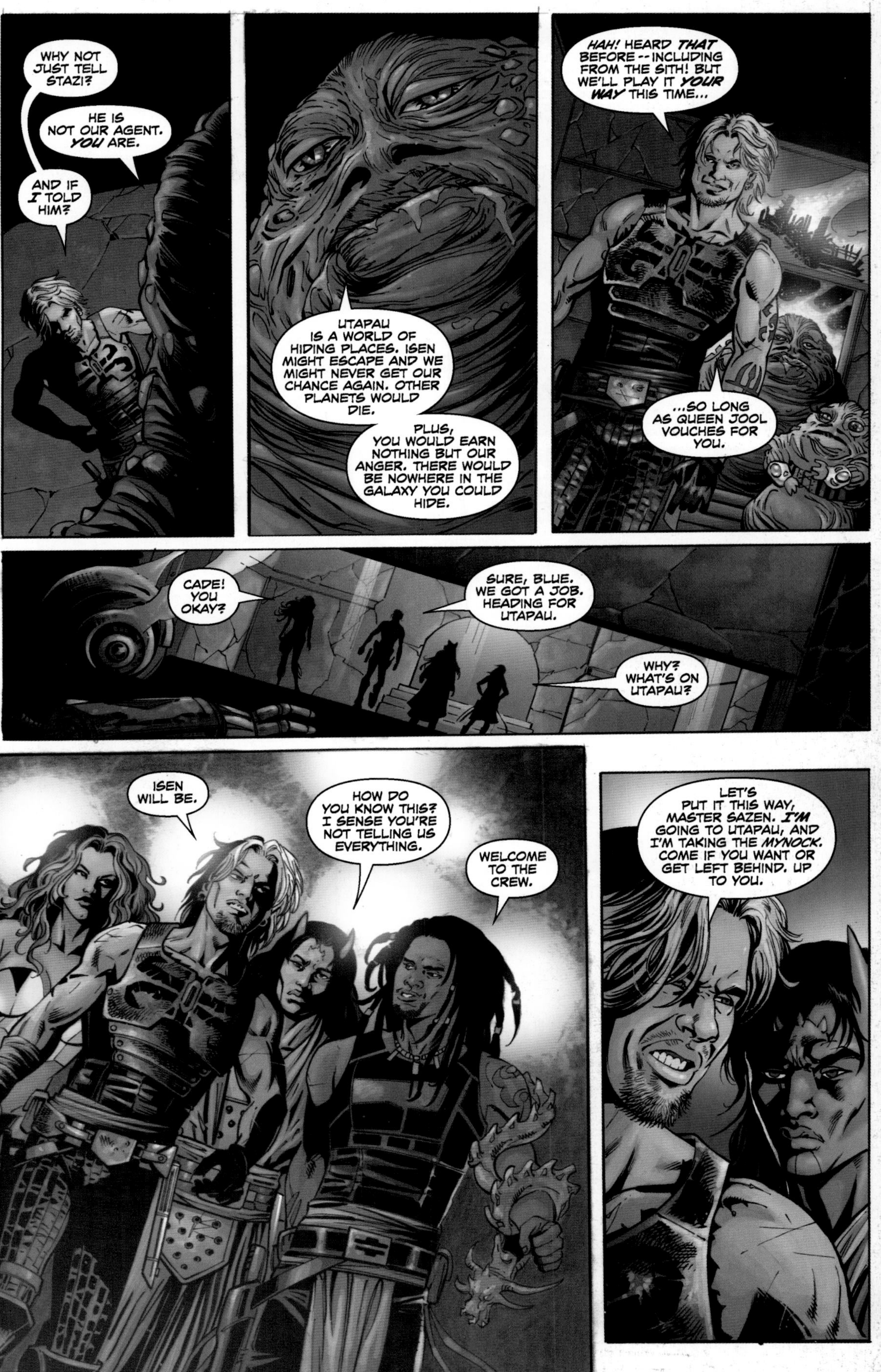
WHY NOT JUST TELL STAZI?
HE IS NOT OUR AGENT. YOU ARE.
AND IF I TOLD HIM?
UTAPAU IS A WORLD OF HIDING PLACES. ISEN MIGHT ESCAPE AND WE MIGHT NEVER GET OUR CHANCE AGAIN. OTHER PLANETS WOULD DIE.
PLUS, YOU WOULD EARN NOTHING BUT OUR ANGER. THERE WOULD BE NOWHERE IN THE GALAXY YOU COULD HIDE.
HAH! HEARD THAT BEFORE--INCLUDING FROM THE SITH! BUT WE'LL PLAY IT YOUR WAY THIS TIME...
...SO LONG AS QUEEN JOOL VOUCHES FOR YOU.
CADE! YOU OKAY?
SURE, BLUE. WE GOT A JOB. HEADING FOR UTAPAU.
WHY? WHAT'S ON UTAPAU?
ISEN WILL BE.
HOW DO YOU KNOW THIS? I SENSE YOU'RE NOT TELLING US EVERYTHING.
WELCOME TO THE CREW.
LET'S PUT IT THIS WAY, MASTER SAZEN. I'M GOING TO UTAPAU, AND I'M TAKING THE MYNOCK. COME IF YOU WANT OR GET LEFT BEHIND. UP TO YOU.

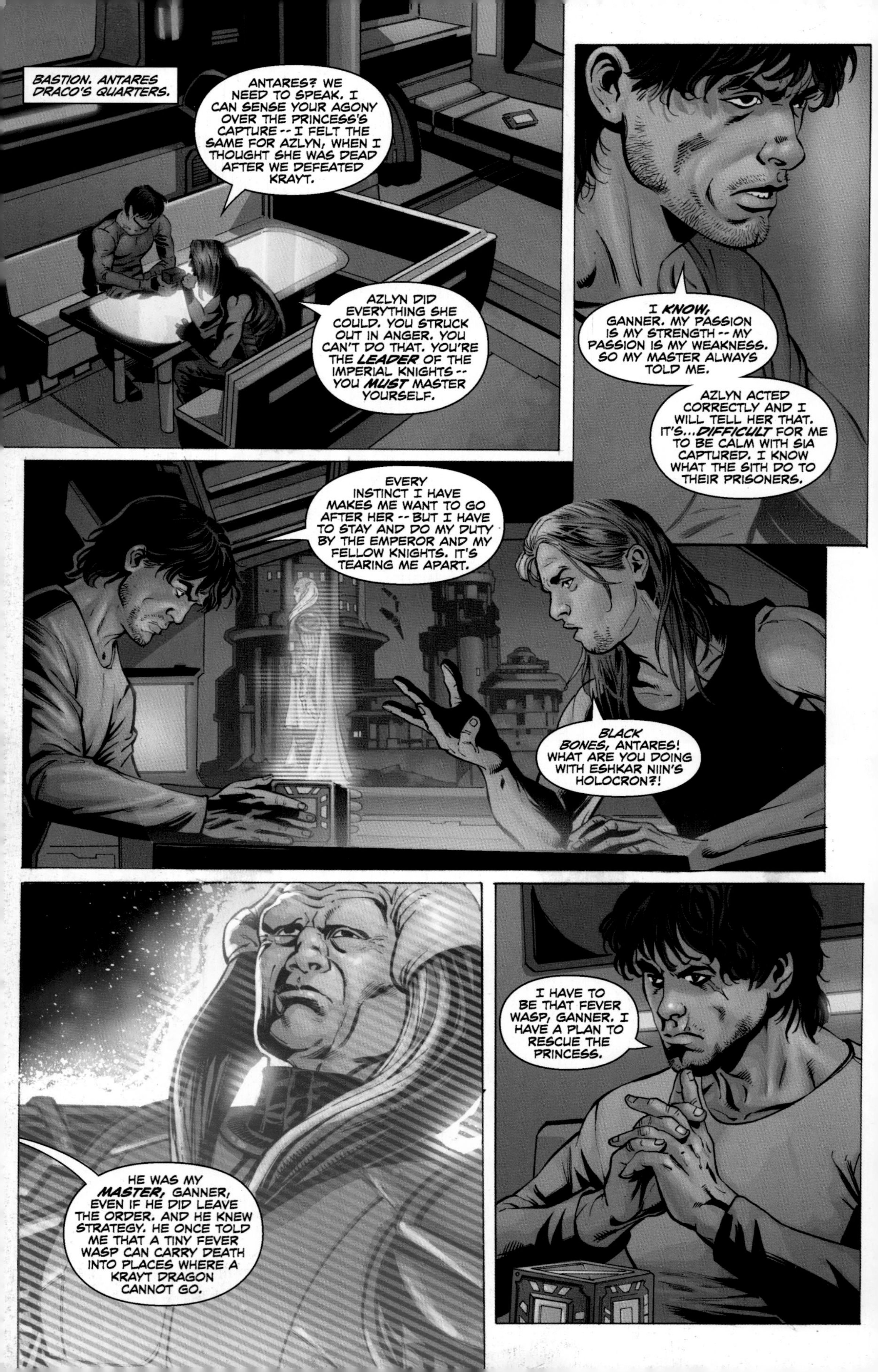
BASTION. ANTARES DRACO'S QUARTERS.
ANTARES? WE NEED TO SPEAK. I CAN SENSE YOUR AGONY OVER THE PRINCESS'S CAPTURE -- I FELT THE SAME FOR AZLYN, WHEN I THOUGHT SHE WAS DEAD AFTER WE DEFEATED KRAYT.
AZLYN DID EVERYTHING SHE COULD. YOU STRUCK OUT IN ANGER. YOU CAN'T DO THAT. YOU'RE THE ***LEADER*** OF THE IMPERIAL KNIGHTS -- YOU ***MUST*** MASTER YOURSELF.
I ***KNOW,*** GANNER. MY PASSION IS MY STRENGTH -- MY PASSION IS MY WEAKNESS. SO MY MASTER ALWAYS TOLD ME.
AZLYN ACTED CORRECTLY AND I WILL TELL HER THAT. IT'S...***DIFFICULT*** FOR ME TO BE CALM WITH SIA CAPTURED. I KNOW WHAT THE SITH DO TO THEIR PRISONERS.
EVERY INSTINCT I HAVE MAKES ME WANT TO GO AFTER HER -- BUT I HAVE TO STAY AND DO MY DUTY BY THE EMPEROR AND MY FELLOW KNIGHTS. IT'S TEARING ME APART.
BLACK BONES, ANTARES! WHAT ARE YOU DOING WITH ESHKAR NIIN'S HOLOCRON?!
HE WAS MY ***MASTER,*** GANNER, EVEN IF HE DID LEAVE THE ORDER. AND HE KNEW STRATEGY. HE ONCE TOLD ME THAT A TINY FEVER WASP CAN CARRY DEATH INTO PLACES WHERE A KRAYT DRAGON CANNOT GO.
I HAVE TO BE THAT FEVER WASP, GANNER. I HAVE A PLAN TO RESCUE THE PRINCESS.

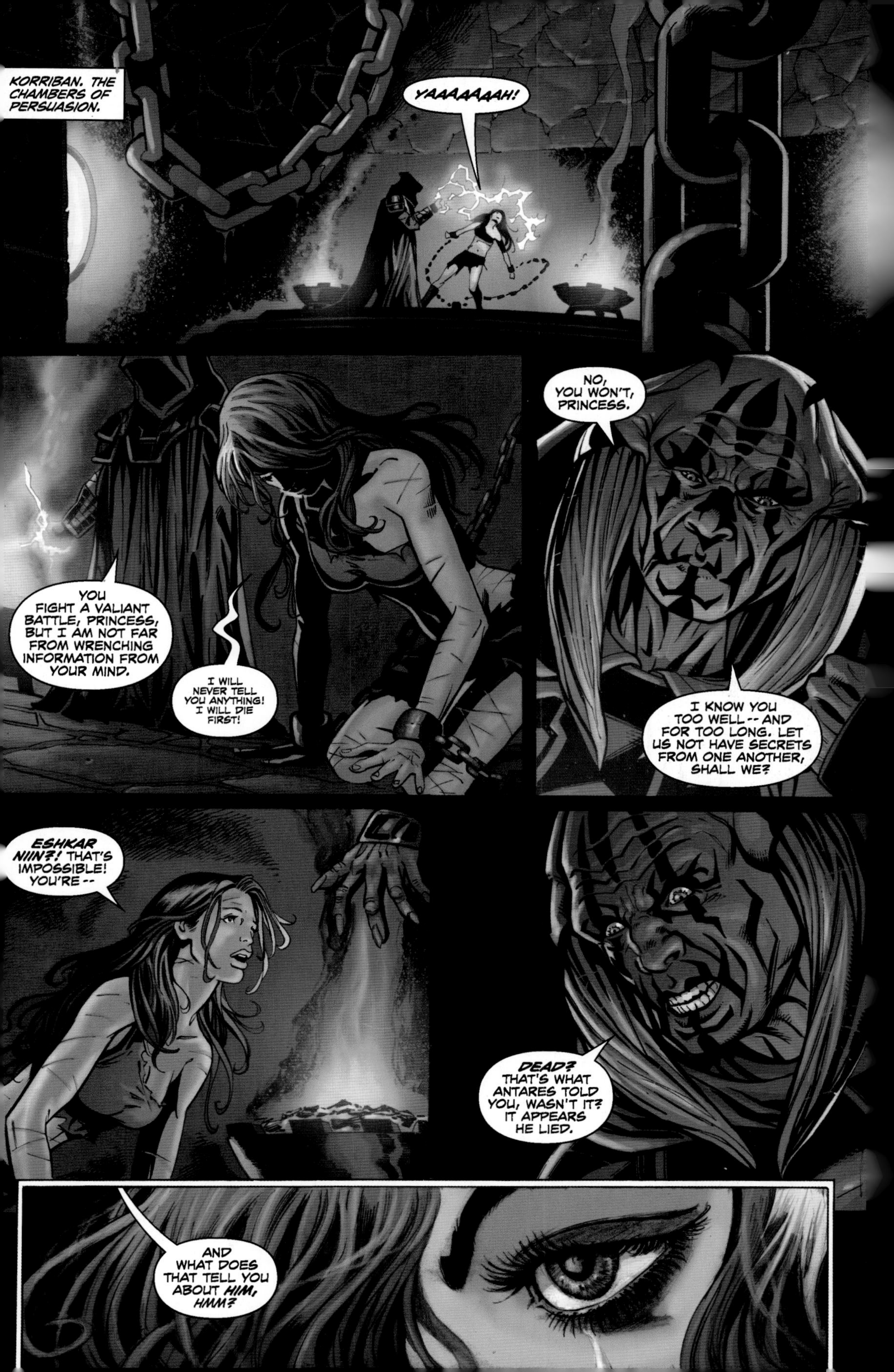

KORRIBAN. THE CHAMBERS OF PERSUASION.
YAAAAAAAH!
YOU FIGHT A VALIANT BATTLE, PRINCESS, BUT I AM NOT FAR FROM WRENCHING INFORMATION FROM YOUR MIND.
I WILL NEVER TELL YOU ANYTHING! I WILL DIE FIRST!
NO, YOU WON'T, PRINCESS.
I KNOW YOU TOO WELL -- AND FOR TOO LONG. LET US NOT HAVE SECRETS FROM ONE ANOTHER, SHALL WE?
ESHKAR NIIN?! THAT'S IMPOSSIBLE! YOU'RE --
DEAD? THAT'S WHAT ANTARES TOLD YOU, WASN'T IT? IT APPEARS HE LIED.
AND WHAT DOES THAT TELL YOU ABOUT HIM, HMM?

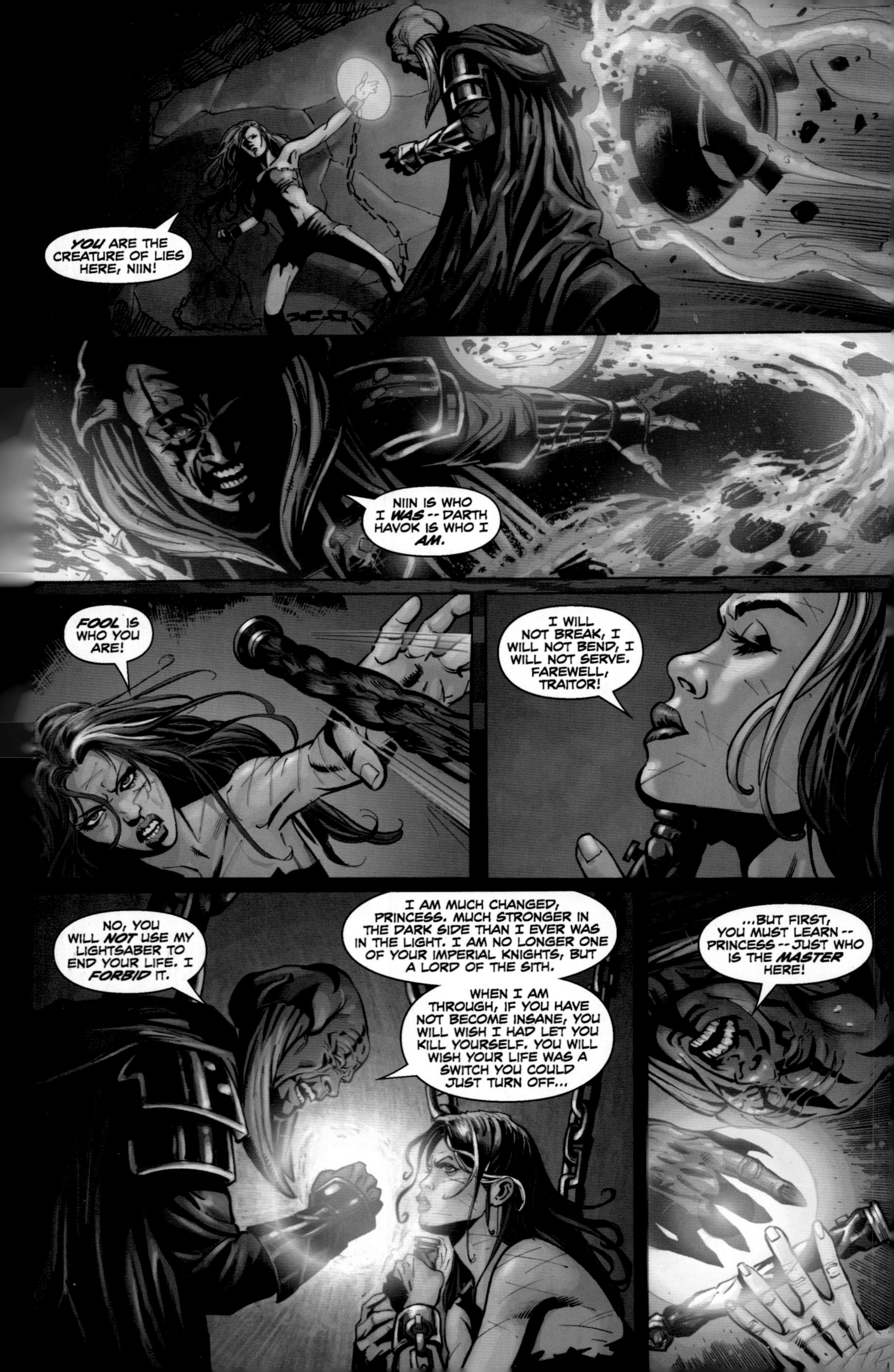
YOU ARE THE CREATURE OF LIES HERE, NIIN!
NIIN IS WHO I WAS -- DARTH HAVOK IS WHO I AM.
FOOL IS WHO YOU ARE!
I WILL NOT BREAK, I WILL NOT BEND, I WILL NOT SERVE. FAREWELL, TRAITOR!
NO, YOU WILL NOT USE MY LIGHTSABER TO END YOUR LIFE. I FORBID IT.
I AM MUCH CHANGED, PRINCESS. MUCH STRONGER IN THE DARK SIDE THAN I EVER WAS IN THE LIGHT. I AM NO LONGER ONE OF YOUR IMPERIAL KNIGHTS, BUT A LORD OF THE SITH.
WHEN I AM THROUGH, IF YOU HAVE NOT BECOME INSANE, YOU WILL WISH I HAD LET YOU KILL YOURSELF. YOU WILL WISH YOUR LIFE WAS A SWITCH YOU COULD JUST TURN OFF...
...BUT FIRST, YOU MUST LEARN -- PRINCESS -- JUST WHO IS THE MASTER HERE!

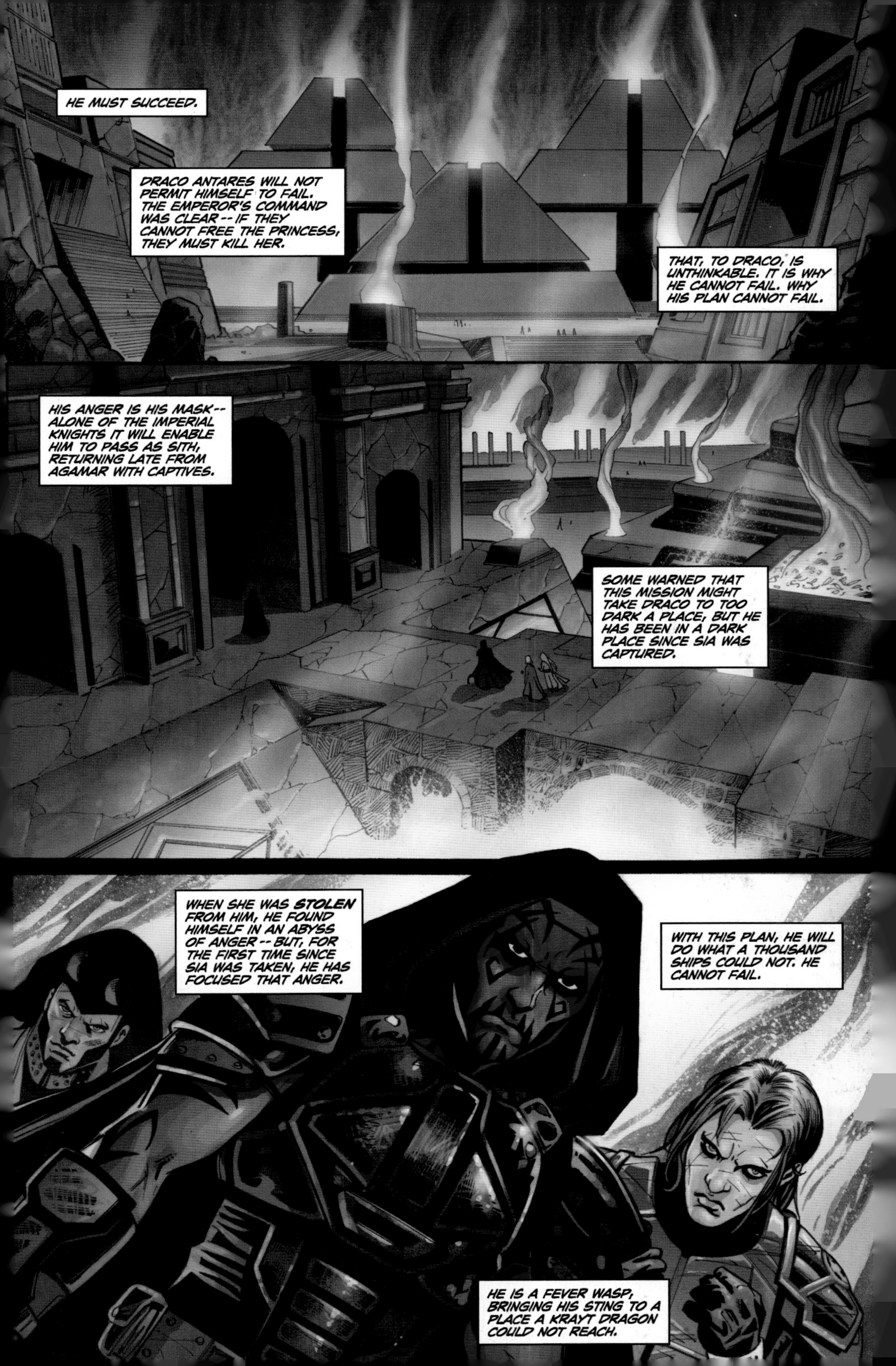
HE MUST SUCCEED.
DRACO ANTARES WILL NOT PERMIT HIMSELF TO FAIL. THE EMPEROR'S COMMAND WAS CLEAR -- IF THEY CANNOT FREE THE PRINCESS, THEY MUST KILL HER.
THAT, TO DRACO, IS UNTHINKABLE. IT IS WHY HE CANNOT FAIL. WHY HIS PLAN CANNOT FAIL.
HIS ANGER IS HIS MASK-- ALONE OF THE IMPERIAL KNIGHTS IT WILL ENABLE HIM TO PASS AS SITH, RETURNING LATE FROM AGAMAR WITH CAPTIVES.
SOME WARNED THAT THIS MISSION MIGHT TAKE DRACO TO TOO DARK A PLACE, BUT HE HAS BEEN IN A DARK PLACE SINCE SIA WAS CAPTURED.
WHEN SHE WAS STOLEN FROM HIM, HE FOUND HIMSELF IN AN ABYSS OF ANGER -- BUT, FOR THE FIRST TIME SINCE SIA WAS TAKEN, HE HAS FOCUSED THAT ANGER.
WITH THIS PLAN, HE WILL DO WHAT A THOUSAND SHIPS COULD NOT. HE CANNOT FAIL.
HE IS A FEVER WASP, BRINGING HIS STING TO A PLACE A KRAYT DRAGON COULD NOT REACH.

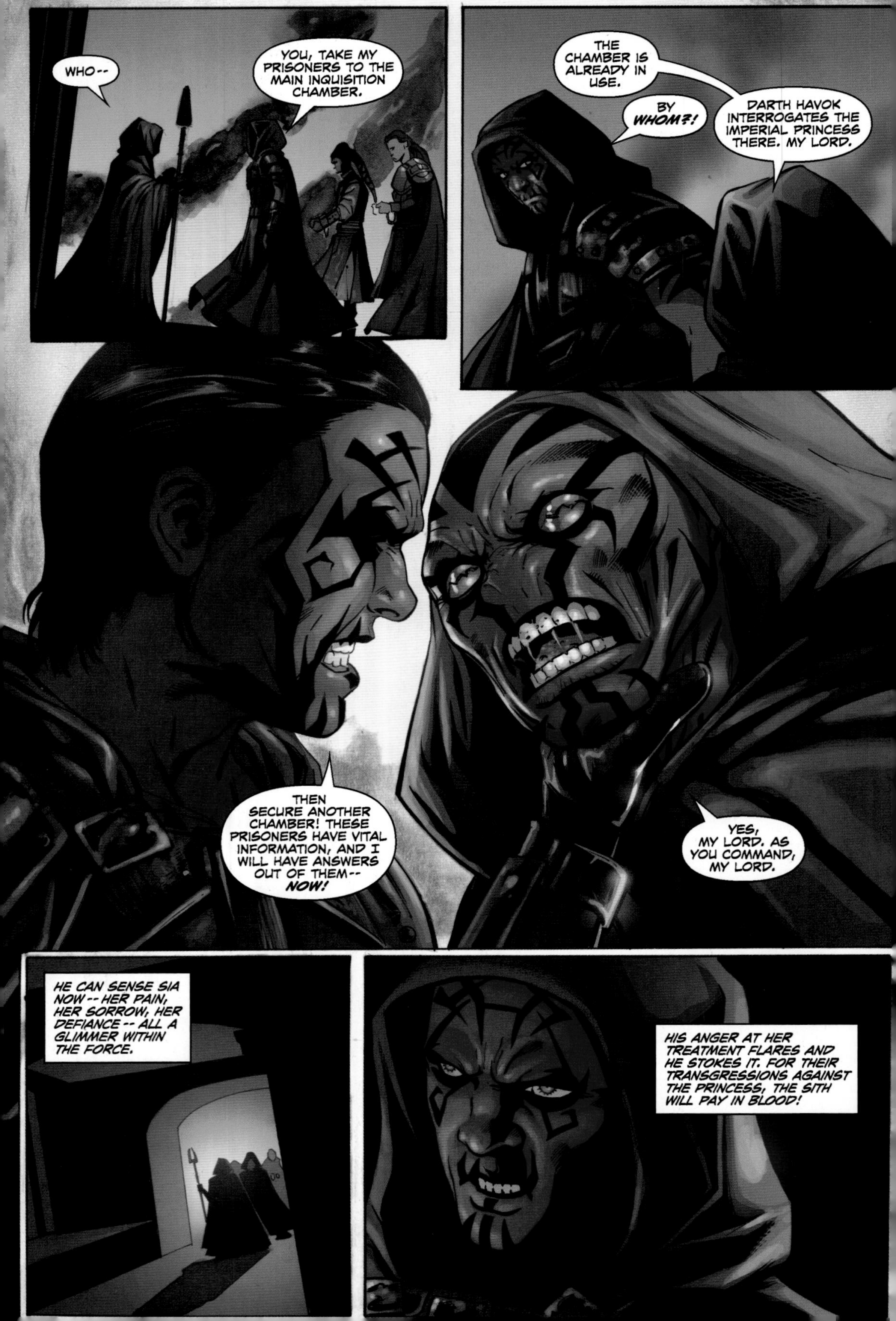
WHO--
YOU, TAKE MY PRISONERS TO THE MAIN INQUISITION CHAMBER.
THE CHAMBER IS ALREADY IN USE.
BY *WHOM?!*
DARTH HAVOK INTERROGATES THE IMPERIAL PRINCESS THERE. MY LORD.
THEN SECURE ANOTHER CHAMBER! THESE PRISONERS HAVE VITAL INFORMATION, AND I WILL HAVE ANSWERS OUT OF THEM-- *NOW!*
YES, MY LORD. AS YOU COMMAND, MY LORD.
HE CAN SENSE SIA NOW--HER PAIN, HER SORROW, HER DEFIANCE--ALL A GLIMMER WITHIN THE FORCE.
HIS ANGER AT HER TREATMENT FLARES AND HE STOKES IT. FOR THEIR TRANSGRESSIONS AGAINST THE PRINCESS, THE SITH WILL PAY IN BLOOD!

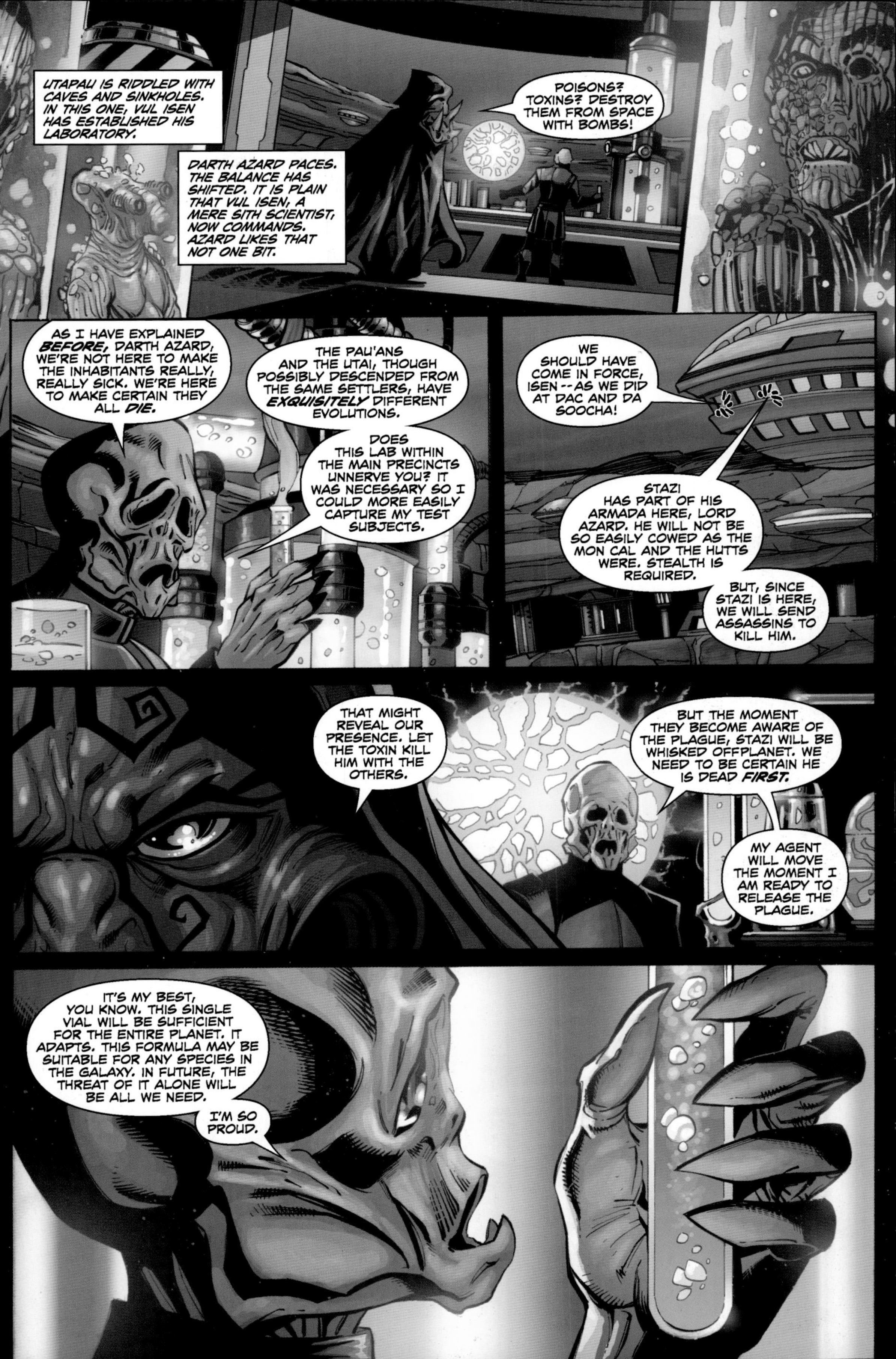
UTAPAU IS RIDDLED WITH CAVES AND SINKHOLES. IN THIS ONE, VUL ISEN HAS ESTABLISHED HIS LABORATORY.
POISONS? TOXINS? DESTROY THEM FROM SPACE WITH BOMBS!
DARTH AZARD PACES. THE BALANCE HAS SHIFTED. IT IS PLAIN THAT VUL ISEN, A MERE SITH SCIENTIST, NOW COMMANDS. AZARD LIKES THAT NOT ONE BIT.
AS I HAVE EXPLAINED BEFORE, DARTH AZARD, WE'RE NOT HERE TO MAKE THE INHABITANTS REALLY, REALLY SICK. WE'RE HERE TO MAKE CERTAIN THEY ALL DIE.
THE PAU'ANS AND THE UTAI, THOUGH POSSIBLY DESCENDED FROM THE SAME SETTLERS, HAVE EXQUISITELY DIFFERENT EVOLUTIONS.
DOES THIS LAB WITHIN THE MAIN PRECINCTS UNNERVE YOU? IT WAS NECESSARY SO I COULD MORE EASILY CAPTURE MY TEST SUBJECTS.
WE SHOULD HAVE COME IN FORCE, ISEN--AS WE DID AT DAC AND DA SOOCHA!
STAZI HAS PART OF HIS ARMADA HERE, LORD AZARD. HE WILL NOT BE SO EASILY COWED AS THE MON CAL AND THE HUTTS WERE. STEALTH IS REQUIRED.
BUT, SINCE STAZI IS HERE, WE WILL SEND ASSASSINS TO KILL HIM.
THAT MIGHT REVEAL OUR PRESENCE. LET THE TOXIN KILL HIM WITH THE OTHERS.
BUT THE MOMENT THEY BECOME AWARE OF THE PLAGUE, STAZI WILL BE WHISKED OFFPLANET. WE NEED TO BE CERTAIN HE IS DEAD FIRST.
MY AGENT WILL MOVE THE MOMENT I AM READY TO RELEASE THE PLAGUE.
IT'S MY BEST, YOU KNOW. THIS SINGLE VIAL WILL BE SUFFICIENT FOR THE ENTIRE PLANET. IT ADAPTS. THIS FORMULA MAY BE SUITABLE FOR ANY SPECIES IN THE GALAXY. IN FUTURE, THE THREAT OF IT ALONE WILL BE ALL WE NEED.
I'M SO PROUD.

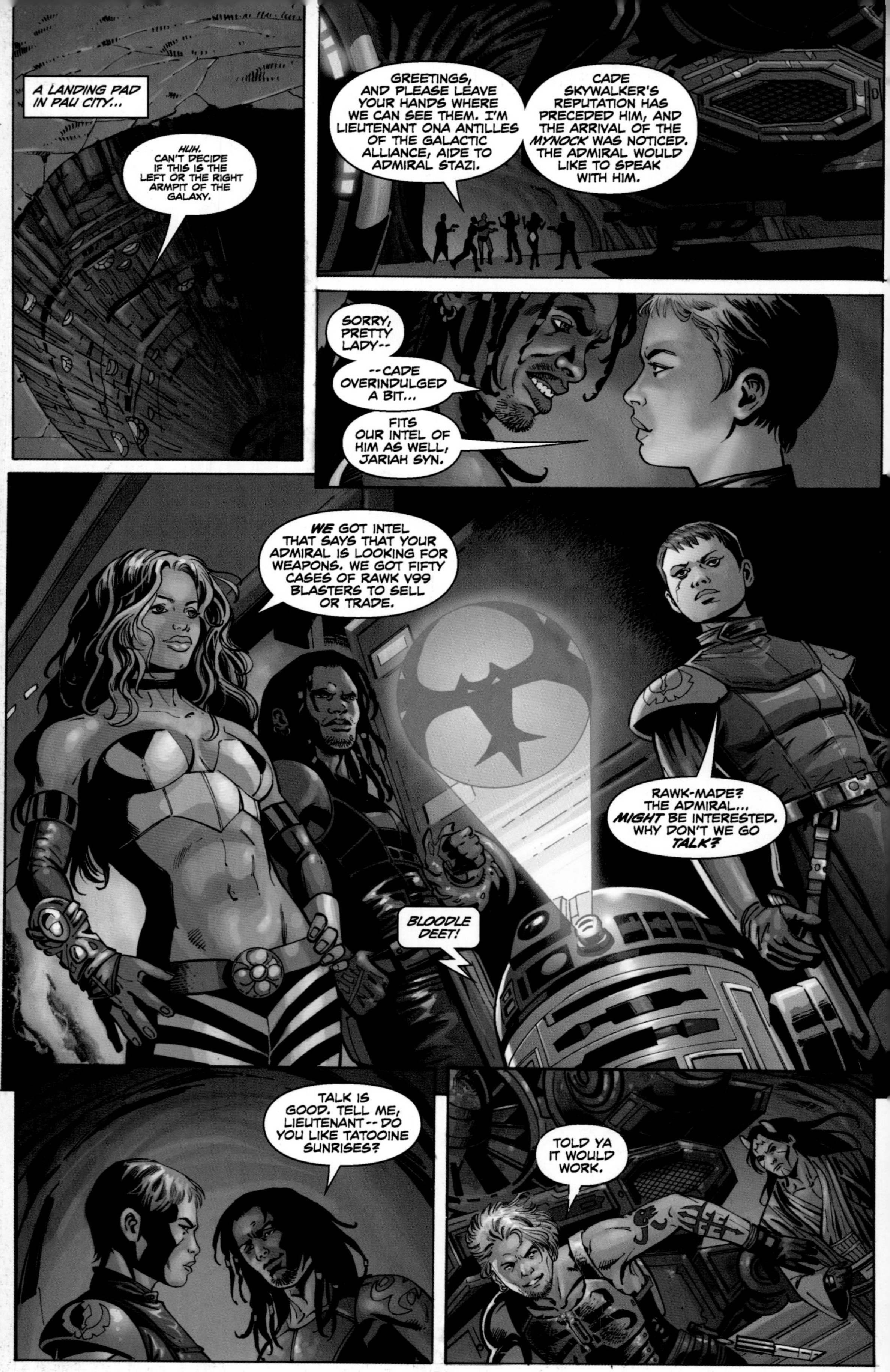
A LANDING PAD IN PAU CITY...
HUH. CAN'T DECIDE IF THIS IS THE LEFT OR THE RIGHT ARMPIT OF THE GALAXY.
GREETINGS, AND PLEASE LEAVE YOUR HANDS WHERE WE CAN SEE THEM. I'M LIEUTENANT ONA ANTILLES OF THE GALACTIC ALLIANCE, AIDE TO ADMIRAL STAZI.
CADE SKYWALKER'S REPUTATION HAS PRECEDED HIM, AND THE ARRIVAL OF THE MYNOCK WAS NOTICED. THE ADMIRAL WOULD LIKE TO SPEAK WITH HIM.
SORRY, PRETTY LADY--
--CADE OVERINDULGED A BIT...
FITS OUR INTEL OF HIM AS WELL, JARIAH SYN.
WE GOT INTEL THAT SAYS THAT YOUR ADMIRAL IS LOOKING FOR WEAPONS. WE GOT FIFTY CASES OF RAWK V99 BLASTERS TO SELL OR TRADE.
RAWK-MADE? THE ADMIRAL... MIGHT BE INTERESTED. WHY DON'T WE GO TALK?
BLOODLE DEET!
TALK IS GOOD. TELL ME, LIEUTENANT-- DO YOU LIKE TATOOINE SUNRISES?
TOLD YA IT WOULD WORK.

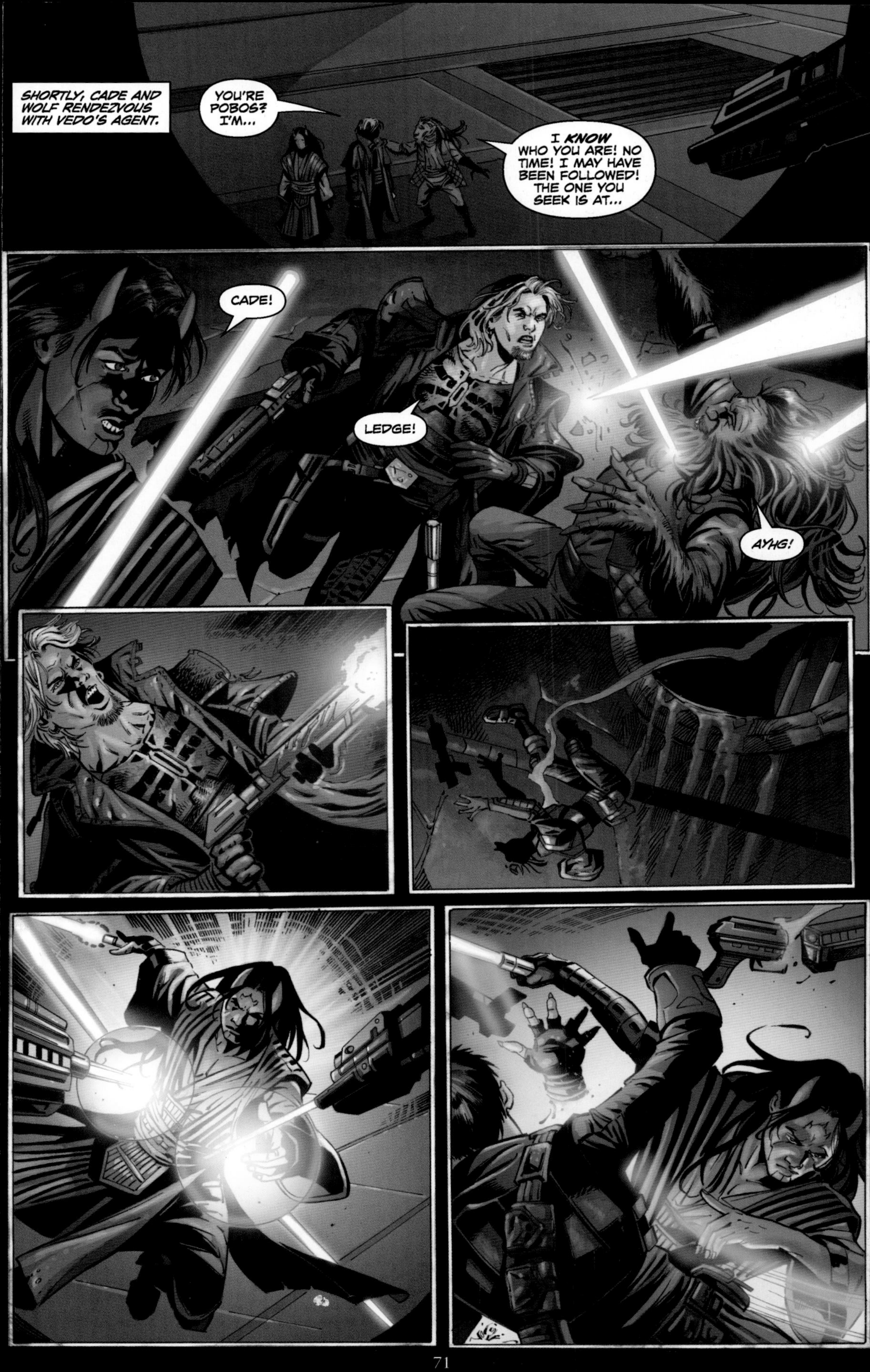
SHORTLY, CADE AND WOLF RENDEZVOUS WITH VEDO'S AGENT.
YOU'RE POBOS? I'M...
I KNOW WHO YOU ARE! NO TIME! I MAY HAVE BEEN FOLLOWED! THE ONE YOU SEEK IS AT...
CADE!
LEDGE!
AYHG!

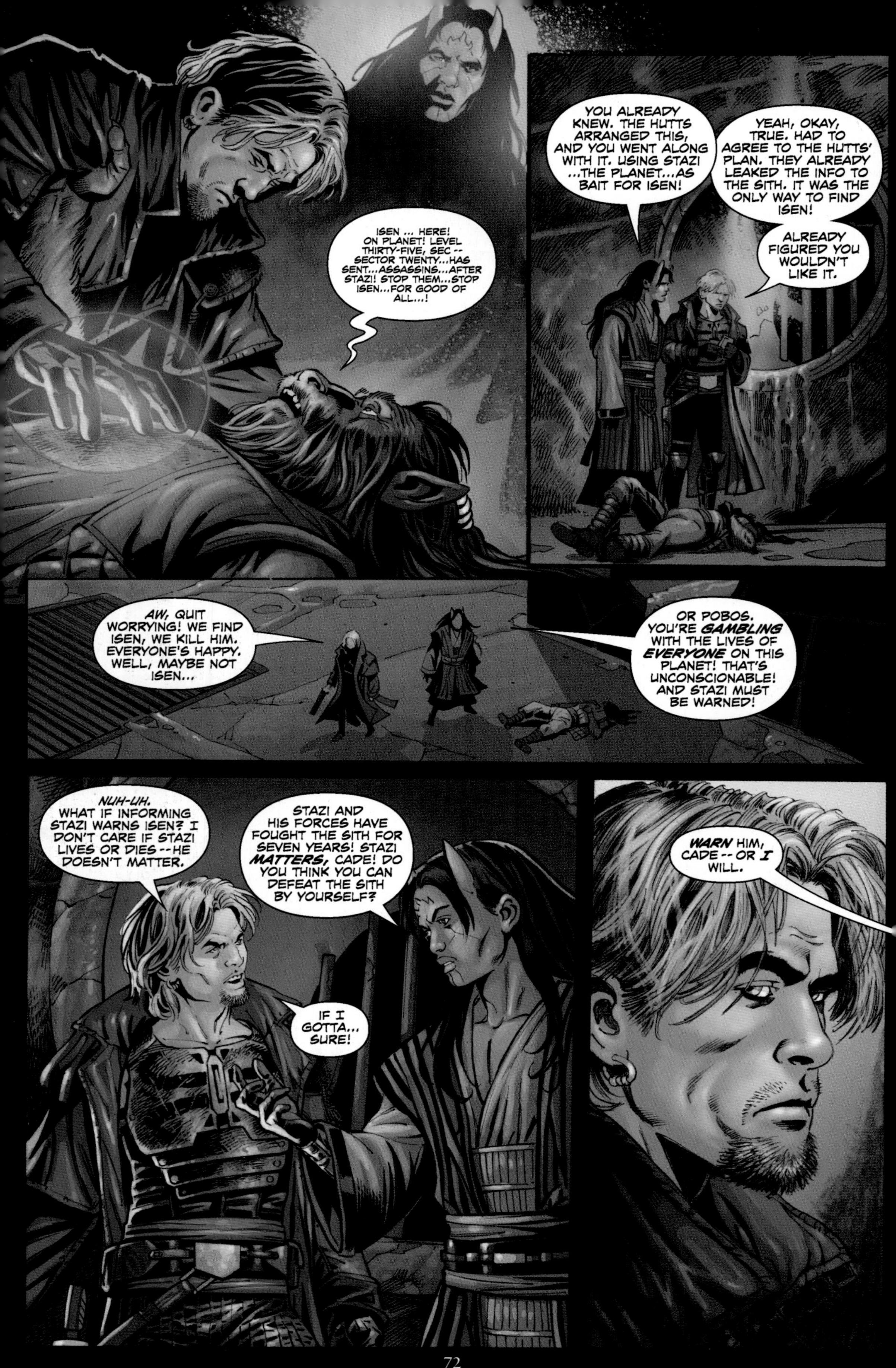
ISEN ... HERE! ON PLANET! LEVEL THIRTY-FIVE, SEC -- SECTOR TWENTY...HAS SENT...ASSASSINS...AFTER STAZI! STOP THEM...STOP ISEN...FOR GOOD OF ALL...!
YOU ALREADY KNEW. THE HUTTS ARRANGED THIS, AND YOU WENT ALONG WITH IT. USING STAZI ...THE PLANET...AS BAIT FOR ISEN!
YEAH, OKAY, TRUE. HAD TO AGREE TO THE HUTTS' PLAN. THEY ALREADY LEAKED THE INFO TO THE SITH. IT WAS THE ONLY WAY TO FIND ISEN!
ALREADY FIGURED YOU WOULDN'T LIKE IT.
AW, QUIT WORRYING! WE FIND ISEN, WE KILL HIM. EVERYONE'S HAPPY. WELL, MAYBE NOT ISEN...
OR POBOS. YOU'RE GAMBLING WITH THE LIVES OF EVERYONE ON THIS PLANET! THAT'S UNCONSCIONABLE! AND STAZI MUST BE WARNED!
NUH-UH. WHAT IF INFORMING STAZI WARNS ISEN? I DON'T CARE IF STAZI LIVES OR DIES--HE DOESN'T MATTER.
STAZI AND HIS FORCES HAVE FOUGHT THE SITH FOR SEVEN YEARS! STAZI MATTERS, CADE! DO YOU THINK YOU CAN DEFEAT THE SITH BY YOURSELF?
IF I GOTTA... SURE!
WARN HIM, CADE--OR I WILL.

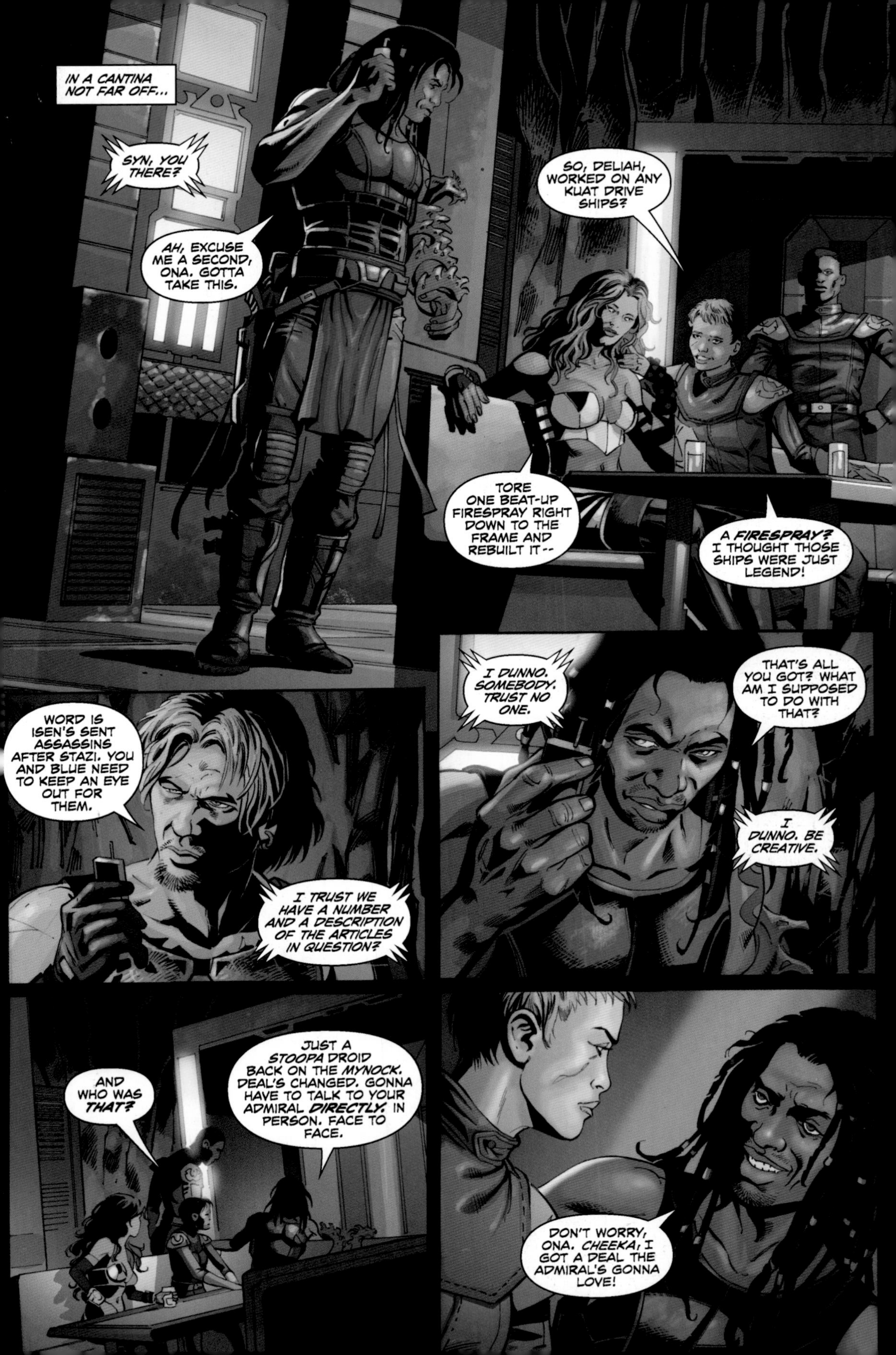
IN A CANTINA NOT FAR OFF...
SYN, YOU THERE?
AH, EXCUSE ME A SECOND, ONA. GOTTA TAKE THIS.
SO, DELIAH, WORKED ON ANY KUAT DRIVE SHIPS?
TORE ONE BEAT-UP FIRESPRAY RIGHT DOWN TO THE FRAME AND REBUILT IT--
A *FIRESPRAY?* I THOUGHT THOSE SHIPS WERE JUST LEGEND!
WORD IS ISEN'S SENT ASSASSINS AFTER STAZI. YOU AND BLUE NEED TO KEEP AN EYE OUT FOR THEM.
I TRUST WE HAVE A NUMBER AND A DESCRIPTION OF THE ARTICLES IN QUESTION?
I DUNNO. SOMEBODY. TRUST NO ONE.
THAT'S ALL YOU GOT? WHAT AM I SUPPOSED TO DO WITH THAT?
I DUNNO. BE CREATIVE.
AND WHO WAS *THAT?*
JUST A *STOOPA* DROID BACK ON THE *MYNOCK*. DEAL'S CHANGED. GONNA HAVE TO TALK TO YOUR ADMIRAL *DIRECTLY.* IN PERSON. FACE TO FACE.
DON'T WORRY, ONA. *CHEEKA*, I GOT A DEAL THE ADMIRAL'S GONNA LOVE!

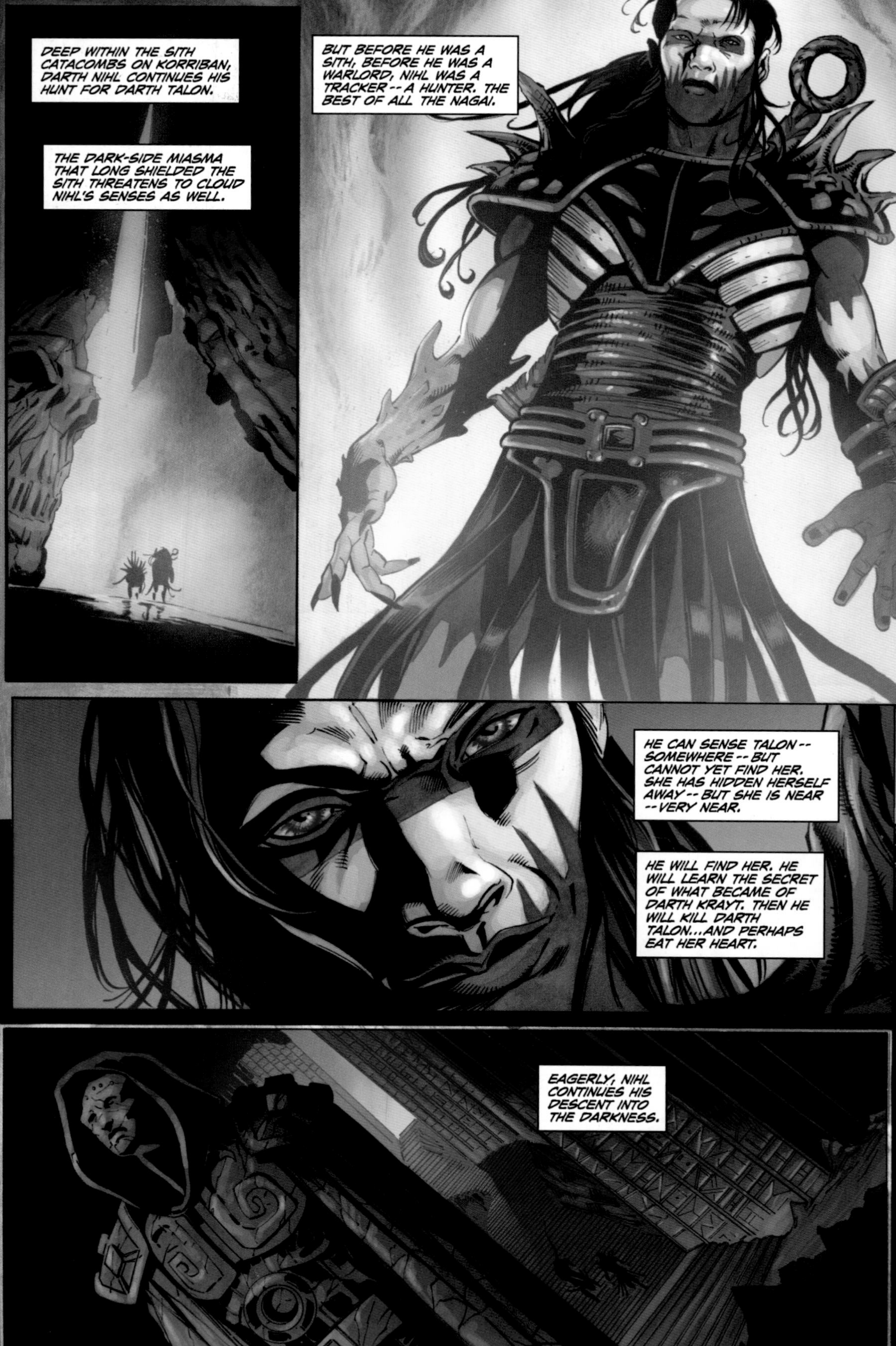
DEEP WITHIN THE SITH CATACOMBS ON KORRIBAN, DARTH NIHL CONTINUES HIS HUNT FOR DARTH TALON.
THE DARK-SIDE MIASMA THAT LONG SHIELDED THE SITH THREATENS TO CLOUD NIHL'S SENSES AS WELL.
BUT BEFORE HE WAS A SITH, BEFORE HE WAS A WARLORD, NIHL WAS A TRACKER -- A HUNTER. THE BEST OF ALL THE NAGAI.
HE CAN SENSE TALON -- SOMEWHERE -- BUT CANNOT YET FIND HER. SHE HAS HIDDEN HERSELF AWAY -- BUT SHE IS NEAR --VERY NEAR.
HE WILL FIND HER. HE WILL LEARN THE SECRET OF WHAT BECAME OF DARTH KRAYT. THEN HE WILL KILL DARTH TALON...AND PERHAPS EAT HER HEART.
EAGERLY, NIHL CONTINUES HIS DESCENT INTO THE DARKNESS.

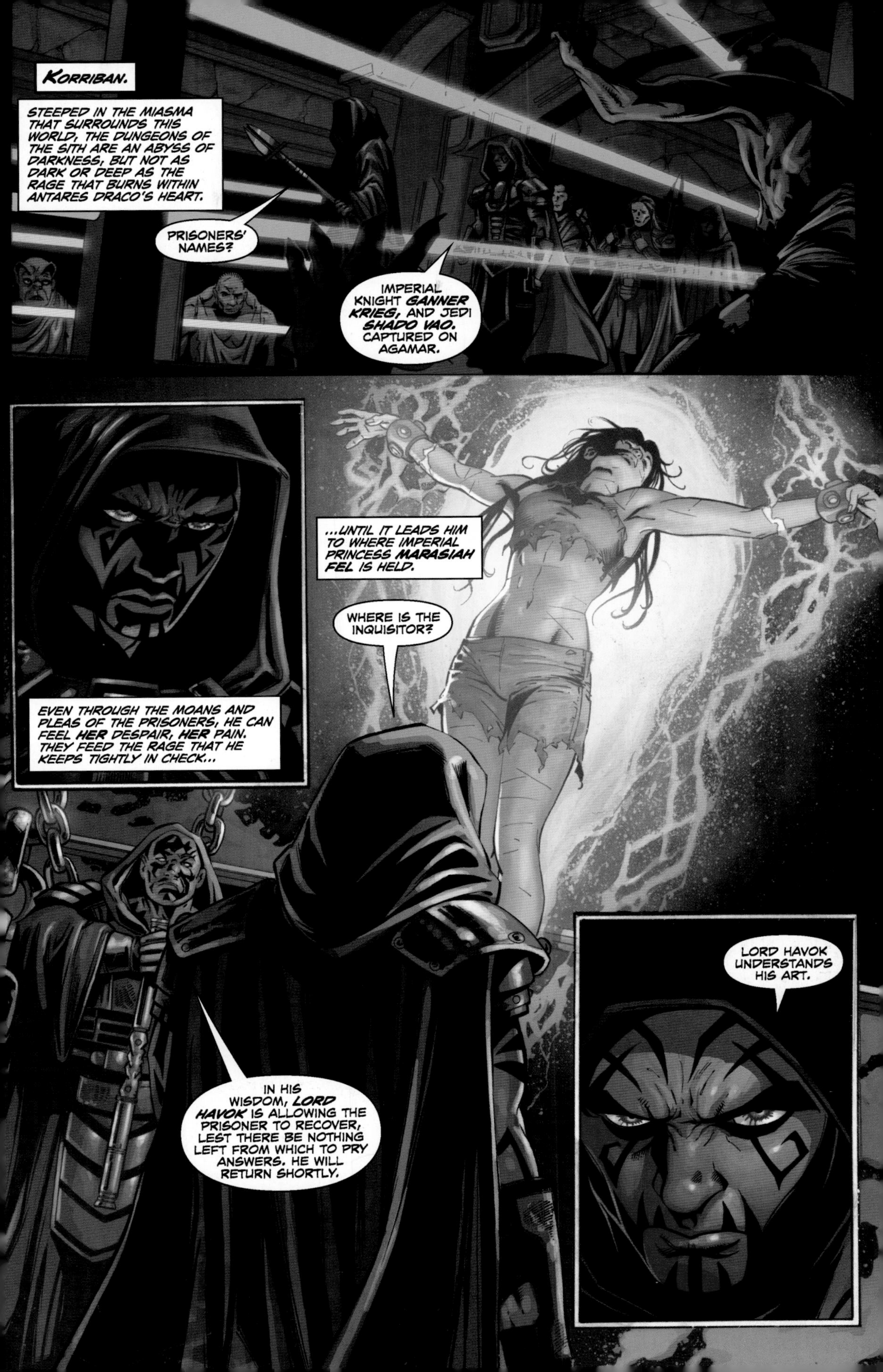
KORRIBAN.
STEEPED IN THE MIASMA THAT SURROUNDS THIS WORLD, THE DUNGEONS OF THE SITH ARE AN ABYSS OF DARKNESS, BUT NOT AS DARK OR DEEP AS THE RAGE THAT BURNS WITHIN ANTARES DRACO'S HEART.
PRISONERS' NAMES?
IMPERIAL KNIGHT GANNER KRIEG, AND JEDI SHADO VAO. CAPTURED ON AGAMAR.
EVEN THROUGH THE MOANS AND PLEAS OF THE PRISONERS, HE CAN FEEL HER DESPAIR, HER PAIN. THEY FEED THE RAGE THAT HE KEEPS TIGHTLY IN CHECK...
...UNTIL IT LEADS HIM TO WHERE IMPERIAL PRINCESS MARASIAH FEL IS HELD.
WHERE IS THE INQUISITOR?
IN HIS WISDOM, LORD HAVOK IS ALLOWING THE PRISONER TO RECOVER, LEST THERE BE NOTHING LEFT FROM WHICH TO PRY ANSWERS. HE WILL RETURN SHORTLY.
LORD HAVOK UNDERSTANDS HIS ART.

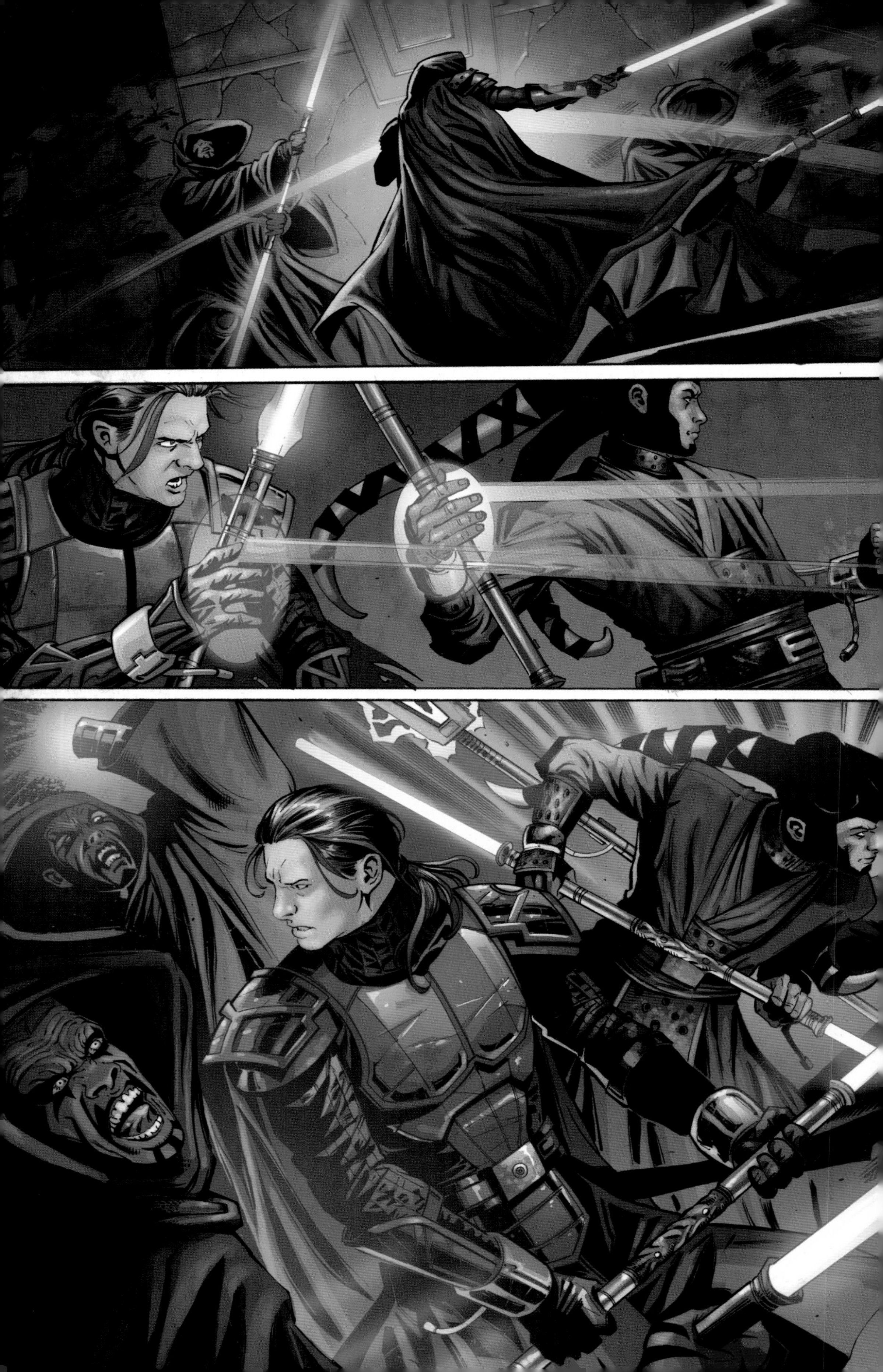

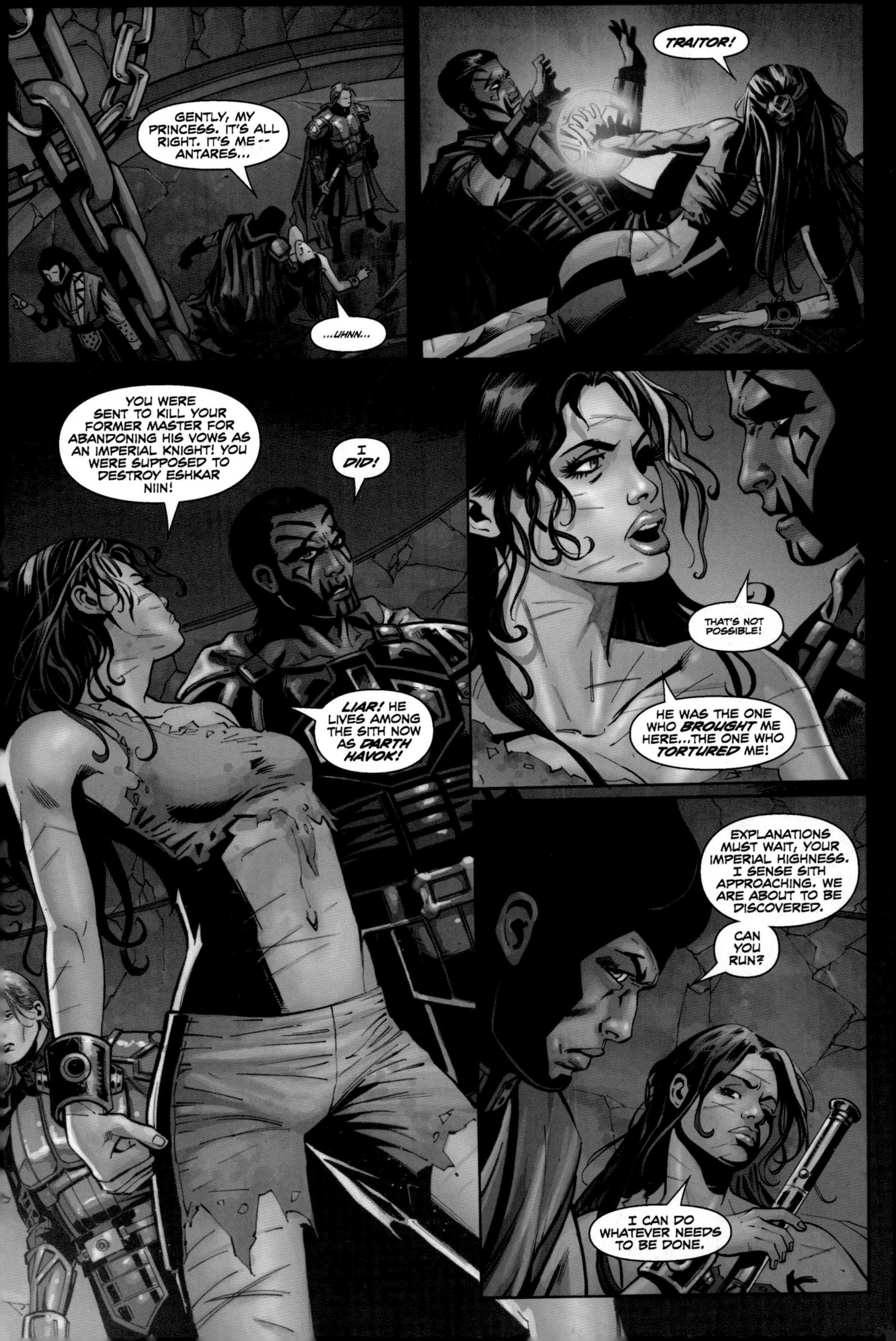
GENTLY, MY PRINCESS. IT'S ALL RIGHT. IT'S ME -- ANTARES...
...UHNN...
TRAITOR!
YOU WERE SENT TO KILL YOUR FORMER MASTER FOR ABANDONING HIS VOWS AS AN IMPERIAL KNIGHT! YOU WERE SUPPOSED TO DESTROY ESHKAR NIIN!
I DID!
LIAR! HE LIVES AMONG THE SITH NOW AS DARTH HAVOK!
THAT'S NOT POSSIBLE!
HE WAS THE ONE WHO BROUGHT ME HERE...THE ONE WHO TORTURED ME!
EXPLANATIONS MUST WAIT, YOUR IMPERIAL HIGHNESS. I SENSE SITH APPROACHING. WE ARE ABOUT TO BE DISCOVERED.
CAN YOU RUN?
I CAN DO WHATEVER NEEDS TO BE DONE.

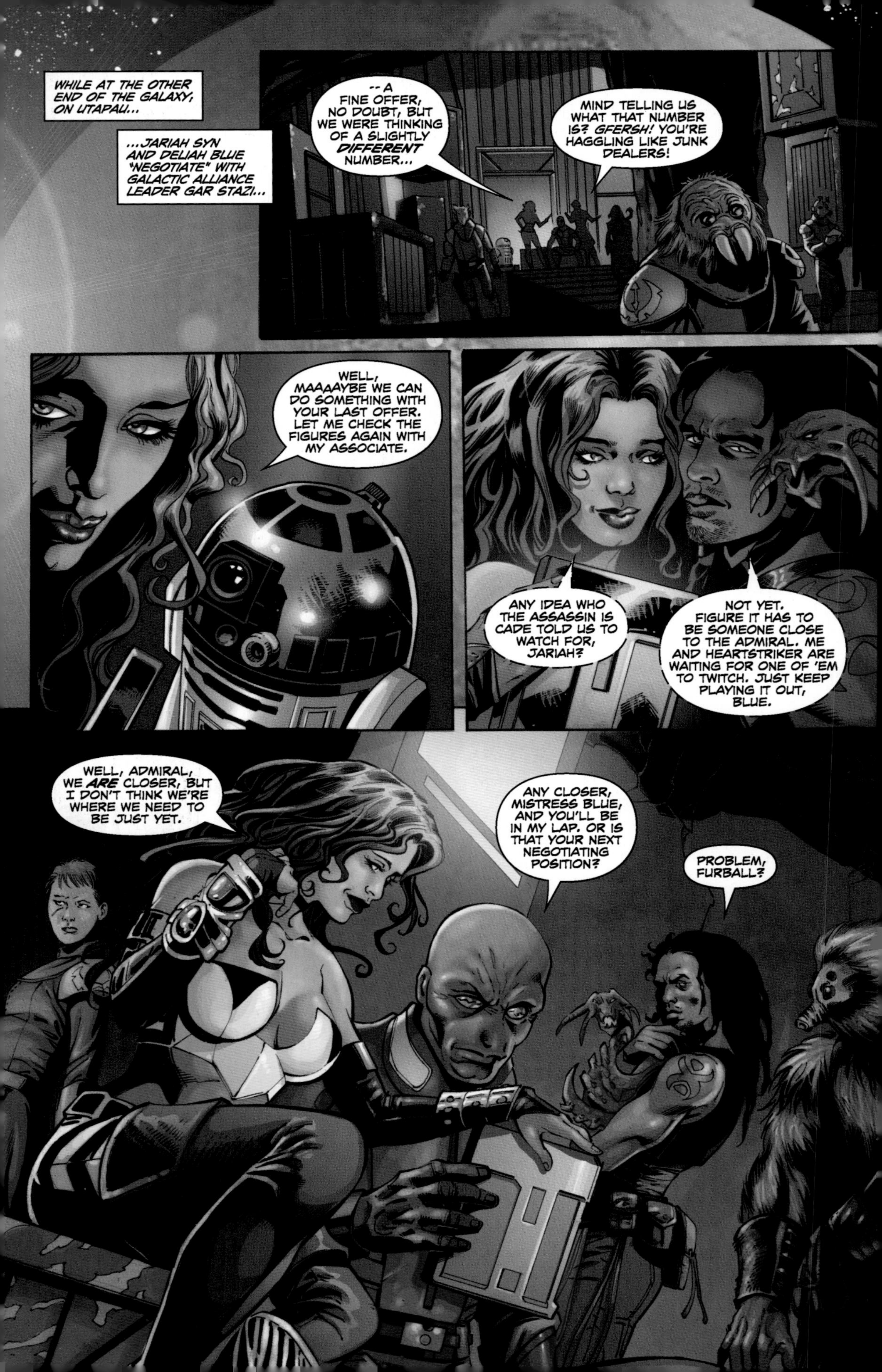
WHILE AT THE OTHER END OF THE GALAXY, ON UTAPAU...
...JARIAH SYN AND DELIAH BLUE "NEGOTIATE" WITH GALACTIC ALLIANCE LEADER GAR STAZI...
--A FINE OFFER, NO DOUBT, BUT WE WERE THINKING OF A SLIGHTLY *DIFFERENT* NUMBER...
MIND TELLING US WHAT THAT NUMBER IS? *GFERSH!* YOU'RE HAGGLING LIKE JUNK DEALERS!
WELL, MAAAAYBE WE CAN DO SOMETHING WITH YOUR LAST OFFER. LET ME CHECK THE FIGURES AGAIN WITH MY ASSOCIATE.
ANY IDEA WHO THE ASSASSIN IS CADE TOLD US TO WATCH FOR, JARIAH?
NOT YET. FIGURE IT HAS TO BE SOMEONE CLOSE TO THE ADMIRAL. ME AND HEARTSTRIKER ARE WAITING FOR ONE OF 'EM TO TWITCH. JUST KEEP PLAYING IT OUT, BLUE.
WELL, ADMIRAL, WE *ARE* CLOSER, BUT I DON'T THINK WE'RE WHERE WE NEED TO BE JUST YET.
ANY CLOSER, MISTRESS BLUE, AND YOU'LL BE IN MY LAP. OR IS THAT YOUR NEXT NEGOTIATING POSITION?
PROBLEM, FURBALL?

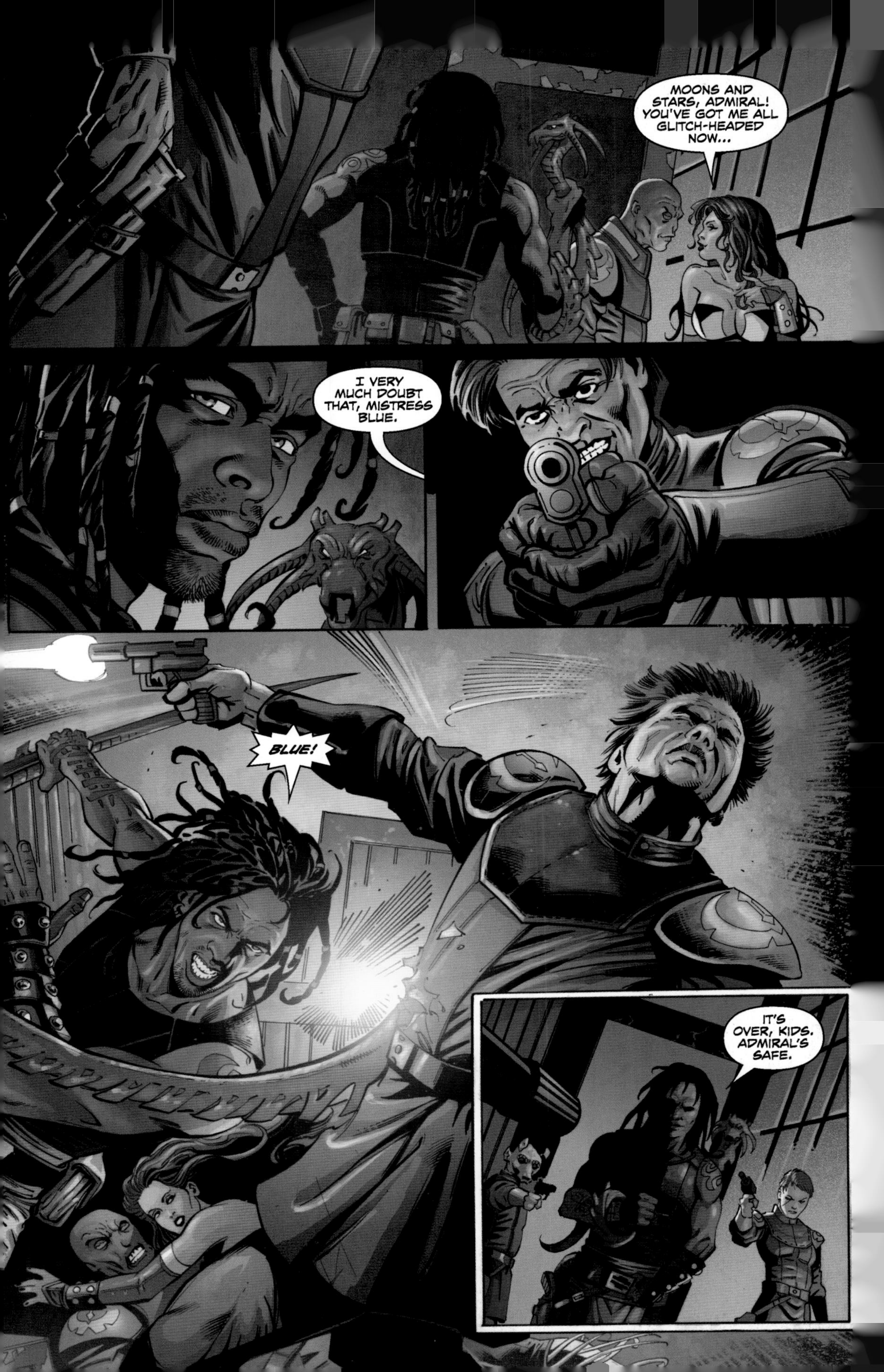
MOONS AND STARS, ADMIRAL! YOU'VE GOT ME ALL GLITCH-HEADED NOW...
I VERY MUCH DOUBT THAT, MISTRESS BLUE.
BLUE!
IT'S OVER, KIDS. ADMIRAL'S SAFE.

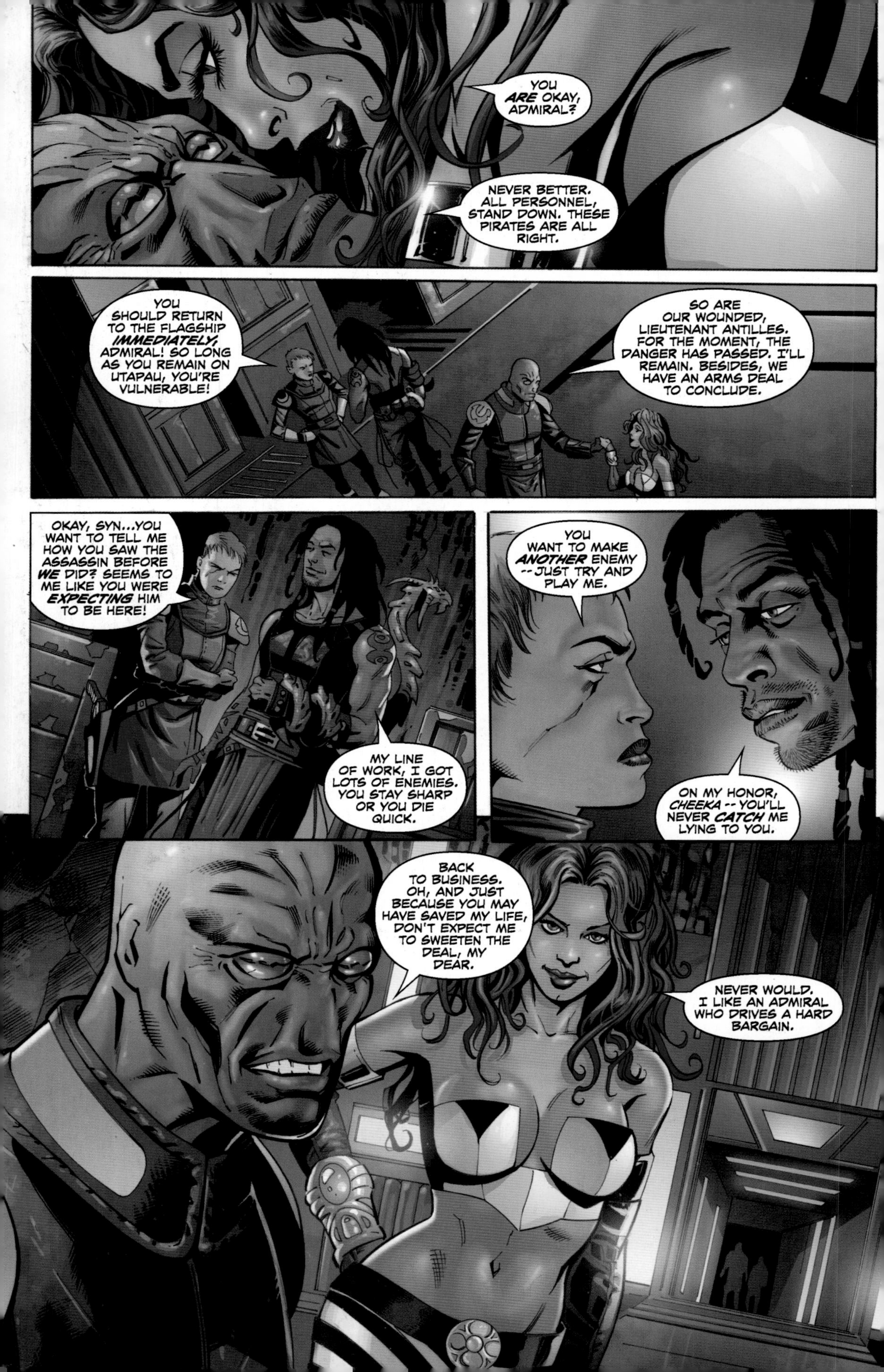
YOU ARE OKAY, ADMIRAL?
NEVER BETTER. ALL PERSONNEL, STAND DOWN. THESE PIRATES ARE ALL RIGHT.
YOU SHOULD RETURN TO THE FLAGSHIP IMMEDIATELY, ADMIRAL! SO LONG AS YOU REMAIN ON UTAPAU, YOU'RE VULNERABLE!
SO ARE OUR WOUNDED, LIEUTENANT ANTILLES. FOR THE MOMENT, THE DANGER HAS PASSED. I'LL REMAIN. BESIDES, WE HAVE AN ARMS DEAL TO CONCLUDE.
OKAY, SYN...YOU WANT TO TELL ME HOW YOU SAW THE ASSASSIN BEFORE WE DID? SEEMS TO ME LIKE YOU WERE EXPECTING HIM TO BE HERE!
MY LINE OF WORK, I GOT LOTS OF ENEMIES. YOU STAY SHARP OR YOU DIE QUICK.
YOU WANT TO MAKE ANOTHER ENEMY --JUST TRY AND PLAY ME.
ON MY HONOR, CHEEKA--YOU'LL NEVER CATCH ME LYING TO YOU.
BACK TO BUSINESS. OH, AND JUST BECAUSE YOU MAY HAVE SAVED MY LIFE, DON'T EXPECT ME TO SWEETEN THE DEAL, MY DEAR.
NEVER WOULD. I LIKE AN ADMIRAL WHO DRIVES A HARD BARGAIN.

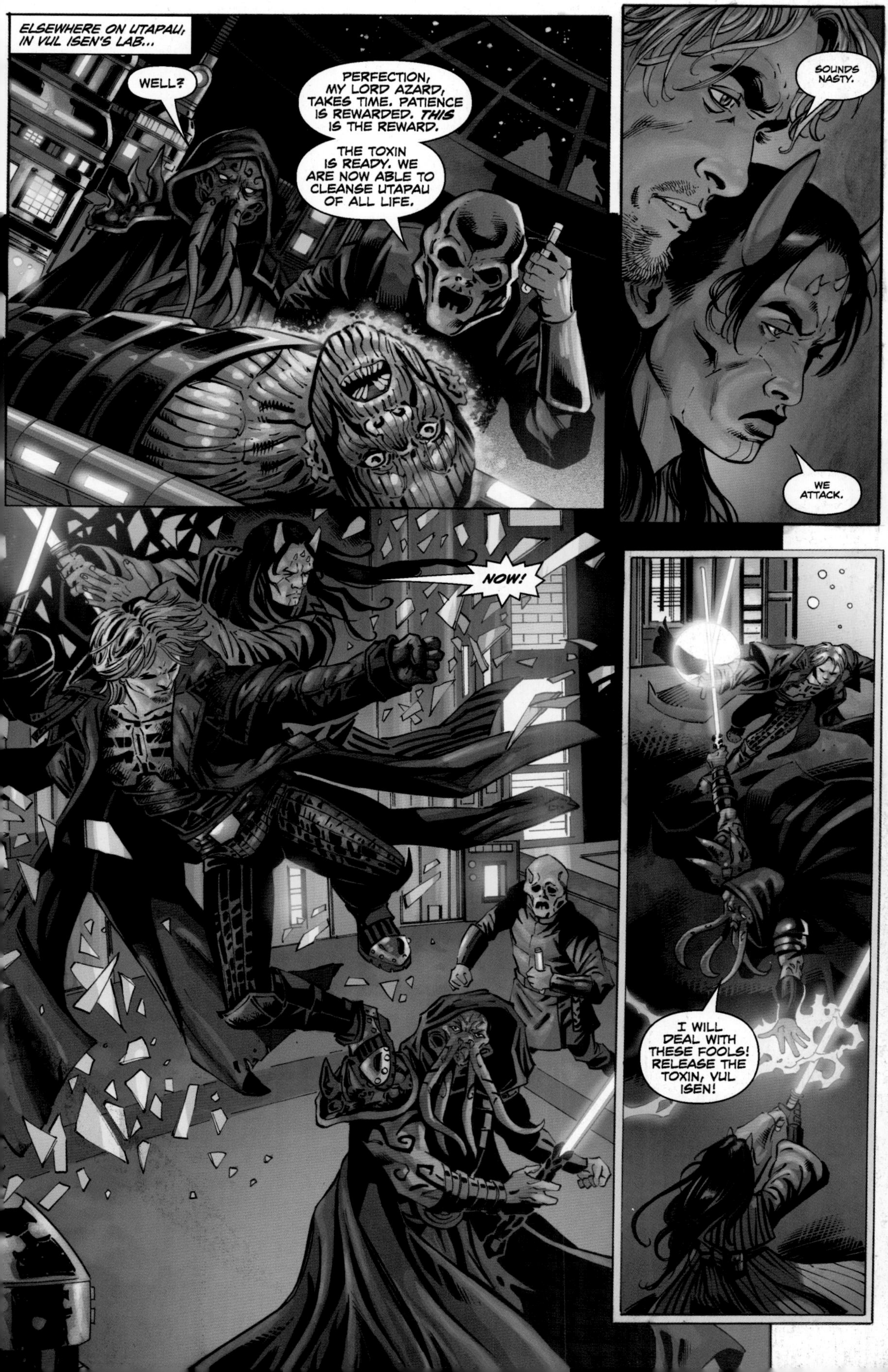

ELSEWHERE ON UTAPAU, IN VUL ISEN'S LAB...
WELL?
PERFECTION, MY LORD AZARD, TAKES TIME. PATIENCE IS REWARDED. *THIS* IS THE REWARD.
THE TOXIN IS READY. WE ARE NOW ABLE TO CLEANSE UTAPAU OF ALL LIFE.
SOUNDS NASTY.
WE ATTACK.
NOW!
I WILL DEAL WITH THESE FOOLS! RELEASE THE TOXIN, VUL ISEN!

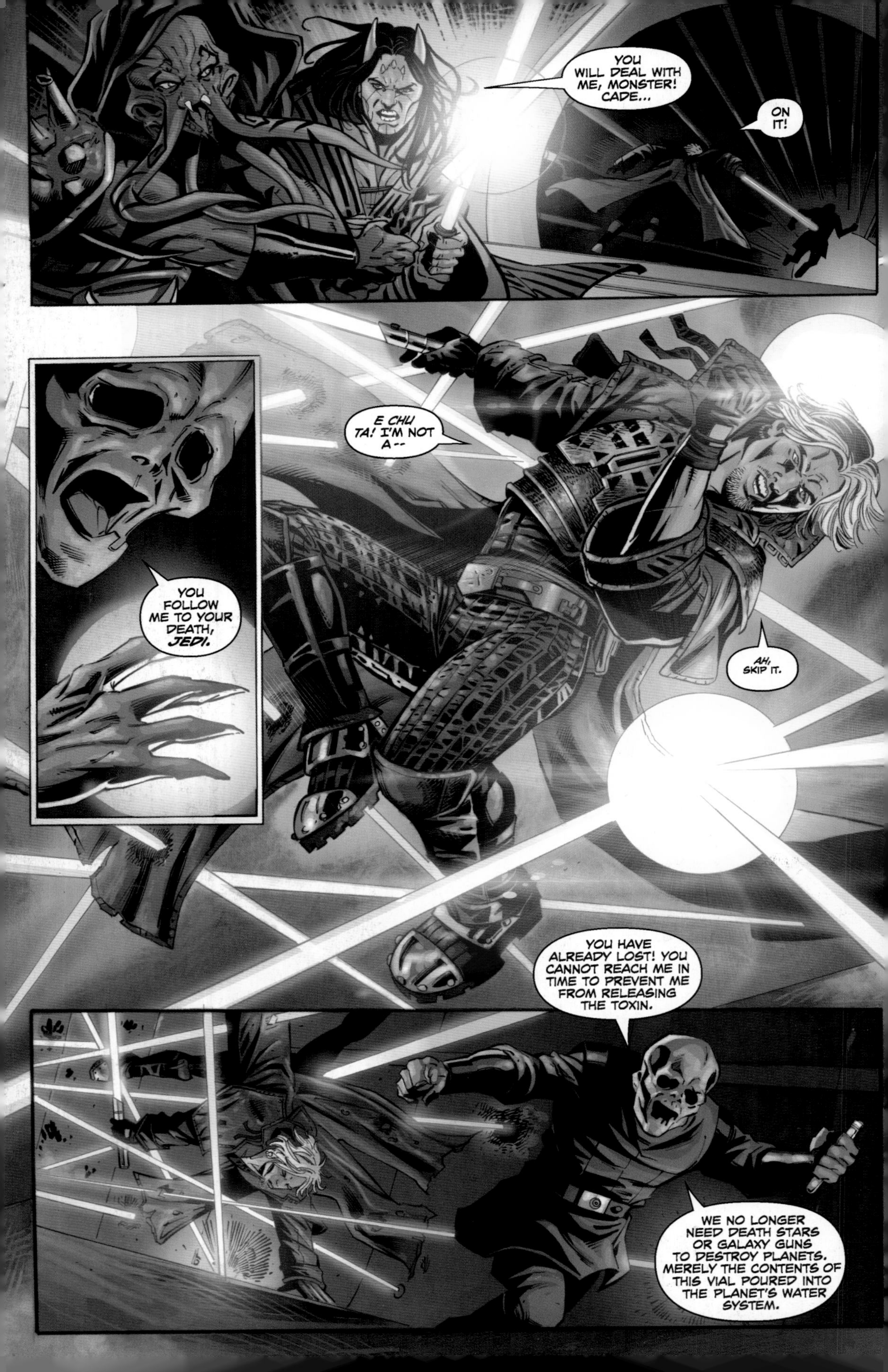
YOU WILL DEAL WITH ME, MONSTER! CADE...
ON IT!
E CHU TA! I'M NOT A--
YOU FOLLOW ME TO YOUR DEATH, *JEDI.*
AH, SKIP IT.
YOU HAVE ALREADY LOST! YOU CANNOT REACH ME IN TIME TO PREVENT ME FROM RELEASING THE TOXIN.
WE NO LONGER NEED DEATH STARS OR GALAXY GUNS TO DESTROY PLANETS. MERELY THE CONTENTS OF THIS VIAL POURED INTO THE PLANET'S WATER SYSTEM.

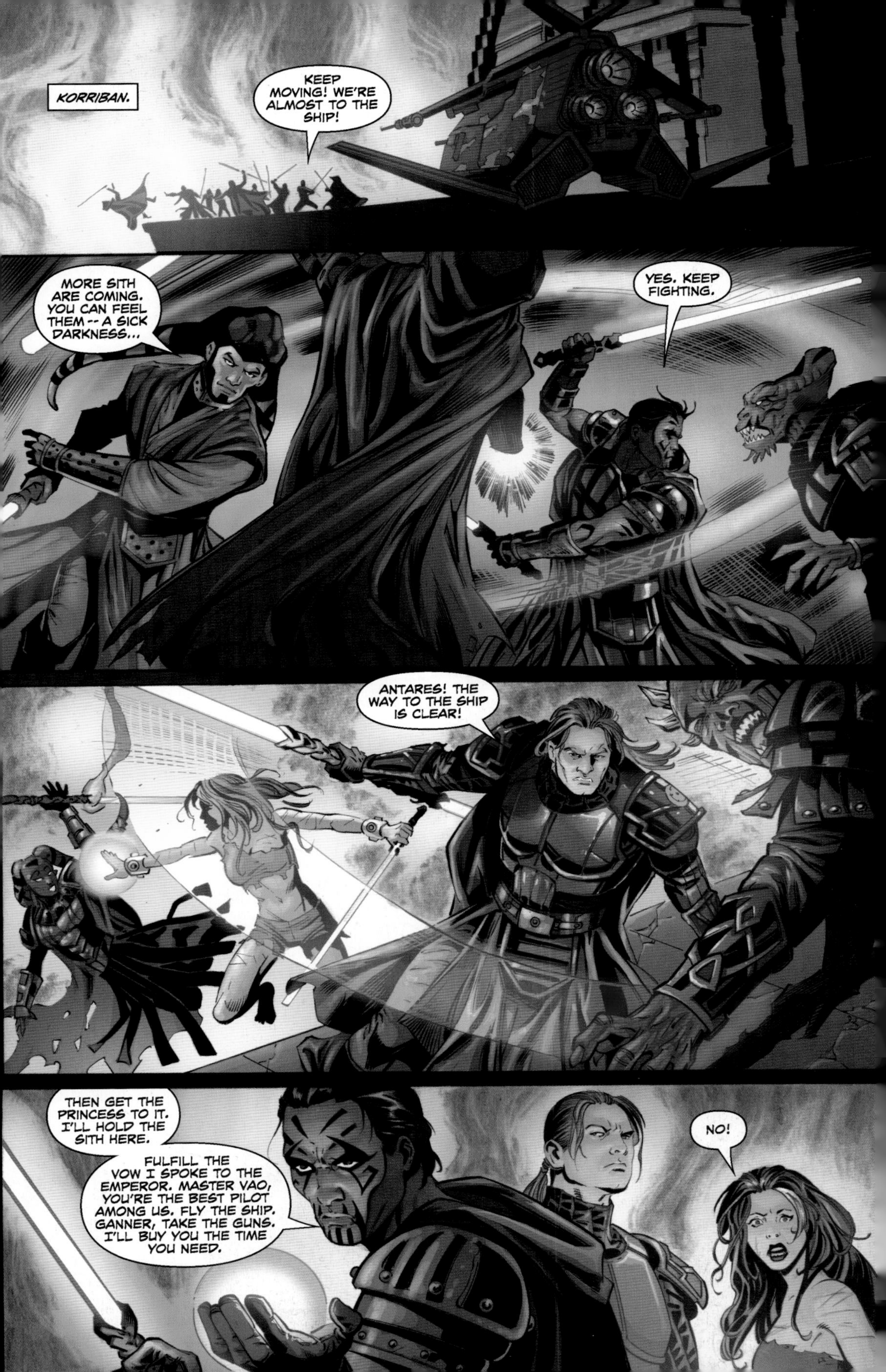
KORRIBAN.
KEEP MOVING! WE'RE ALMOST TO THE SHIP!
MORE SITH ARE COMING. YOU CAN FEEL THEM -- A SICK DARKNESS...
YES. KEEP FIGHTING.
ANTARES! THE WAY TO THE SHIP IS CLEAR!
THEN GET THE PRINCESS TO IT. I'LL HOLD THE SITH HERE.
FULFILL THE VOW I SPOKE TO THE EMPEROR. MASTER VAO, YOU'RE THE BEST PILOT AMONG US. FLY THE SHIP. GANNER, TAKE THE GUNS. I'LL BUY YOU THE TIME YOU NEED.
NO!

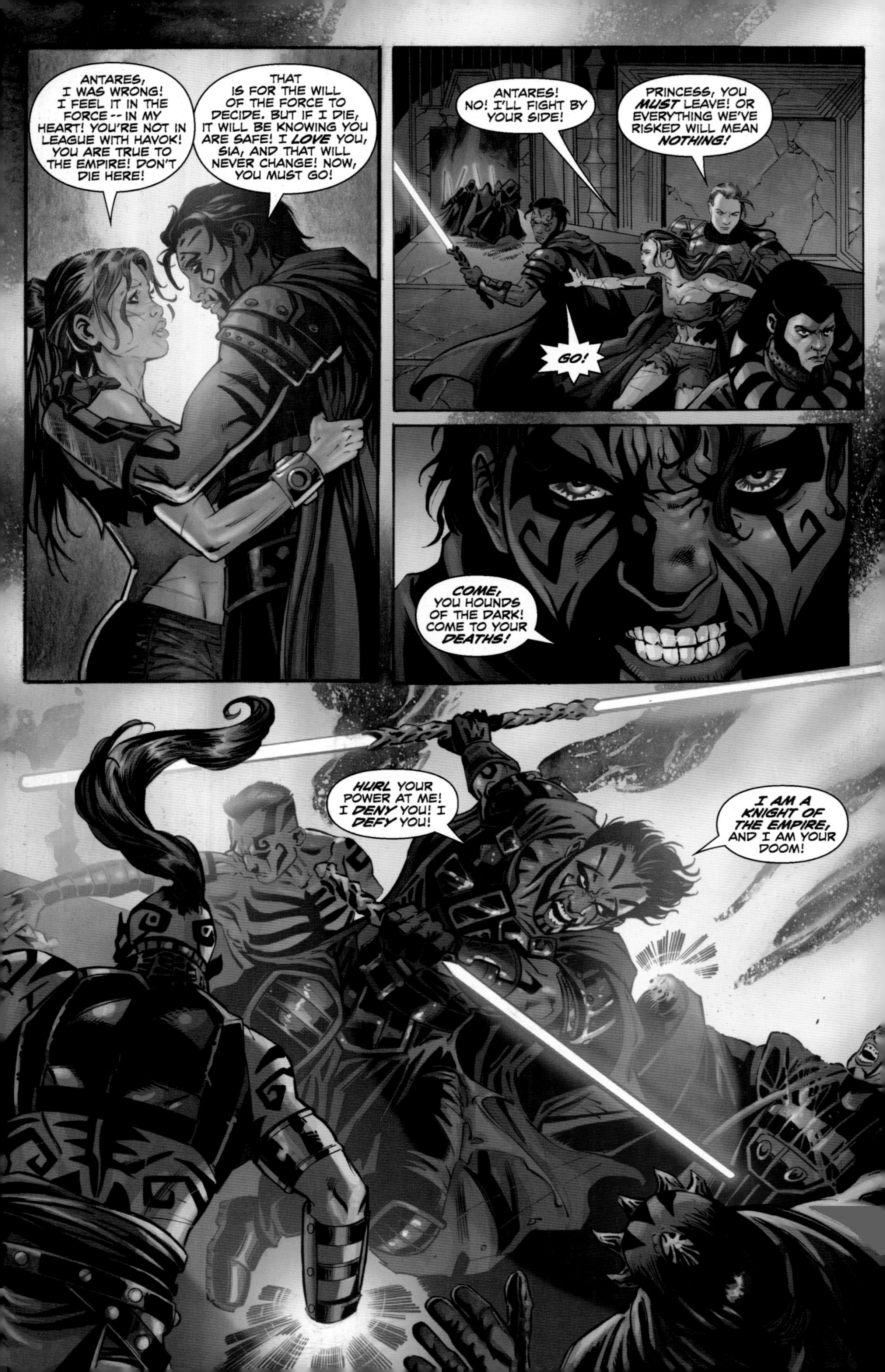
ANTARES, I WAS WRONG! I FEEL IT IN THE FORCE -- IN MY HEART! YOU'RE NOT IN LEAGUE WITH HAVOK! YOU ARE TRUE TO THE EMPIRE! DON'T DIE HERE!
THAT IS FOR THE WILL OF THE FORCE TO DECIDE. BUT IF I DIE, IT WILL BE KNOWING YOU ARE SAFE! I *LOVE* YOU, SIA, AND THAT WILL NEVER CHANGE! NOW, YOU MUST GO!
ANTARES! NO! I'LL FIGHT BY YOUR SIDE!
PRINCESS, YOU *MUST* LEAVE! OR EVERYTHING WE'VE RISKED WILL MEAN *NOTHING!*
GO!
COME, YOU HOUNDS OF THE DARK! COME TO YOUR *DEATHS!*
HURL YOUR POWER AT ME! I *DENY* YOU! I *DEFY* YOU!
I AM A KNIGHT OF THE EMPIRE, AND I AM YOUR DOOM!

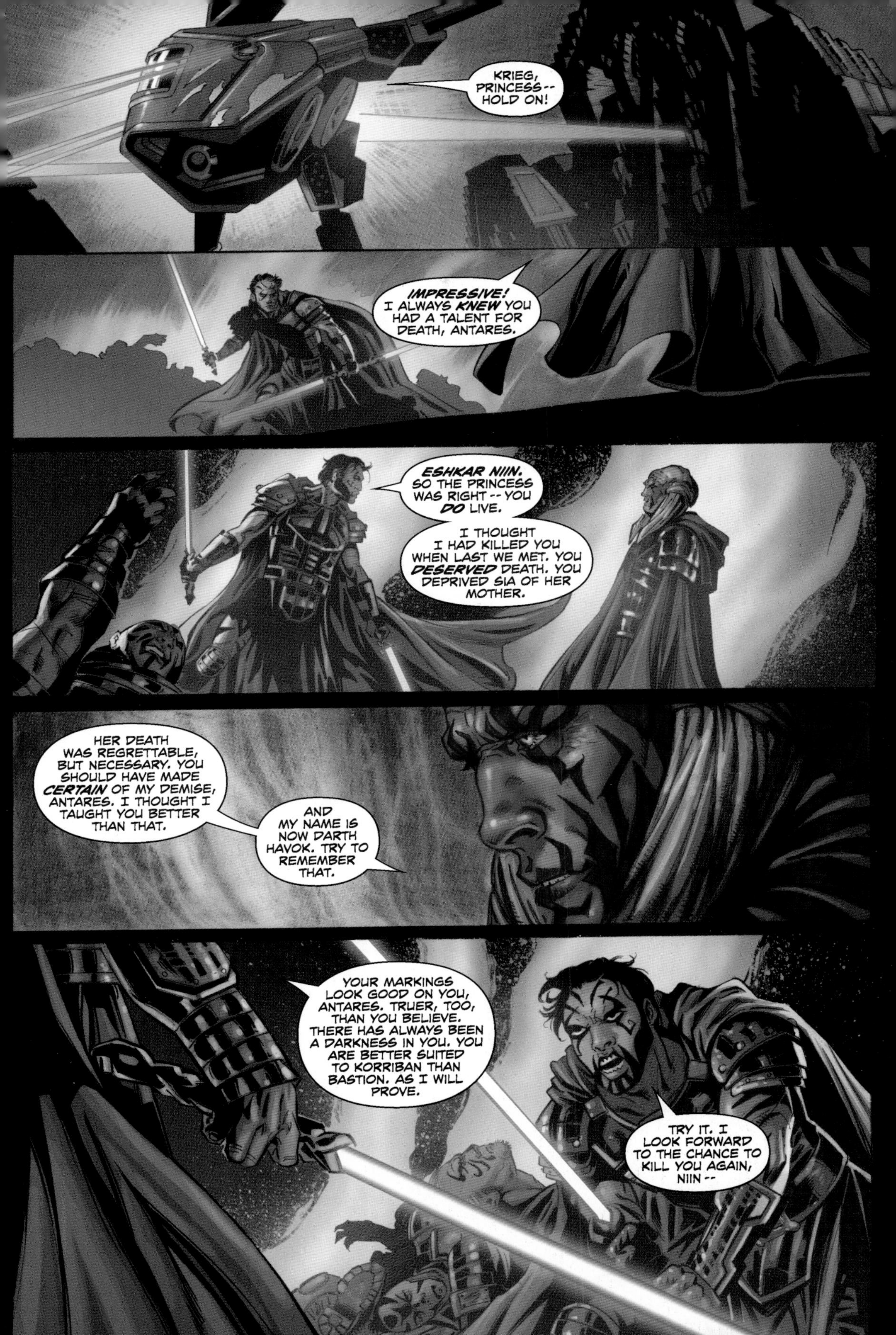
KRIEG, PRINCESS-- HOLD ON!
IMPRESSIVE! I ALWAYS KNEW YOU HAD A TALENT FOR DEATH, ANTARES.
ESHKAR NIIN. SO THE PRINCESS WAS RIGHT -- YOU DO LIVE.
I THOUGHT I HAD KILLED YOU WHEN LAST WE MET. YOU DESERVED DEATH. YOU DEPRIVED SIA OF HER MOTHER.
HER DEATH WAS REGRETTABLE, BUT NECESSARY. YOU SHOULD HAVE MADE CERTAIN OF MY DEMISE, ANTARES. I THOUGHT I TAUGHT YOU BETTER THAN THAT.
AND MY NAME IS NOW DARTH HAVOK. TRY TO REMEMBER THAT.
YOUR MARKINGS LOOK GOOD ON YOU, ANTARES. TRUER, TOO, THAN YOU BELIEVE. THERE HAS ALWAYS BEEN A DARKNESS IN YOU. YOU ARE BETTER SUITED TO KORRIBAN THAN BASTION. AS I WILL PROVE.
TRY IT. I LOOK FORWARD TO THE CHANCE TO KILL YOU AGAIN, NIIN --

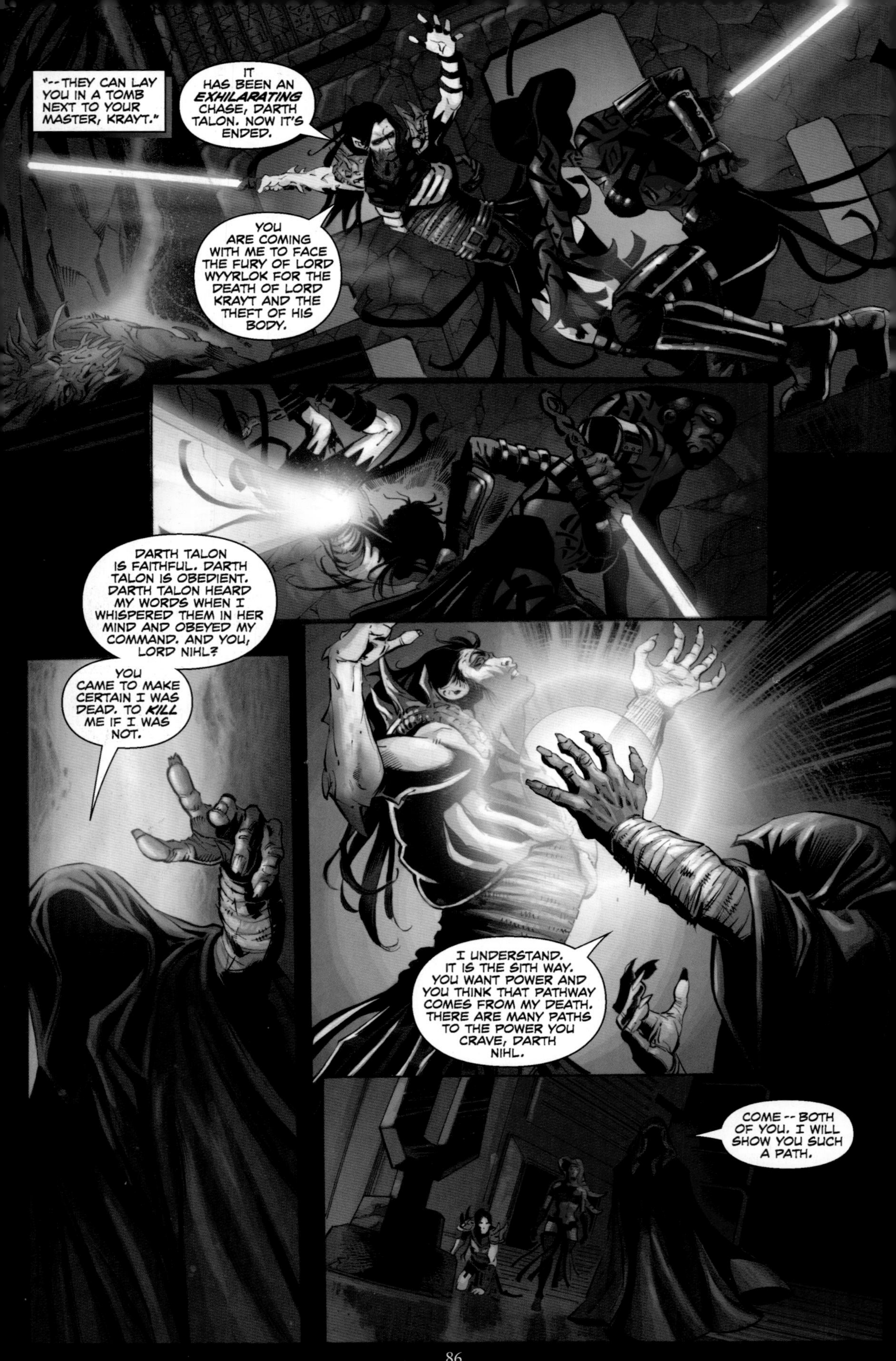
"--THEY CAN LAY YOU IN A TOMB NEXT TO YOUR MASTER, KRAYT."
IT HAS BEEN AN EXHILARATING CHASE, DARTH TALON. NOW IT'S ENDED.
YOU ARE COMING WITH ME TO FACE THE FURY OF LORD WYYRLOK FOR THE DEATH OF LORD KRAYT AND THE THEFT OF HIS BODY.
DARTH TALON IS FAITHFUL. DARTH TALON IS OBEDIENT. DARTH TALON HEARD MY WORDS WHEN I WHISPERED THEM IN HER MIND AND OBEYED MY COMMAND. AND YOU, LORD NIHL?
YOU CAME TO MAKE CERTAIN I WAS DEAD. TO KILL ME IF I WAS NOT.
I UNDERSTAND. IT IS THE SITH WAY. YOU WANT POWER AND YOU THINK THAT PATHWAY COMES FROM MY DEATH. THERE ARE MANY PATHS TO THE POWER YOU CRAVE, DARTH NIHL.
COME -- BOTH OF YOU. I WILL SHOW YOU SUCH A PATH.

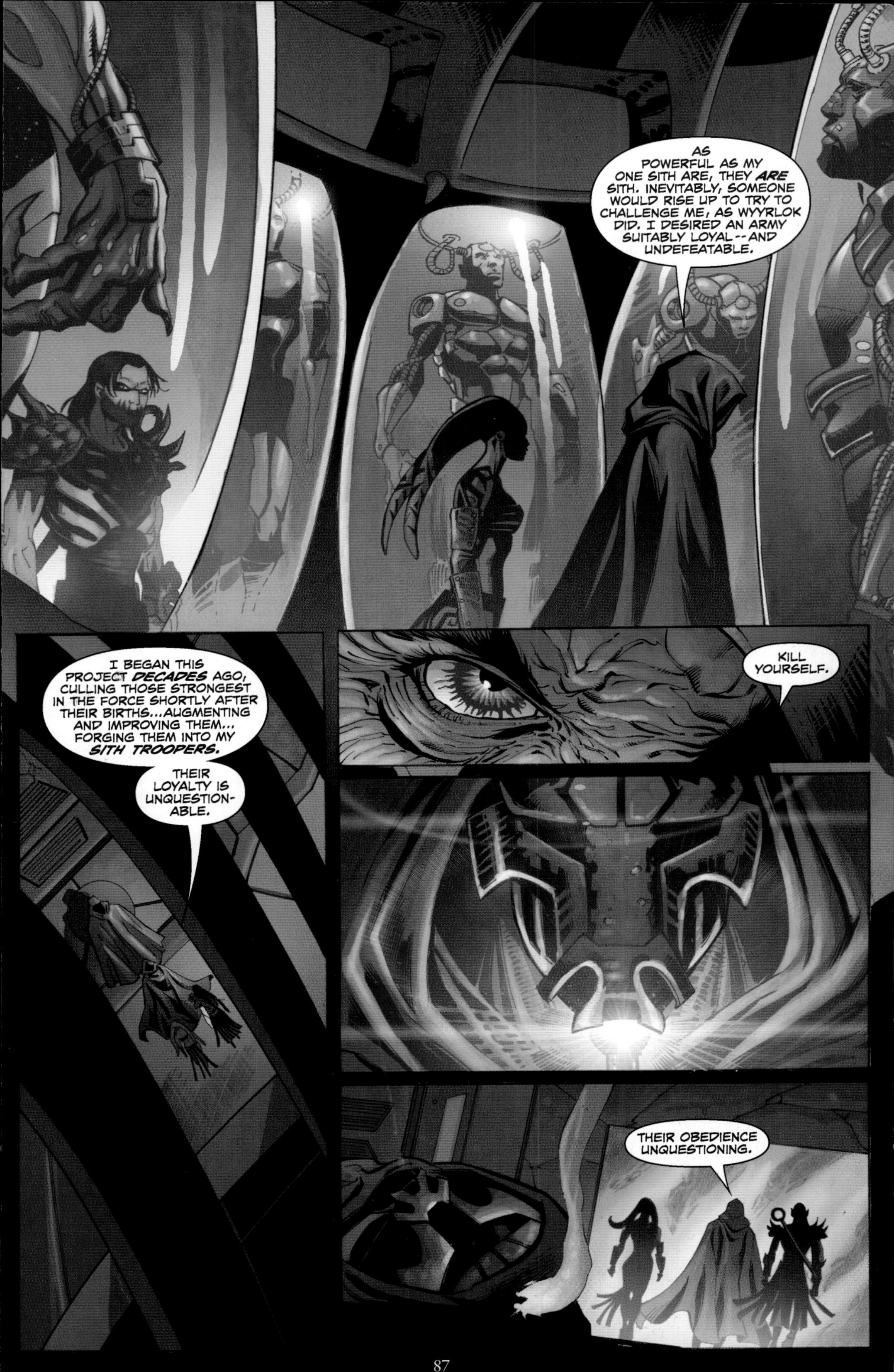
AS POWERFUL AS MY ONE SITH ARE, THEY ARE SITH. INEVITABLY, SOMEONE WOULD RISE UP TO TRY TO CHALLENGE ME, AS WYYRLOK DID. I DESIRED AN ARMY SUITABLY LOYAL--AND UNDEFEATABLE.
I BEGAN THIS PROJECT DECADES AGO, CULLING THOSE STRONGEST IN THE FORCE SHORTLY AFTER THEIR BIRTHS...AUGMENTING AND IMPROVING THEM... FORGING THEM INTO MY SITH TROOPERS.
THEIR LOYALTY IS UNQUESTION-ABLE.
KILL YOURSELF.
THEIR OBEDIENCE UNQUESTIONING.

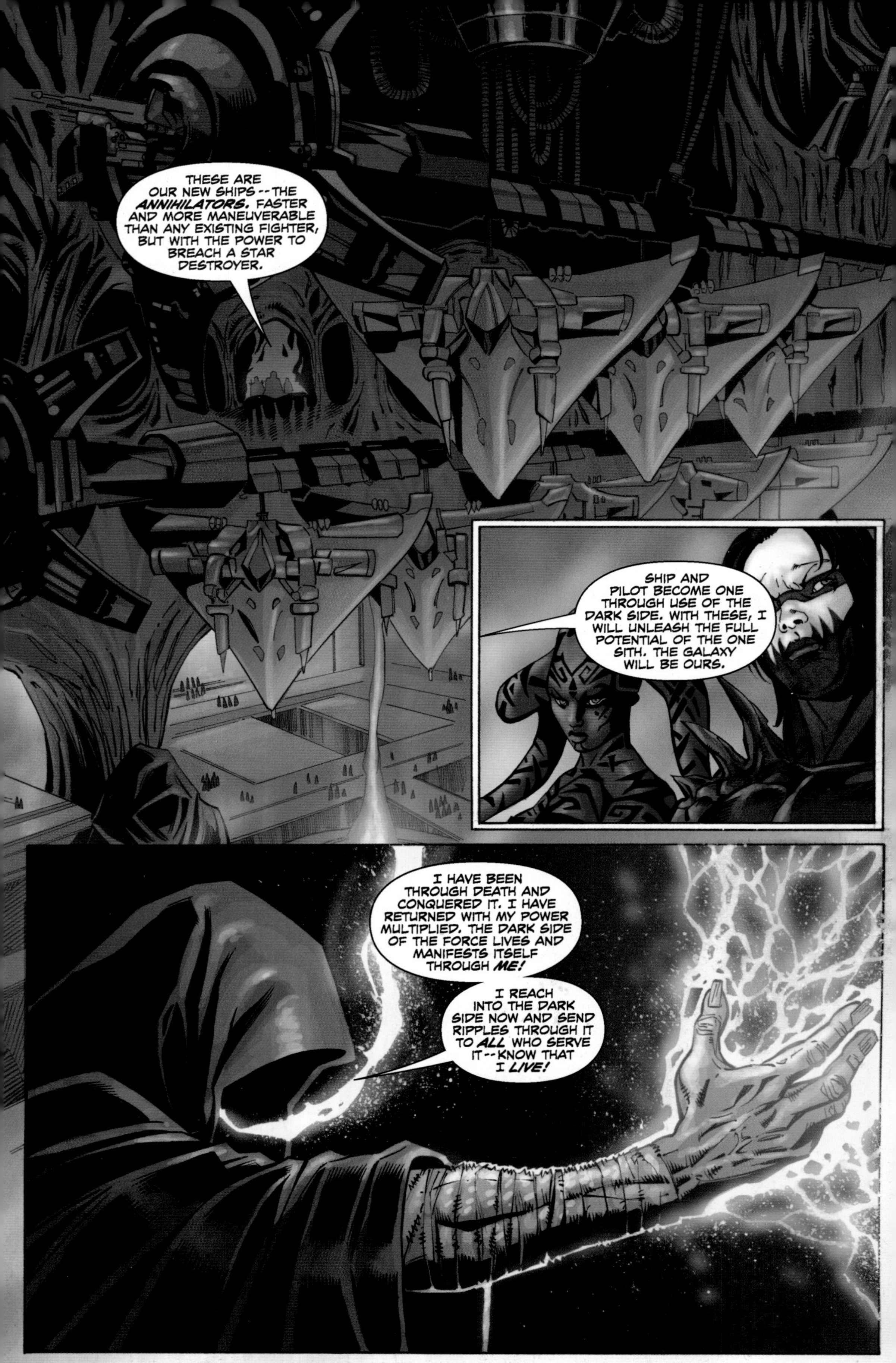

THESE ARE OUR NEW SHIPS -- THE ANNIHILATORS. FASTER AND MORE MANEUVERABLE THAN ANY EXISTING FIGHTER, BUT WITH THE POWER TO BREACH A STAR DESTROYER.
SHIP AND PILOT BECOME ONE THROUGH USE OF THE DARK SIDE. WITH THESE, I WILL UNLEASH THE FULL POTENTIAL OF THE ONE SITH. THE GALAXY WILL BE OURS.
I HAVE BEEN THROUGH DEATH AND CONQUERED IT. I HAVE RETURNED WITH MY POWER MULTIPLIED. THE DARK SIDE OF THE FORCE LIVES AND MANIFESTS ITSELF THROUGH ME!
I REACH INTO THE DARK SIDE NOW AND SEND RIPPLES THROUGH IT TO ALL WHO SERVE IT -- KNOW THAT I LIVE!

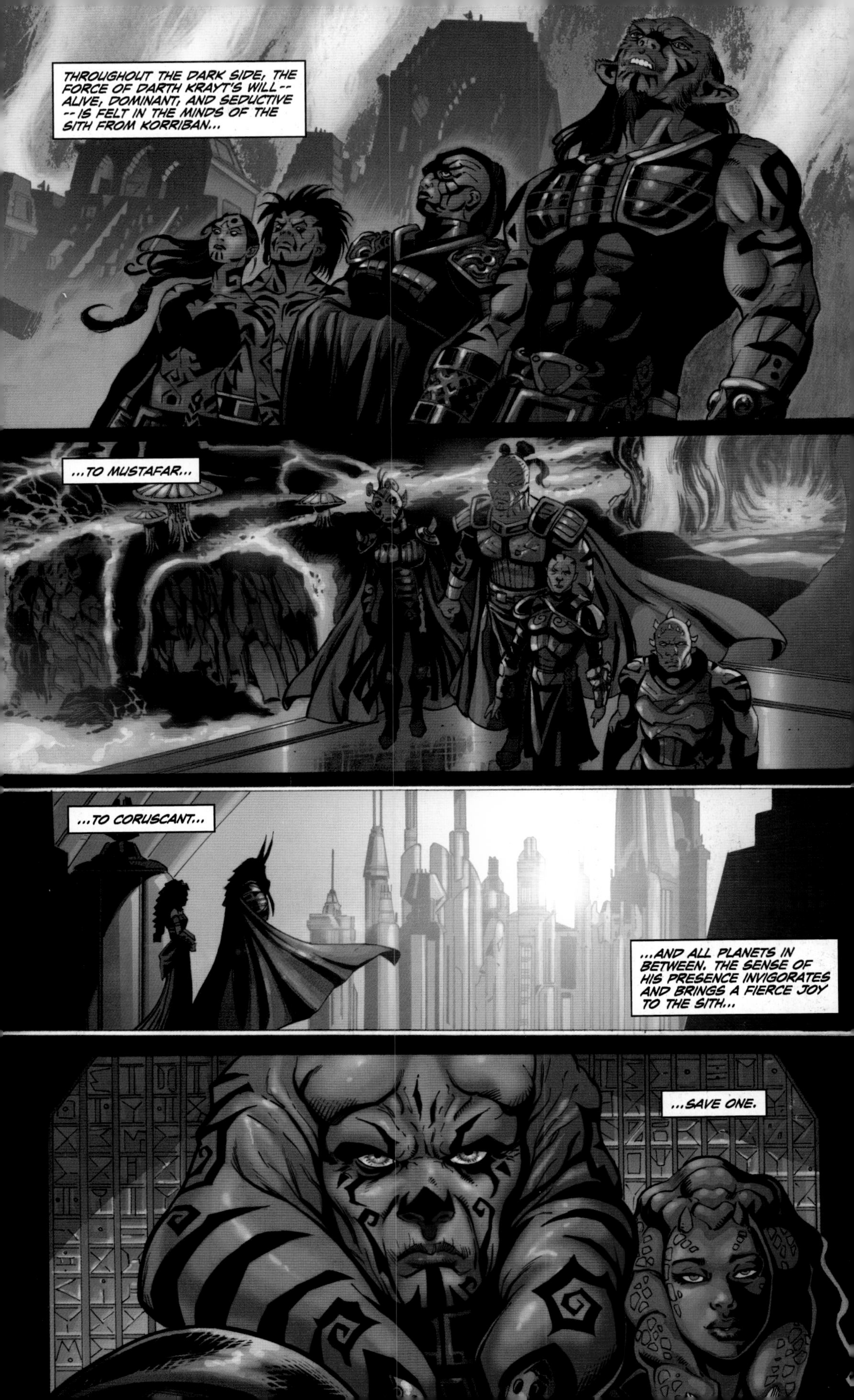
THROUGHOUT THE DARK SIDE, THE FORCE OF DARTH KRAYT'S WILL -- ALIVE, DOMINANT, AND SEDUCTIVE -- IS FELT IN THE MINDS OF THE SITH FROM KORRIBAN...
...TO MUSTAFAR...
...TO CORUSCANT...
...AND ALL PLANETS IN BETWEEN. THE SENSE OF HIS PRESENCE INVIGORATES AND BRINGS A FIERCE JOY TO THE SITH...
...SAVE ONE.

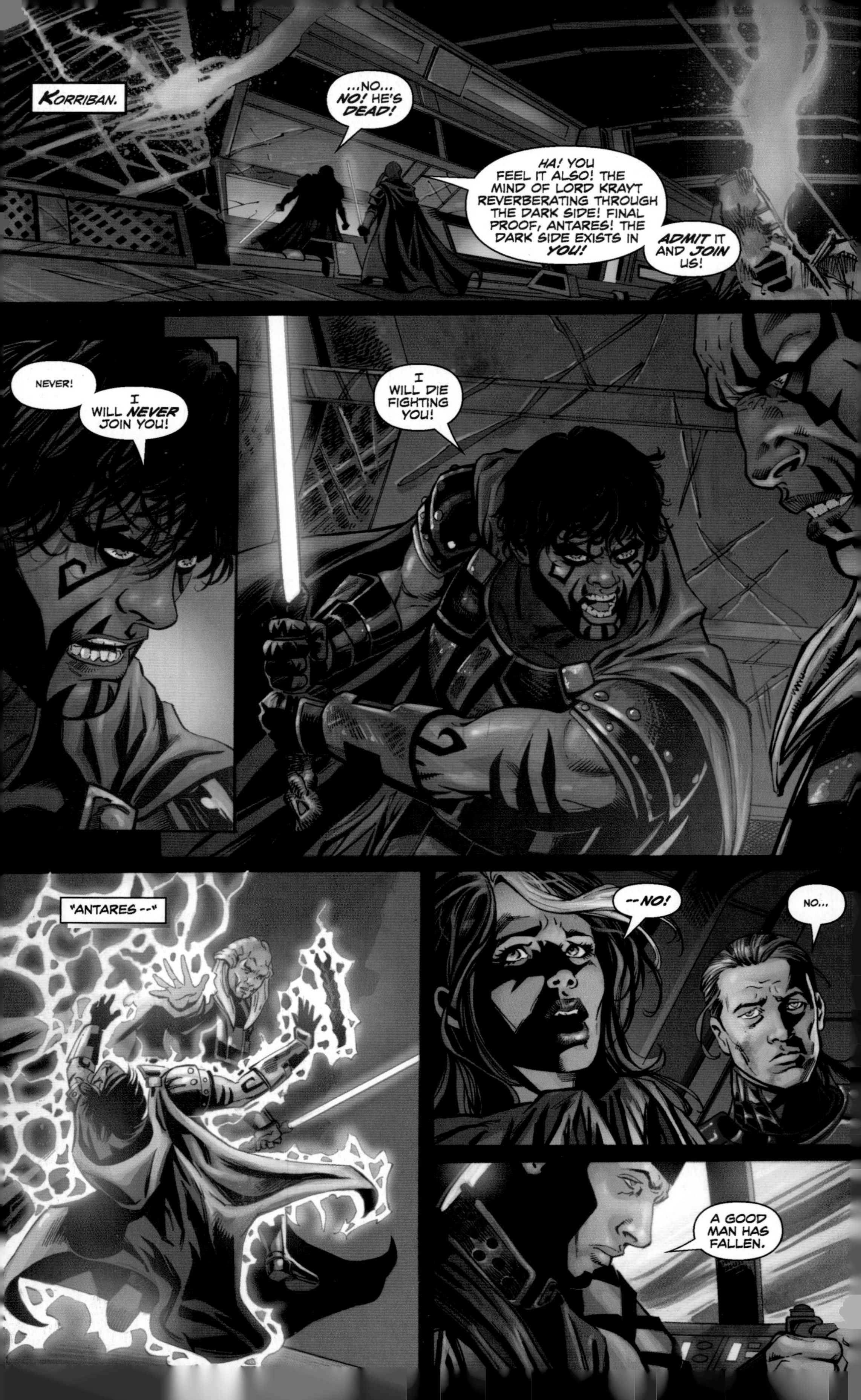

Korriban.
...NO... NO! HE'S DEAD!
HA! YOU FEEL IT ALSO! THE MIND OF LORD KRAYT REVERBERATING THROUGH THE DARK SIDE! FINAL PROOF, ANTARES! THE DARK SIDE EXISTS IN YOU!
ADMIT IT AND JOIN US!
NEVER!
I WILL NEVER JOIN YOU!
I WILL DIE FIGHTING YOU!
"ANTARES --"
--NO!
NO...
A GOOD MAN HAS FALLEN.

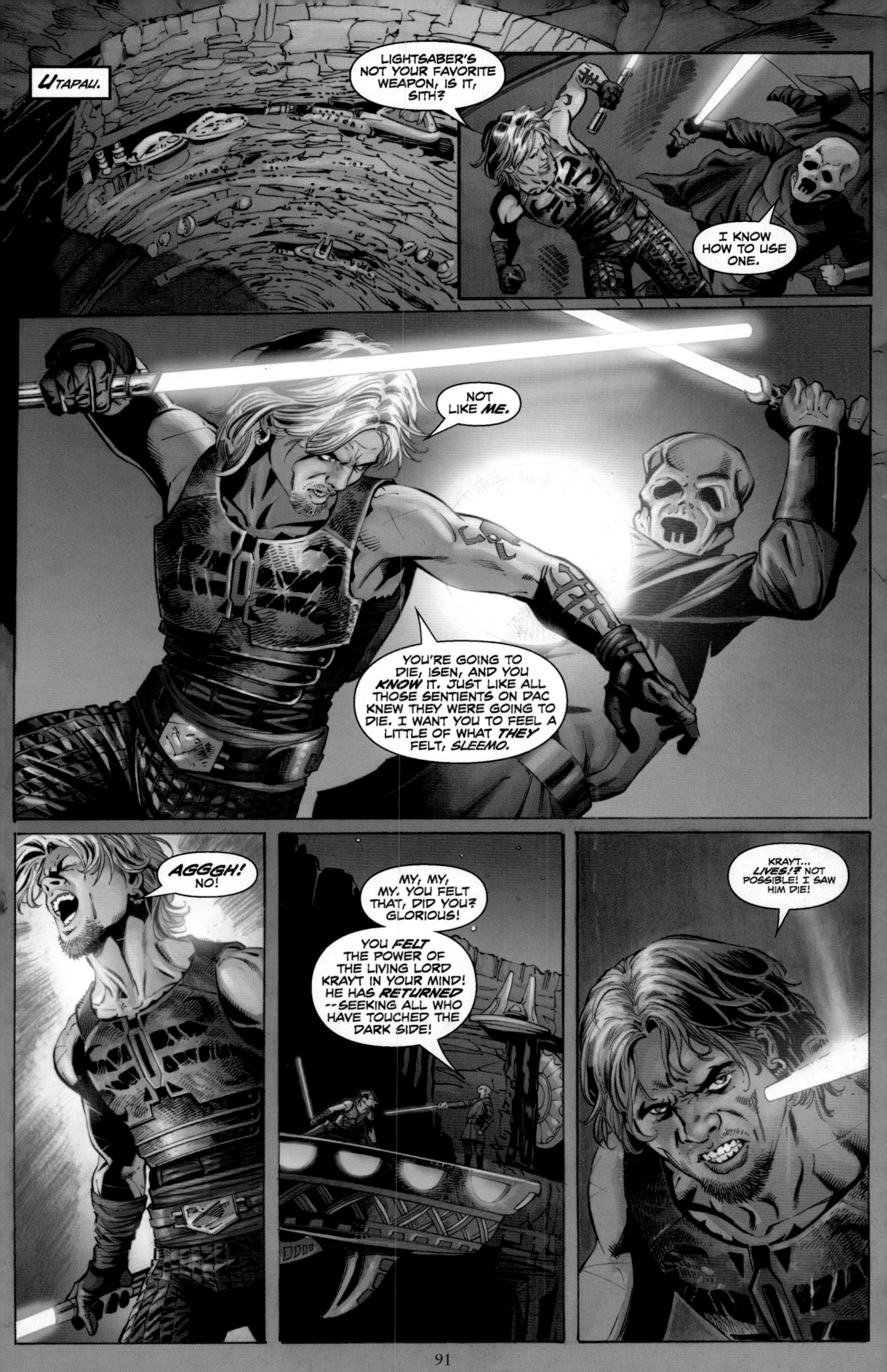
UTAPAU.
LIGHTSABER'S NOT YOUR FAVORITE WEAPON, IS IT, SITH?
I KNOW HOW TO USE ONE.
NOT LIKE *ME.*
YOU'RE GOING TO DIE, ISEN, AND YOU *KNOW* IT. JUST LIKE ALL THOSE SENTIENTS ON DAC KNEW THEY WERE GOING TO DIE. I WANT YOU TO FEEL A LITTLE OF WHAT *THEY* FELT, *SLEEMO.*
AGGGH! NO!
MY, MY, MY. YOU FELT THAT, DID YOU? GLORIOUS!
YOU *FELT* THE POWER OF THE LIVING LORD KRAYT IN YOUR MIND! HE HAS *RETURNED* --SEEKING ALL WHO HAVE TOUCHED THE DARK SIDE!
KRAYT... *LIVES!?* NOT POSSIBLE! I SAW HIM DIE!

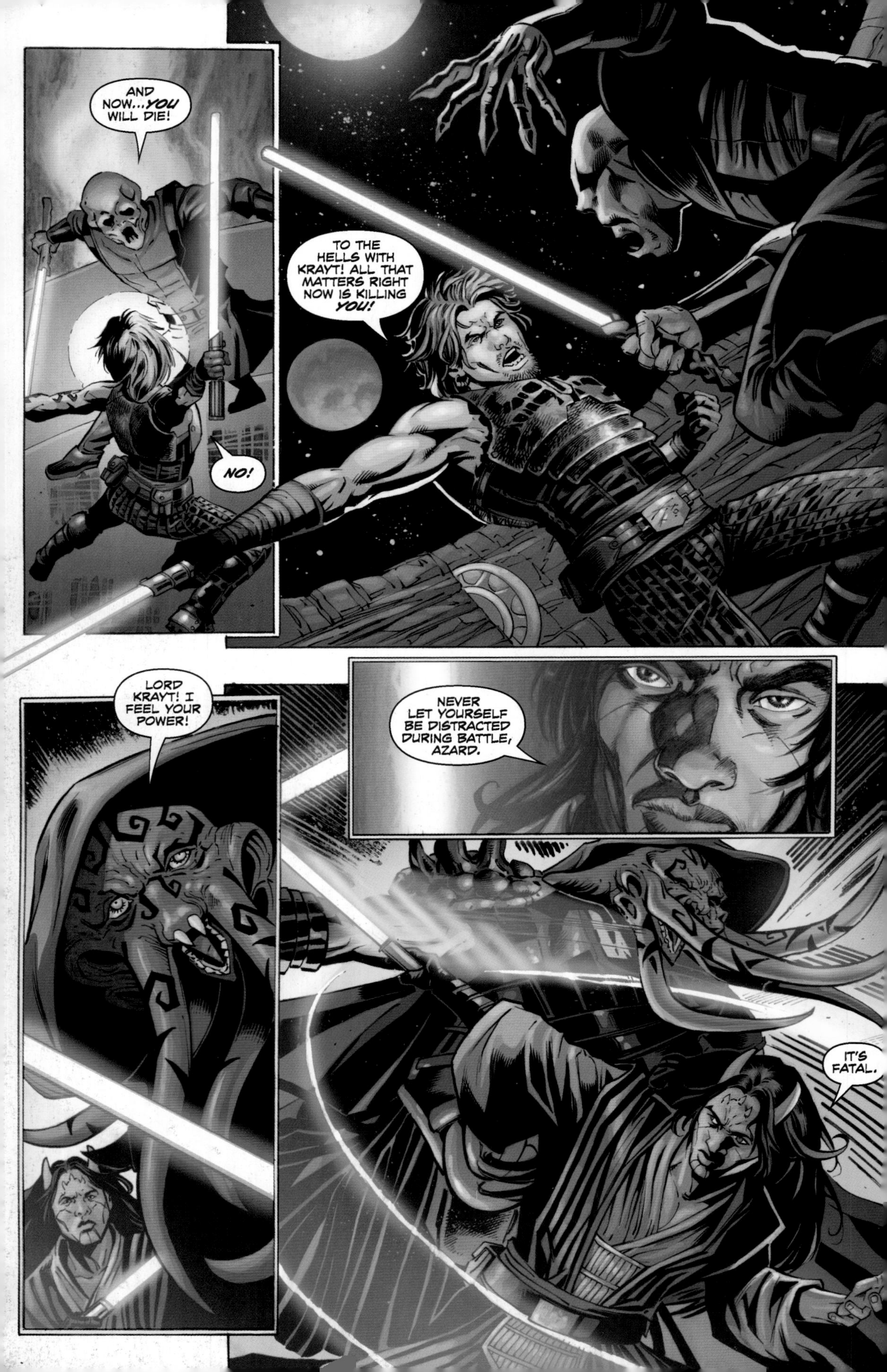
AND NOW...YOU WILL DIE!
NO!
TO THE HELLS WITH KRAYT! ALL THAT MATTERS RIGHT NOW IS KILLING YOU!
LORD KRAYT! I FEEL YOUR POWER!
NEVER LET YOURSELF BE DISTRACTED DURING BATTLE, AZARD.
IT'S FATAL.

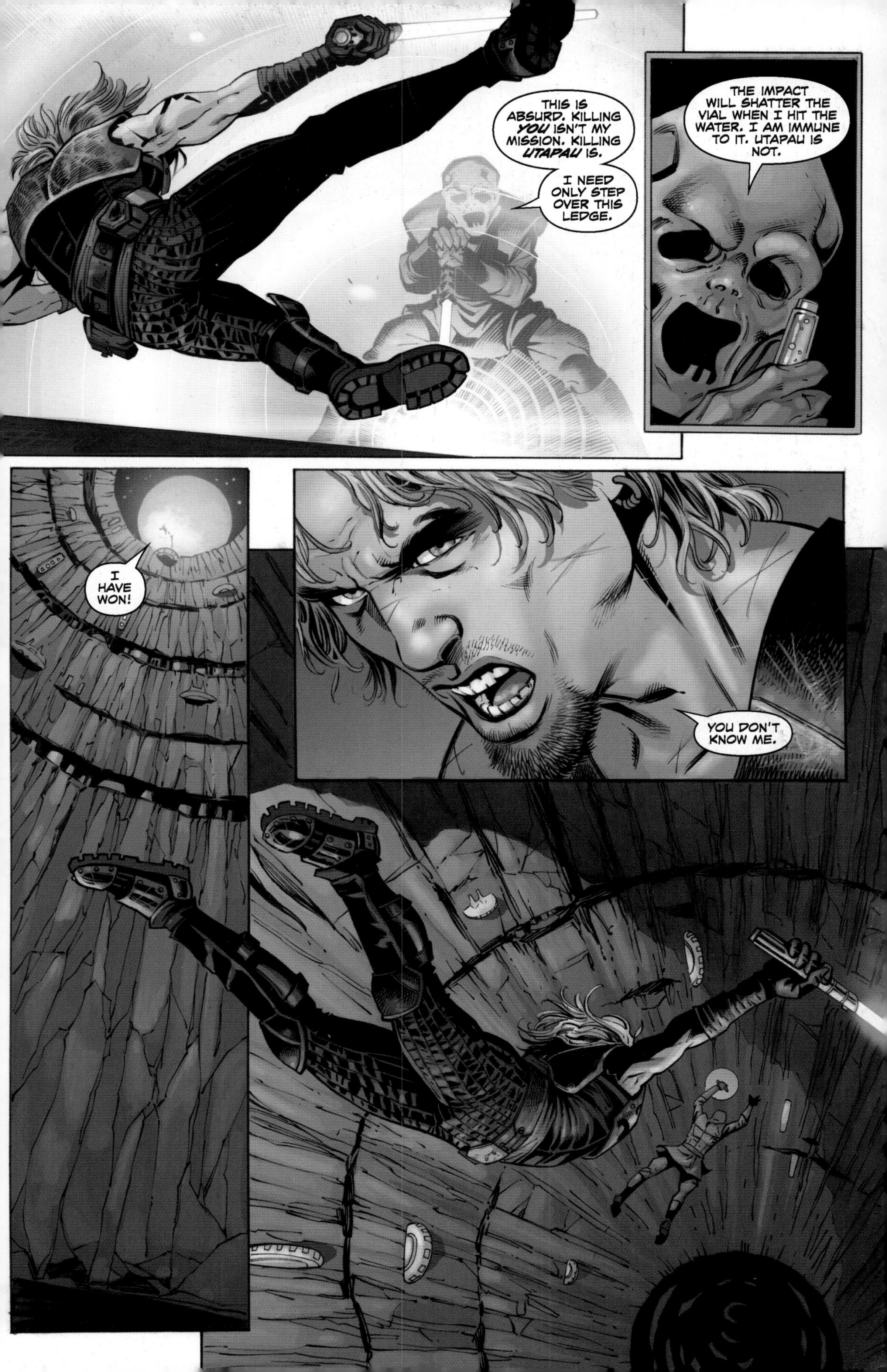
THIS IS ABSURD. KILLING YOU ISN'T MY MISSION. KILLING UTAPAU IS.
I NEED ONLY STEP OVER THIS LEDGE.
THE IMPACT WILL SHATTER THE VIAL WHEN I HIT THE WATER. I AM IMMUNE TO IT. UTAPAU IS NOT.
I HAVE WON!
YOU DON'T KNOW ME.

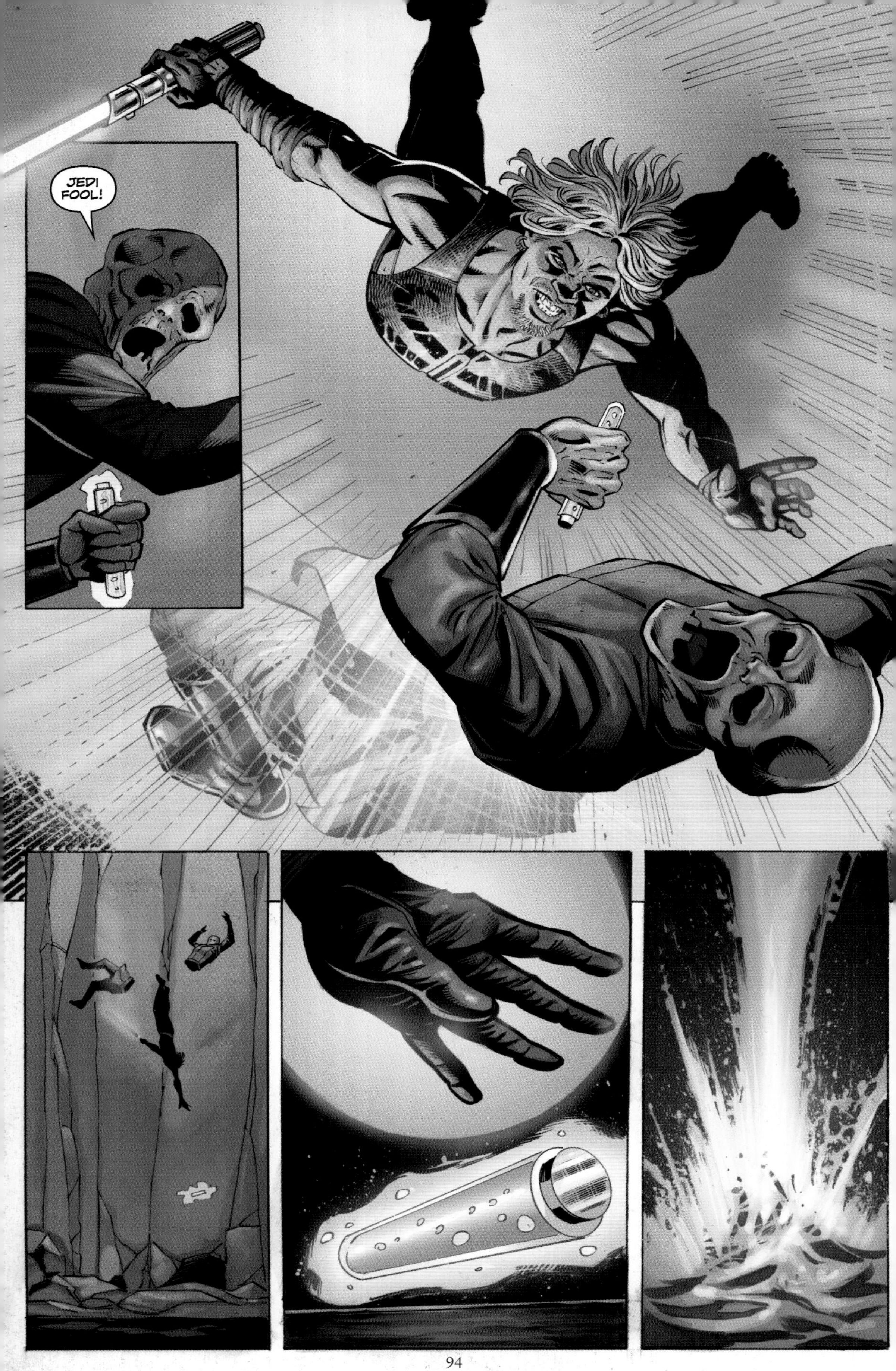
JEDI FOOL!

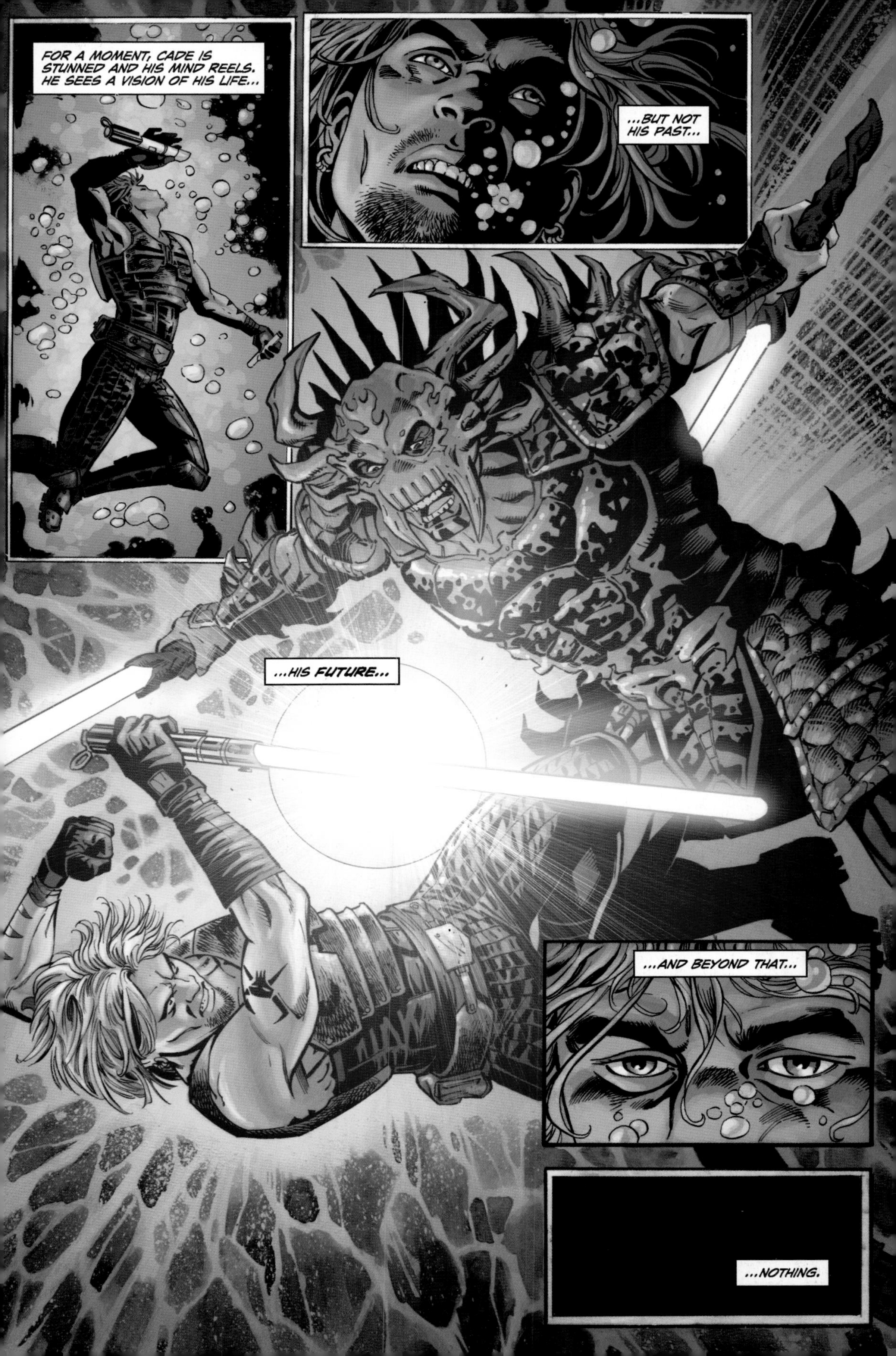
FOR A MOMENT, CADE IS STUNNED AND HIS MIND REELS. HE SEES A VISION OF HIS LIFE...
...BUT NOT HIS PAST...
...HIS FUTURE...
...AND BEYOND THAT...
...NOTHING.

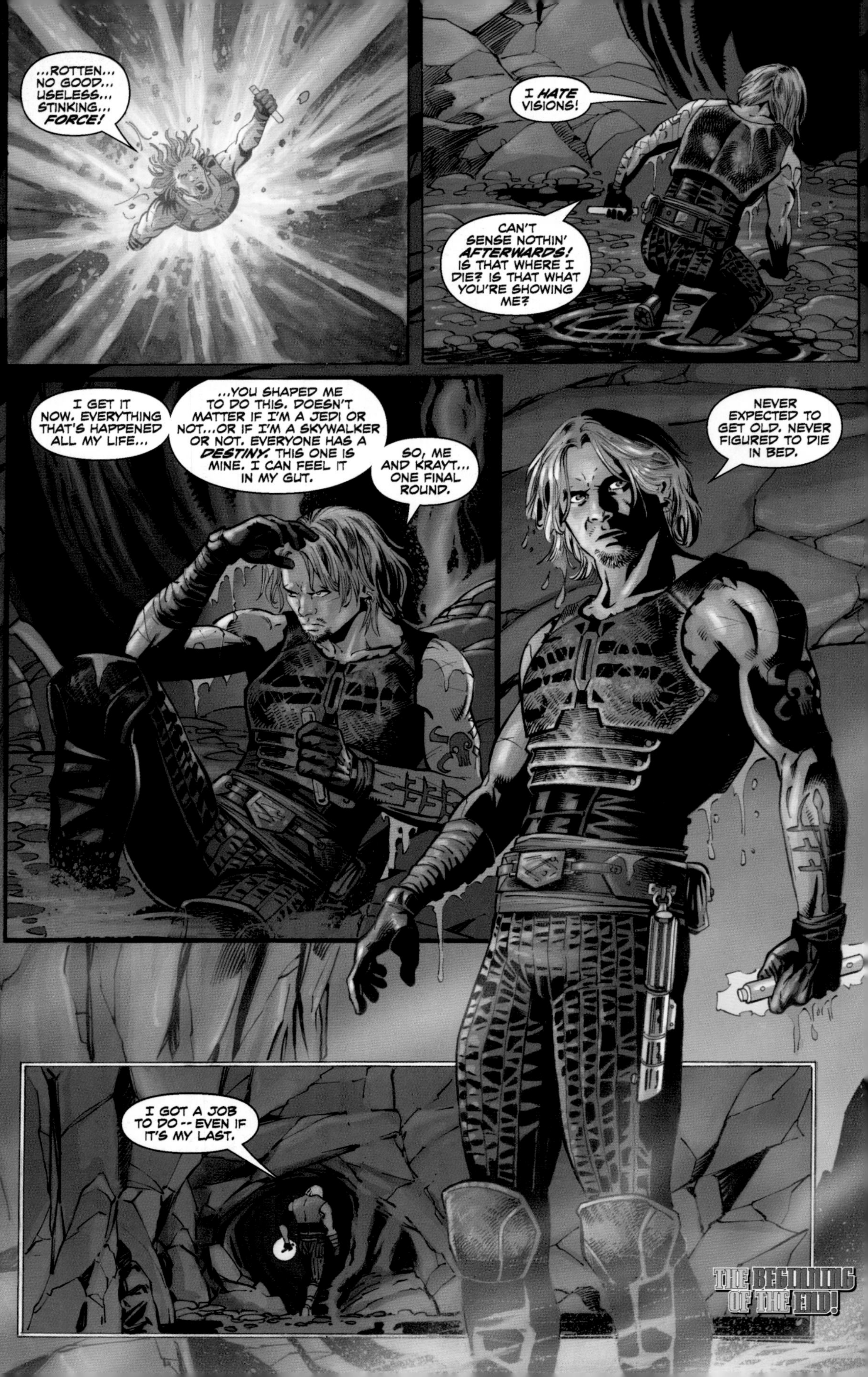
...ROTTEN... NO GOOD... USELESS... STINKING... FORCE!
I HATE VISIONS!
CAN'T SENSE NOTHIN' AFTERWARDS! IS THAT WHERE I DIE? IS THAT WHAT YOU'RE SHOWING ME?
I GET IT NOW. EVERYTHING THAT'S HAPPENED ALL MY LIFE...
...YOU SHAPED ME TO DO THIS. DOESN'T MATTER IF I'M A JEDI OR NOT...OR IF I'M A SKYWALKER OR NOT. EVERYONE HAS A DESTINY. THIS ONE IS MINE. I CAN FEEL IT IN MY GUT.
SO, ME AND KRAYT... ONE FINAL ROUND.
NEVER EXPECTED TO GET OLD. NEVER FIGURED TO DIE IN BED.
I GOT A JOB TO DO -- EVEN IF IT'S MY LAST.
THE BEGINNING OF THE END!

GLOSSARY

champio: champion
cheeka: woman
chobaso: welcome
dopa-meekie: double-dealing
E chu ta!: exclamation
gaggalak mursto: worm-eating liar
grancha: very good
koochoo: idiot
pateesa: friend; term of affection
pyroman/boomer: demolitions expert
sleemo: slimeball
sweets patogga: sweetie pie

STAR WARS GRAPHIC NOVEL TIMELINE (IN YEARS)

Omnibus: Tales of the Jedi—5,000–3,986 BSW4

Knights of the Old Republic (9 volumes)—3,964 BSW4

Jedi vs. Sith—1,000 BSW4

Omnibus: Rise of the Sith—33 BSW4

Episode I: The Phantom Menace—32 BSW4

Omnibus: Emissaries and Assassins—32 BSW4

Bounty Hunters—31 BSW4

Omnibus: Quinlan Vos – Jedi in Darkness—31–28 BSW4

Omnibus: Menace Revealed—31–22 BSW4

Honor and Duty—24 BSW4

Episode II: Attack of the Clones—22 BSW4

Clone Wars (9 volumes)—22–19 BSW4

Clone Wars Adventures (10 volumes)—22–19 BSW4

The Clone Wars (7 volumes)—22–19 BSW4

General Grievous—20 BSW4

Episode III: Revenge of the Sith—19 BSW4

Dark Times (4 volumes)—19 BSW4

Omnibus: Droids—3 BSW4

Omnibus: Boba Fett—3–1 BSW4, 0–10 ASW4

The Force Unleashed—2 BSW4

Adventures (4 volumes)—1–0 BSW4, 0–3 ASW4

Episode IV: A New Hope—SW4

Classic Star Wars—0–3 ASW4

A Long Time Ago… (7 volumes)—0–4 ASW4

Empire (6 volumes)—0 ASW4

Rebellion (3 volumes)—0 ASW4

Omnibus: Early Victories—0–1 ASW4

Jabba the Hutt: The Art of the Deal—1 ASW4

Episode V: The Empire Strikes Back—3 ASW4

Omnibus: Shadows of the Empire—3.5–4.5 ASW4

Episode VI: Return of the Jedi—4 ASW4

Omnibus: X-Wing Rogue Squadron—4–5 ASW4

The Thrawn Trilogy—9 ASW4

Dark Empire—10 ASW4

Crimson Empire—11 ASW4

Jedi Academy: Leviathan—13 ASW4

Union—20 ASW4

Chewbacca—25 ASW4

Legacy (10 volumes)—130 ASW4

Old Republic Era
25,000 – 1000 years before
Star Wars: A New Hope

Rise of the Empire Era
1000 – 0 years before
Star Wars: A New Hope

Rebellion Era
0 – 5 years after
Star Wars: A New Hope

New Republic Era
5 – 25 years after
Star Wars: A New Hope

New Jedi Order Era
25+ years after
Star Wars: A New Hope

Legacy Era
130+ years after
Star Wars: A New Hope

Infinities
Does not apply to timeline

Sergio Aragonés Stomps Star Wars
Star Wars Tales
Star Wars Infinities
Tag and Bink
Star Wars Visionaries

BSW4 = before *Episode IV: A New Hope*. ASW4 = after *Episode IV: A New Hope*.

STAR WARS

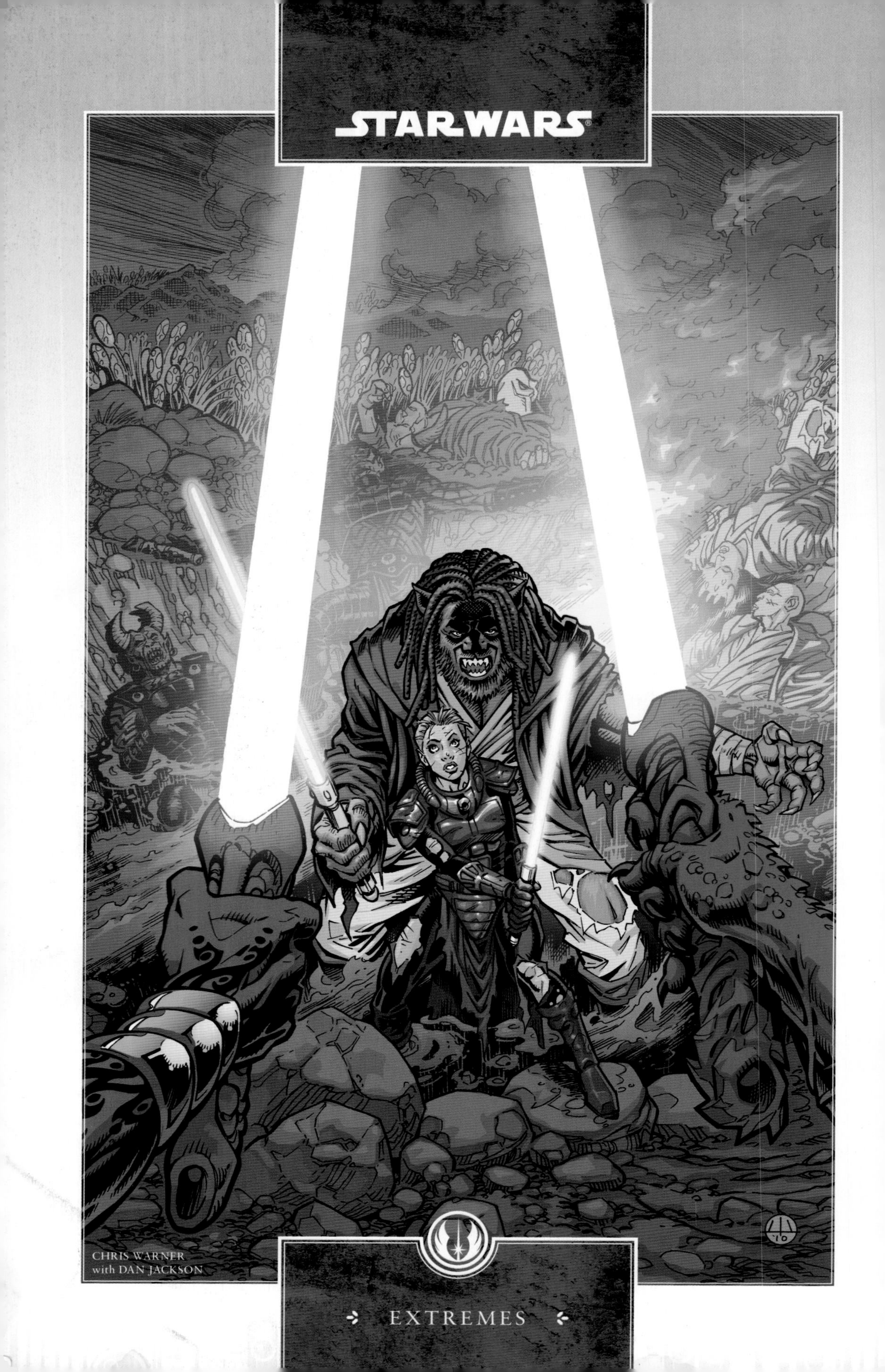
CHRIS WARNER
with DAN JACKSON

EXTREMES

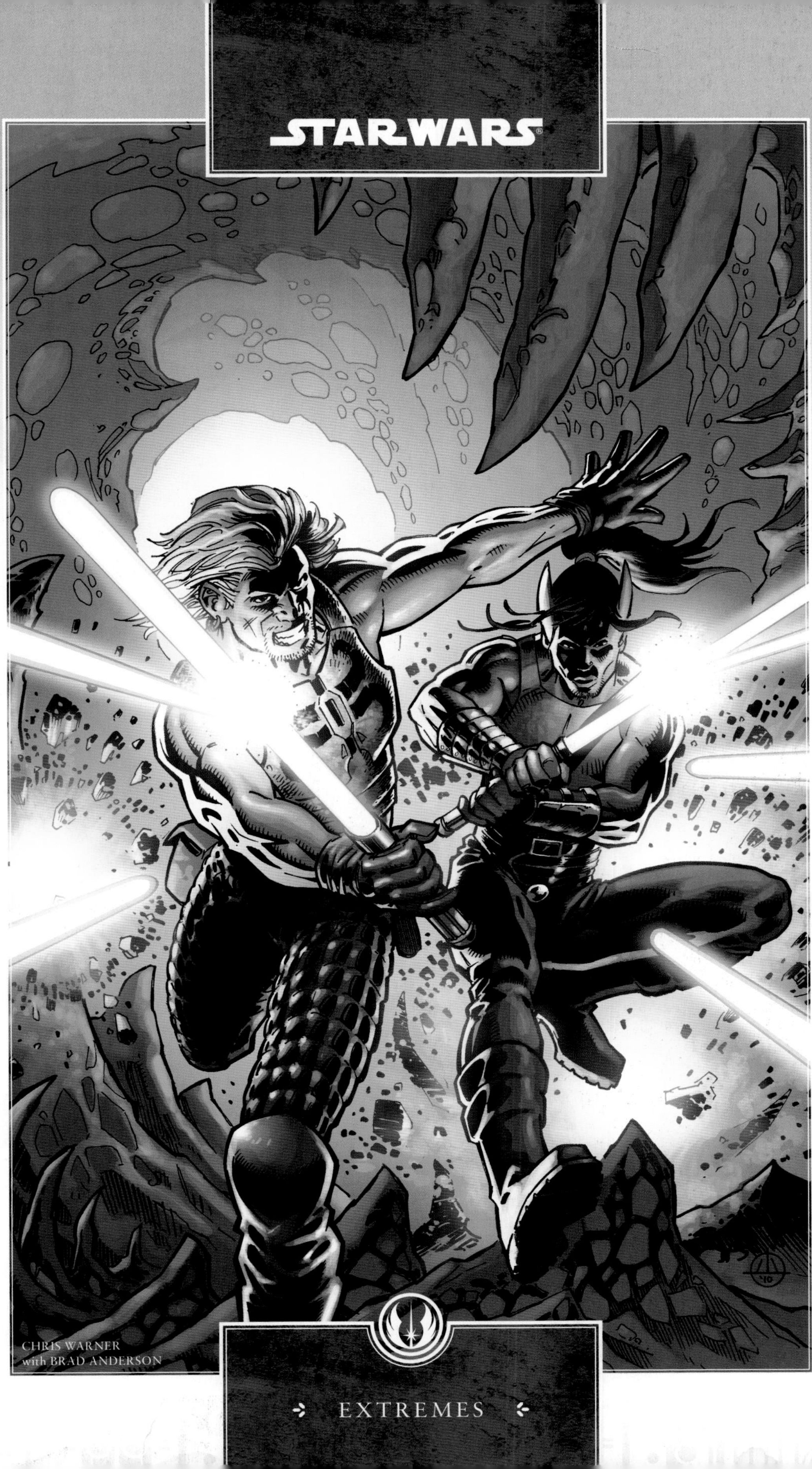
STAR WARS
CHRIS WARNER
with BRAD ANDERSON
EXTREMES

STAR WARS®
LEGACY

Volume 1: Broken
$17.99
ISBN 978-1-59307-716-7

Volume 2: Shards
$19.99
ISBN 978-1-59307-879-9

Volume 3: Claws of the Dragon
$17.99
ISBN 978-1-59307-946-8

Volume 4: Alliance
$15.99
ISBN 978-1-59582-223-9

Volume 5: The Hidden Temple
$15.99
ISBN 978-1-59582-224-6

Volume 6: Vector Volume 2
$17.99
ISBN 978-1-59582-227-7

Volume 7: Storms
$17.99
ISBN 978-1-59582-350-2

Volume 8: Tatooine
$17.99
ISBN 978-1-59582-414-1

Volume 9: Monster
$17.99
ISBN 978-1-59582-485-1

More than one hundred years have passed since the events in *Return of the Jedi* and the days of the New Jedi Order. There is new evil gripping the galaxy, shattering a resurgent Empire, and seeking to destroy the last of the Jedi. Even as their power is failing, the Jedi hold onto one final hope . . . the last remaining heir to the Skywalker legacy.

AVAILABLE AT YOUR LOCAL COMICS SHOP OR BOOKSTORE

STAR WARS®
KNIGHTS OF THE OLD REPUBLIC

Volume 1: Commencement
ISBN 978-1-59307-640-5 | $18.99

Volume 2: Flashpoint
ISBN 978-1-59307-761-7 | $18.99

**Volume 3: Days of Fear,
Nights of Anger**
ISBN 978-1-59307-867-6 | $18.99

**Volume 4: Daze of Hate,
Knights of Suffering**
ISBN 978-1-59582-208-6 | $18.99

Volume 5: Vector
ISBN 978-1-59582-227-7 | $17.99

Volume 6: Vindication
ISBN 978-1-59582-274-1 | $19.99

Volume 7: Dueling Ambitions
ISBN 978-1-59582-348-9 | $18.99

Volume 8: Destroyer
ISBN 978-1-59582-419-6 | $17.99

Volume 9: Demon
ISBN 978-1-59582-476-9 | $16.99

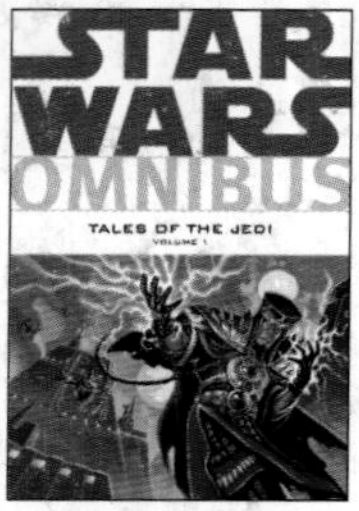
STAR WARS
OMNIBUS
TALES OF THE JEDI
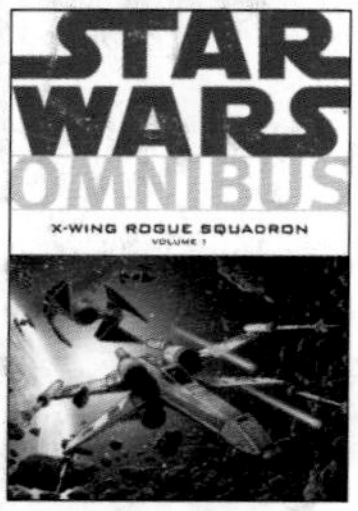
STAR WARS
OMNIBUS
X-WING ROGUE SQUADRON
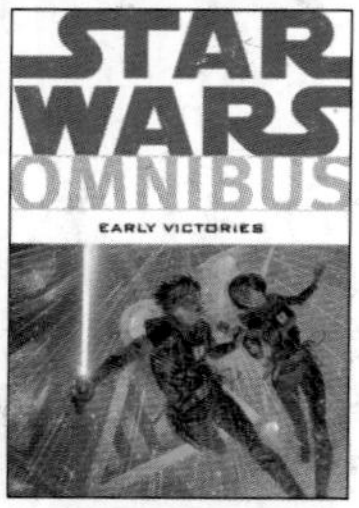
STAR WARS
OMNIBUS
EARLY VICTORIES
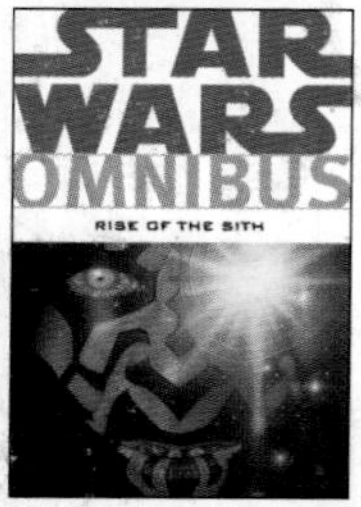
STAR WARS
OMNIBUS
RISE OF THE SITH
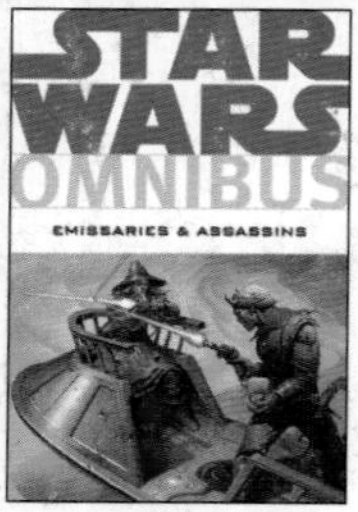
STAR WARS
OMNIBUS
EMISSARIES & ASSASSINS
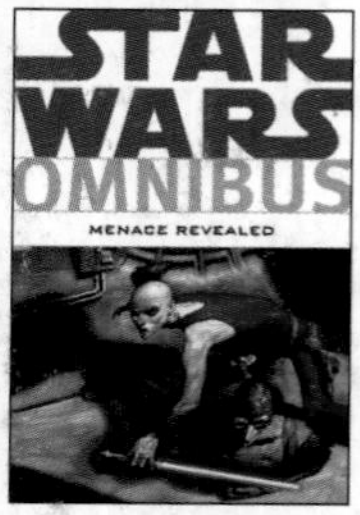
STAR WARS
OMNIBUS
MENACE REVEALED
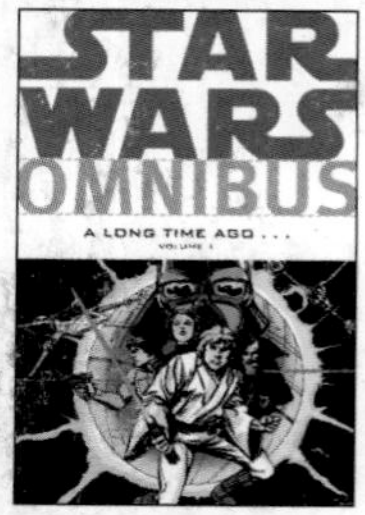
STAR WARS
OMNIBUS
A LONG TIME AGO . . .

STAR WARS OMNIBUS COLLECTIONS

STAR WARS: TALES OF THE JEDI

Including the *Tales of the Jedi* stories "The Golden Age of the Sith," "The Freedon Nadd Uprising," and "Knights of the Old Republic," these huge omnibus editions are the ultimate introduction to the ancient history of the *Star Wars* universe!

Volume 1 ISBN 978-1-59307-830-0 | $24.99 **Volume 2 ISBN 978-1-59307-911-6 | $24.99**

STAR WARS: X-WING ROGUE SQUADRON

The greatest starfighters of the Rebel Alliance become the defenders of a new Republic in this massive collection of stories featuring Wedge Antilles, hero of the Battle of Endor, and his team of ace pilots known throughout the galaxy as Rogue Squadron.

Volume 1 ISBN 978-1-59307-572-9 | $24.99 **Volume 2 ISBN 978-1-59307-619-1 | $24.99**

Volume 3 ISBN 978-1-59307-776-1 | $24.99

STAR WARS: BOBA FETT

Boba Fett, the most feared, most respected, and most loved bounty hunter in the galaxy, now has all of his comics stories collected into one massive volume!

ISBN 978-1-59582-418-9 | $24.99

STAR WARS: EARLY VICTORIES

Following the destruction of the first Death Star, Luke Skywalker is the new, unexpected hero of the Rebellion. But the galaxy hasn't been saved yet–Luke and Princess Leia find there are many more battles to be fought against the Empire and Darth Vader!

ISBN 978-1-59582-172-0 | $24.99

STAR WARS: RISE OF THE SITH

Before the name of Skywalker–or Vader–achieved fame across the galaxy, the Jedi Knights had long preserved peace and justice . . . as well as preventing the return of the Sith. These thrilling tales illustrate the events leading up to *The Phantom Menace*.

ISBN 978-1-59582-228-4 | $24.99

STAR WARS: EMISSARIES AND ASSASSINS

Discover more stories featuring Anakin Skywalker, Amidala, Obi-Wan, and Qui-Gon set during the time of Episode I: *The Phantom Menace* in this mega collection!

ISBN 978-1-59582-229-1 | $24.99

STAR WARS: MENACE REVEALED

This is our largest omnibus of never-before-collected and out-of-print *Star Wars* stories. Included here are one-shot adventures, short story arcs, specialty issues, and early Dark Horse Extra comic strips! All of these tales take place after Episode I: *The Phantom Menace*, and lead up to Episode II: *Attack of the Clones*.

ISBN 978-1-59582-273-4 | $24.99

STAR WARS: SHADOWS OF THE EMPIRE

Featuring all your favorite characters from the *Star Wars* trilogy—Luke Skywalker, Princess Leia, and Han Solo—this volume includes stories written by acclaimed novelists Timothy Zahn and Steve Perry!

ISBN 978-1-59582-434-9 | $24.99

STAR WARS: A LONG TIME AGO. . . .

Star Wars: A Long Time Ago. . . . omnibus volumes feature classic *Star Wars* stories not seen in over twenty years! Originally printed by Marvel Comics, these stories have been recolored and are sure to please *Star Wars* fans both new and old.

Volume 1: ISBN 978-1-59582-486-8 | $24.99 **Volume 2: ISBN 978-1-59582-554-4 | $24.99**

AVAILABLE AT YOUR LOCAL COMICS SHOP OR BOOKSTORE!

To find a comics shop in your area, call 1-888-266-4226

For more information or to order direct: • On the web: darkhorse.com

• E-mail: mailorder@darkhorse.com • Phone: 1-800-862-0052 Mon.–Fri. 9 AM to 5 PM Pacific Time